TWELVE TURNING POINTS OF THE SECOND WORLD WAR

TWELVE TURNING POINTS OF THE SECOND WORLD WAR

P.M.H. BELL

YALE UNIVERSITY PRESS
NEW HAVEN AND LONDON

For information about this and other Yale University Press publications, please contact:
U.S. Office: sales.press@yale.edu   www.yalebooks.com
Europe Office: sales @yaleup.co.uk   www.yalebooks.co.uk

Set in Adobe Caslon Pro by IDSUK (DataConnection) Ltd
Printed in the United States of America

Library of Congress Cataloging-in-Publication Data

Bell, P.M.H. (Philip Michael Hett), 1930-
    Twelve turning points of the Second World War / P.M.H. Bell.
    p. cm.
    ISBN 978-0-300-14885-5 (cl:alk. paper)
    1.   World War, 1939–1945—Campaigns. . I. Title.
    D743.B393 2011
    940.54—dc22
                                                                2010051189

A catalogue record for this book is available from the British Library.

10 9 8 7 6 5 4 3 2 1

This book is dedicated to David Dutton, in long friendship.

CONTENTS

ILLUSTRATIONS

MAPS

INTRODUCTION

When the hurly-burly's done,
When the battle's lost and won.
(William Shakespeare, *Macbeth*, Act I, scene 1)

The Second World War still holds a magnetic attraction for many of us, as an incessant stream of books, television programmes and films testifies. It dominates the history of the twentieth century, towering over even the First World War and the Cold War, and its fascination seems endless. The war's sheer length is impressive. In Europe it began with the German invasion of Poland in September 1939 and ended with the defeat of Germany in May 1945. In East Asia and the Pacific it lasted even longer, starting with the Japanese attack on China in July 1937 (or 1931, if we take the occupation of Manchuria as the beginning of hostilities) and ending with the downfall of Japan in August 1945. In scope it grew from limited wars in the Far East and Europe to conflicts that engulfed the whole of Europe, North Africa, eastern Asia and the Pacific. By the time it was over, the war had affected every continent in one way or another.

This conflict included just about every form of warfare known to man. Armies of millions fought immense battles on the Russian Front, while others grappled in the strange surroundings of the North African desert and the jungles of Burma. Amphibious warfare took new forms in the Normandy landings and the struggle for Iwo Jima in the Pacific. Naval war ranged from the long and bitter U-boat campaign in the Atlantic to fleet actions where the opposing warships never sighted one another, and the fighting was done by carrier-borne aircraft. Aerial bombardment grew to an unprecedented scale, culminating in the atomic bombs that were dropped on Japan in 1945. At the same time, resistance movements all over Europe brought irregular warfare to new heights of intensity. In the background, a hidden competition in secret intelligence, code-breaking, science and technology was pursued with a remarkable combination of brilliance and persistence.

The cost of the war in death and destruction was immense, and almost beyond calculation. One authoritative estimate produces figures of about 22 million military and 26 million civilian deaths, including some 6 million Jews who were annihilated in the Nazi death camps, symbolised by Auschwitz and Mauthausen. Numbers for those who were maimed in the conflict, or died of disease or starvation, are unknown. The war also brought about vast movements of people, especially in Europe – at the end of the war there were somewhere between 16 and 30 million refugees in western Europe, most of whom never returned to their homes in eastern Europe. Many cities across the world, from Europe to Japan, were reduced to ruin.

Yet despite this record of death, suffering and destruction, there remains a firm conviction in many countries – notably in Britain, the United States and Russia – that the Second World War was in a real sense a 'good war', or at the very least a necessary war. In the English-speaking world there has been no reaction against the Second World War like that which has dominated sentiment about the First World War, which is often regarded as sheer waste. In Russia much of the admiration that still surrounds the name of Stalin arises from his reputation as the organiser of victory against Germany. In Europe, there was at the time (and has been since) no serious doubt that Hitler's Germany simply had to be defeated; no half-measures were possible. During the war itself, this struggle was highly personalised, and to a large degree it remains so. Hitler himself was the enemy, and he is still a demonic figure unlike any other in modern history. In the Pacific the war was less personalised, but after the shock of Pearl Harbor on 7 December 1941, the Americans were utterly determined to defeat Japan.

So we look back, after many years, on a war that still grips our attention. We are appalled by the death and destruction. We admire the courage of the fighting men and the endurance of the civilian populations. We are fascinated by the stories of code-breaking, intelligence and resistance. But there is a downside to this fascination. The story is so gigantic and complex that it is hard for us to *understand* the war as well as being amazed or awestruck by it. The mass of events we call the Second World War is so vast and complicated that we cannot grasp it. There is too much hurly-burly for us to make sense of it. We need a key to the puzzle. This sometimes emerges as a general impression that the war was a long and rocky road to an inevitable Allied victory; but this is misleading, because there were times when victory was far from certain and events might have turned out very differently. It is better to adopt the idea of *turning points* as a way of understanding this vast conflict.

A turning point is simply a point at which a decisive or important change takes place. The main turning points in the Second World War are mostly battles lost and won – or not quite won, which can be equally important. Sometimes they are less dramatic and clear-cut than a battle, but instead contests decided in factories and shipyards, or in the manoeuvres of diplomacy and international conferences. When we examine these turning points, it becomes plain that the war followed a shape and pattern. There were three main phases. First, in 1940 and 1941, there came the initial triumphs of the Axis powers. Germany defeated France completely in an astonishing six weeks in May and June 1940; and then came close to beating Britain too, but failed at the last, so that the victory in the west was incomplete. For Germany, the Battle of France was won, but the Battle of Britain was not. In 1941 this pattern was repeated, first in Europe and then in the Pacific. The German invasion of the Soviet Union in June 1941 began with prodigious victories, but was finally brought to a halt. The Germans did not reach Moscow, and the Soviet Union and its armies survived. In the Pacific, the Japanese scored a remarkable success in their attack on Pearl Harbor in December 1941, and then went on to conquer the whole of South-East Asia; but the Americans and their allies held on, and only a few months later stemmed the tide with a victory at Midway Island. The pattern of these events was almost uncannily similar. The Germans and Japanese won one battle after another, but failed to clinch the final victory.

There followed a period of recovery by the Allied powers, from the end of 1942 to 1943, in which the balance began to swing against Germany and Japan. At the turn of the years 1942–43 Soviet forces first checked a German offensive at Stalingrad, and then launched a counter-attack which first trapped and then destroyed a whole German army. At sea, the Battle of the Atlantic, which had swayed to and fro for some three years, was suddenly won by the Allies in the space of a month – May 1943. In the background to these events, and largely hidden from the public gaze, the contest in war production shifted decisively in the Allies' favour in the last part of 1942 and the start of 1943.

The third and final stage of the war, from 1943 to 1945, brought the complete victory of the Allied powers over their enemies. In this phase, the Germans still had a slender chance of avoiding defeat. They might have managed to stem the Soviet drive on the Eastern Front, perhaps keeping German territory intact. In the west, they might have defeated the Anglo-American invasion of France in 1944, and thrown the landing forces back into the sea. Politically, they hoped that the alliance against them of Britain, the USA and the Soviet Union might break up, allowing Germany to escape defeat by playing its enemies off one against another. In the event, none of these possible scenarios came about. The Soviet Union maintained its successes on the Eastern Front, though at a heavy cost. The Allied invasion of France was sometimes a close-run thing, but ended in decisive victory. On the diplomatic front, the three-power conferences at Teheran (November 1943) and Yalta (February 1945) kept the Grand Alliance intact and maintained the unity that was the key to victory.

In East Asia and the Pacific, the final phase of the war saw Japan defeated in one campaign after another, on land, at sea and in the air. The Japanese economy was strangled by an American blockade, and Japanese cities were ruined by incendiary bombing. The sole remaining hope for Japan was that it could put up such a fierce defence of the home islands that the Americans would prefer to make peace rather than suffer the casualties which would be inflicted during an invasion. In the event, the atomic bombs that were dropped on Hiroshima and Nagasaki in August 1945, together with the Soviet Union's entry into the war in massive strength, destroyed this slender hope, and Japan was compelled to surrender. This proved a turning point not only in the war but in human history. The Second World War ended, and the nuclear age began.

This approach to the history of the war requires a choice of particular turning points that is bound to be difficult and controversial – as I soon found when I mentioned this project to my friends. As rivals to the twelve turning points selected for this book, others come readily to mind. The Nazi-Soviet Pact of August 1939 decided the shape and course of the war in unexpected ways for nearly two years, and would make a fascinating study. The determination of the Poles to stand and fight in 1939, rather than yield to German threats, was decisive in starting the shooting war in Europe – otherwise, there would surely have been another Munich, and war would have been postponed. In 1940–41 President Roosevelt took the decisive step of providing help to the British, first by the destroyers-for-bases deal, and later by the lend-lease programme which allowed Britain to maintain its imports from America even when it could no longer pay for them. These two actions were not as dramatic as battles, but crucial events none the less. On the Eastern Front, where the decisive land battles of the war took place and the German Army suffered fatal losses, the great conflicts at Moscow in December 1941 and Kursk in July 1943 have a strong claim to stand beside Stalingrad (July 1942–February 1943) among the turning points of the war. In the Mediterranean theatre of war, the British victory at El Alamein (October–November 1942) and the Anglo-American landings in French North Africa (November 1942) brought a conclusive end to the war in Africa and opened the Mediterranean to Allied shipping, and would appear in many lists of turning points. After all, Winston Churchill himself wrote that 'It may almost be said, "Before Alamein we never had a victory. After Alamein we never had a defeat."' That in itself is a strong claim!

Among all these rivals for selection as turning points, we may well speculate as to which would appear in *everyone's* list. Surely the Battle of Britain in 1940, the German invasion of the Soviet Union in June 1941, and the Japanese attack on Pearl Harbor in December 1941 could not be left out. They certainly figure in my list for this book, along with others that make up a round dozen. In any case, whichever turning points we choose, this approach to the history of the Second World War offers a way of understanding that vast and confused conflict. It sets the decisive events (battles, conferences, war production) in their context. It brings out the roles played by the great leaders – Churchill, Roosevelt and Stalin on one side, and Hitler on the other. The Allied leaders had their disputes and difficulties, but held together at the crucial points. On the German side, Hitler began the war as a wonder-worker, and in 1940–41 it seemed that everything he touched turned to gold; but from 1942 onwards his interventions often proved disastrous. In 1942–43 he condemned a whole German army to death at Stalingrad; and in 1944 he so misdirected the Normandy campaign that an American general was moved to comment that 'One's imagination boggled at what the German army might have done to us without Hitler working so effectively for our side.' There were times, in fact, when Hitler was more valuable to the Allies alive than dead.

In this way, the book sets out to offer the interested reader a fresh look at the main outlines of the Second World War, and how that great conflict was lost and won. Of course it is not the whole story, but it may serve as a beginning.

TWELVE TURNING POINTS
OF THE SECOND WORLD WAR

CHAPTER ONE

HITLER'S TRIUMPH

THE COLLAPSE OF FRANCE, MAY–JUNE 1940

At 11.15 on the morning of 3 September 1939 the British Prime Minister, Neville Chamberlain, announced on the radio that 'this country is at war with Germany'. No sooner had he finished his broadcast than the air-raid sirens wailed across London, and people took refuge in underground shelters. It seemed that the long-expected Armageddon of bombardment from the air was about to start. In the event, it proved a false alarm. John Colville, a civil servant in the newly formed Ministry of Economic Warfare, played a rubber of bridge with his colleagues in the basement of the London School of Economics, and then emerged to find that nothing had happened. It was in this anticlimactic fashion that Britain entered a war that was to last for six years.

It was a war that had been likely since Adolf Hitler took power in Germany in January 1933, and had become almost inevitable by 1939. Nazi Germany had been rearming rapidly since 1935, and there was no doubt that these armaments were to be used to establish German predominance in Europe, and perhaps more widely than that. In 1938–39 the advance of German power was speeding up. In March 1938 Hitler annexed Austria. In September the same year, the Germans took over the Sudeten areas of Czechoslovakia, and in March 1939 they broke up the rest of the country. On all these occasions the German advance had been unopposed, and indeed had been encouraged by the policy of appeasement pursued by Britain and France. But from March 1939 all this changed. Hitler's next proposed victim was Poland, but the Poles could be neither persuaded nor bullied into surrendering their independence. Moreover, the British and French had reluctantly decided that Germany was aiming at the domination of Europe, and would have to be resisted, if necessary by force. So unless Hitler was willing to call a halt, or the Poles chose to give way, or the British and French returned to a policy of appeasement, war was certain. None of these events came about, and war began. Germany attacked Poland in the early hours of 1 September 1939; and on the 3rd, Britain and France declared war on Germany.

The campaign in Poland was over in five weeks. The Polish air force was destroyed almost at once, and the army resisted the German tanks bravely but in vain. The Soviet Union delivered a deadly blow by invading from the east on 19 September, following the Nazi-Soviet Pact of 23 August. Warsaw was bombed for ten days before surrendering on 27 September. In the face of these disasters, the Polish government did not surrender but took refuge in France to continue the struggle in exile, with new armed forces formed from units that had escaped from Poland. Meanwhile, both the Germans and the Soviets began programmes of massacre and deportation, opposed by an underground resistance movement which came into being almost immediately.

The contrast between anticlimax in Britain and total war in Poland could not have been sharper. But when the Poles were defeated, a strange quietness descended over Europe. *Blitzkrieg*, lightning war, in Poland was followed by *sitzkrieg*, a sit-down war, in the west. France and Britain were content to stand on the defensive, planning for a long war in which they would build up their forces while strangling Germany by economic blockade – a strategy that became sadly unreal when the Soviet Union, under a commercial agreement following the Nazi-Soviet Pact, undertook to supply Germany with vast quantities of oil and raw materials, opening a gap in the blockade that the western Allies could not hope to close. Germany, by contrast, was determined on attack, but failed to get started. Hitler first ordered an offensive against France, Belgium and Holland to start as early as 12 November 1939, barely a month after the end of the Polish campaign; but the operation was repeatedly postponed – no fewer than 29 times in all – due to unreadiness or bad weather.

The result was the 'phoney war' – a war that was declared but not waged, except at sea and by propaganda. In this time of inactivity, both sides made plans. The French, who provided by far the greater part of the Allied armies in the west and therefore took command, had built an elaborate system of fortifications from Switzerland to Belgium – the famous Maginot Line, which was thought to be impregnable to any form of attack. The French did not extend their fortifications to the Channel coast, partly on grounds of cost but also because they intended to advance into Belgium in the event of a German attack. They anticipated that the Germans would repeat their strategy of 1914, and strike against northern France by way of Belgium and perhaps the Netherlands. The French high command proposed to meet such an attack by advancing into Belgium to the River Dyle, which could be held as a defensive line; and also by a rapid move into the southern Netherlands at Breda – the so-called 'Breda variant' on the main plan, which was eventually to assume vital, and indeed disastrous, importance. The French strategy was thus to advance to meet the Germans like a door swinging on its hinge. The hinge itself was in the Ardennes, an area of forest and hills, generally believed on the French side to be impassable for tanks, as Marshal Pétain – the famous hero of the Great War – had declared when he was Minister of War in 1935. French strategic thinking was therefore far from being static and defensive, but combined defence along the Maginot Line with an advance to meet the Germans in the Low Countries.

The Germans for their part were determined on attack, but changed their minds several times as to the exact form and location of their offensive. Eventually, by February 1940, they settled on the daring concept of an assault through the supposedly impassable Ardennes, to be followed by a rapid advance to cut off the Allied forces in Belgium and northern France. Hitler's original idea had been for a limited operation which would defeat part of the French army and capture territory to enable him to attack Britain by air and sea. But General von Manstein, a remarkably able and unorthodox staff officer, conceived instead the daring concept of a complete and rapid victory through the destruction of the Allied armies.

In this way each side laid its plans, but meanwhile the phoney war continued. The British and French had declared war, but then almost nothing happened. A long, hard winter passed in a state of suspended animation. The contrast was all the greater when the Germans opened their offensive in the west on 10 May 1940, advancing (as the Allies had anticipated) into Belgium and Holland. But the real shock came elsewhere, as the Germans struck their main blow, with a mass of Panzer divisions, through the Ardennes forest and across the River Meuse at Sedan. The risks were enormous. At one stage, on the 12th, the Germans had managed to create 'the biggest known traffic jam in Europe'. If Allied bombers had found this splendid target, the German advance might have been halted that very day, and the rest of the campaign transformed. But the traffic jam remained unobserved.

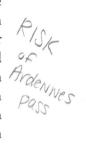

In the event, the next two days decided the issue of this first battle in favour of the Germans. On 13 May the Luftwaffe launched a series of devastating attacks on French forces defending the line of the Meuse.

1 The biggest traffic jam in Europe, 12 May 1940. German vehicles stuck on a narrow road through the Ardennes forest.

Something like 1,500 German aircraft, including 250 dive-bombers, made incessant attacks for four or five hours. The total French casualties eventually turned out to be no more than 56, but French communications (which depended on land-lines laid in the open) were disrupted beyond repair, and above all the French infantry were reduced to a state of paralysis by the constant assaults. At one stage the 55th Infantry Division, which had sustained the worst of the air bombardment, suffered an attack of mass panic – the so-called 'panic of Bulson' – in which troops fled, shouting that they had seen German tanks when in fact there was not a single tank in the area. The division effectively dissolved before the first German tanks arrived.

The next day, 14 May, opened with the French high command in a state of despair. Captain André Beaufre, a junior staff officer and later to be a distinguished general, visited the headquarters of General Georges, the Commander-in-Chief on the Allied north-eastern front, at about 3 o'clock in the morning – never the best of times. The scene was burned on to his memory:

> The room was barely half-lit. . . . The atmosphere was that of a family in which there has been a death. Georges got up quickly and came to

Doumenc [a French general]. He was terribly pale. 'Our front has been broken at Sedan! There has been a collapse . . .' He flung himself into a chair and burst into tears.

The Germans were in fact across the Meuse, and later that day a projected French counter-attack, using a force of some 300 tanks, failed to get under way because the heavy French vehicles had only small fuel tanks and quickly ran out of petrol, and there were very few radios so that communication was impossible. In the next few days, the 2nd French Armoured Division fell to pieces because it was ordered to move in different directions in rapid succession, in each case without regard for actual conditions on the ground. In contrast to this paralysis and confusion, the Germans advanced with astonishing confidence and speed, and their armoured divisions reached the Channel at the mouth of the River Somme on 20 May. They covered the 200 miles from Sedan to the coast in six days. It was a burst of speed that left their opponents bewildered.

Meanwhile, the northern French armies and most of the British Expeditionary Force (BEF) advanced into Belgium, following their own long-laid plans. In what proved a disastrous development of those plans, the French Seventh Army, under General Giraud, was ordered to dash forward into the southern Netherlands at Breda to help the Dutch. To form the Seventh Army for this operation, General Gamelin, the French Commander-in-Chief, had used up the whole of his strategic reserve. When Churchill, who had become British Prime Minister on 10 May, went to Paris on the 16th to confer with the French, he asked Gamelin: 'Où est la masse de manoeuvre?' ('Where is the strategic reserve?'). Gamelin shrugged his shoulders and replied 'Aucune' ('There is none'). This was true, but not the whole truth. In fact the strategic reserve had existed, but had been used up in the advance to Breda, where it arrived only in time to beat a hasty retreat. So it came about that the whole Allied force in northern France moved into the Low Countries, according to plan, only to find themselves cut off as the Germans made their dash to the Channel.

[margin note: realized there were NO mobile reserves]

The first phase of this astonishing campaign ended with large Allied armies cut off in the north, though separated from the forces to the south by a German-occupied corridor that itself was extremely slender. At this point, on 20 May, Paul Reynaud, the French Premier, dismissed Gamelin and replaced him with General Weygand, a vigorous 73-year-old who had won a high reputation in the Great War and had been recalled to service on the outbreak of war. Weygand made an ineffectual visit by air to the northern

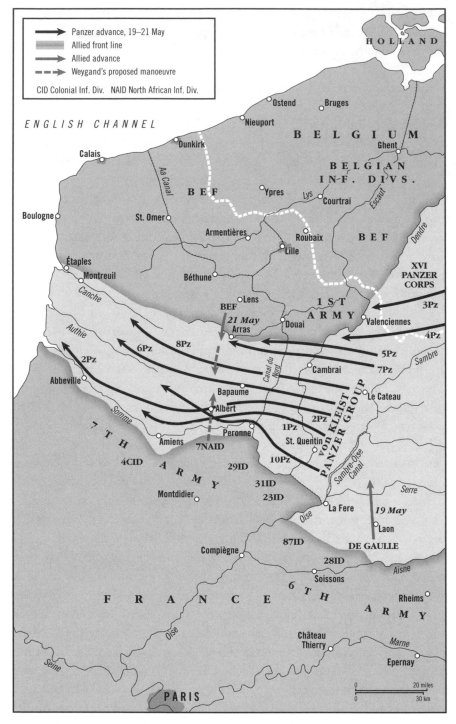

Map 1 The Panzer 'Corridor' (18–21 May).

forces, and then came up with the fairly obvious idea that the best course would be to cut the German corridor and reunite the Allied armies by a combined attack from north and south. This seemed simple in theory but proved virtually impossible in practice. The French armies in the south could not be quickly organised for an offensive, while the forces in the north were fighting for their lives, and could only summon the strength for a small-scale British attack near Arras on 21–23 May, which took the Germans by surprise at the start but was soon halted by German anti-tank guns.

The key question in the next phase of the battle soon became not whether the Allies could mount a counter-offensive, but whether the armies cut off in the north could save anything at all from the wreck of defeat. In their extremity they were aided by an unexpected stroke of good fortune. On 24 May German tanks were only ten miles from Dunkirk, the only port still available for an Allied escape. At that point the Germans stopped. Already during the night of 23–24 May, General von Rundstedt, the German commander, had ordered one wing of his forces to halt, so that following troops could close up with those ahead. He at first intended this to apply for only one day, but on the 24th Hitler visited von Rundstedt's headquarters and confirmed a further 'halt order', which was not countermanded until the afternoon of the 26th. This meant that the German advance resumed only at 08.00 hours on the 27th, after a delay of three days in all, during which the Panzers remained inactive. Contrary to later legend, the 'halt order' of the 24th was not imposed by Hitler in person, but was only a confirmation and extension of the earlier order of 23–24 May. Von Rundstedt was afraid that his forces were overextended, and wanted time to consolidate; and Hitler agreed with him. Nor was the 'halt order' the result of any desire on Hitler's part to allow the British to escape as a way of making peace with them, as another legend later asserted. On the contrary, Hitler's Directive No. 13, drafted on the 24th, laid down that the next objective was to annihilate the French and British forces surrounded in the north. Hermann Goering tele-phoned Hitler personally to say that the Luftwaffe could finish off the forces around Dunkirk by itself – the army would only need to occupy the ground – and it appears that Hitler believed him.

Whatever the reasons behind it, the 'halt order' brought the Germans to a standstill for three days. This was another might-have-been. If the Germans had kept up their advance, they might well have captured or destroyed most of the BEF, with disastrous consequences for Britain. As it was, the German delay gave the British time to save themselves. On 25 May Field Marshal Lord Gort, the commander of the BEF, decided on

2 British troops under constant air attack waiting to be evacuated from the beaches near Dunkirk. In the course of nine days, 224,000 British troops were rescued to form the nucleus of a new army.

his own responsibility to give up Weygand's plan for an offensive and to fall back on Dunkirk in the hope of saving his army by sea. The next day the British gave the order to start Operation DYNAMO, the code name for a sea borne evacuation, which got under way in the early hours of the 27th. At first, the British naval commander (Admiral Ramsay) expected to take off no more than about 45,000 men out of a total of some 250,000 British troops. In fact, in the course of nine days, 224,000 British troops and 111,000 others (mostly French) were evacuated, though they left behind nearly all their artillery and heavy equipment. For the British, this was a mixture of disaster and triumph. The disaster was that the BEF had been defeated and driven out of France – something the Germans never managed to achieve in 1914–18. The triumph was that such a large number of men got away, to form the basis for another army in the future. Churchill wisely warned the House of Commons, and his fellow countrymen, that wars were not won by evacuations; but Dunkirk made its mark in the popular mind as a tremendous national achievement. For the French, alas, it was a defeat on the way to other defeats.

In the event, the French Army fought a last battle with a bravery and determination that have been too little remembered. They formed new defensive positions along the rivers Somme and Aisne, turning villages into 'hedgehogs', with orders to hold out even when surrounded. By prodigious efforts, the surviving French armoured divisions were re-equipped with new tanks. Above all, morale was high and fighting spirit revived. An infantryman wrote to his parents: 'We're very tired, but we hold on, they shall not pass, we'll get them.' (The French phrases, 'ils ne passeront pas, on les aura', were echoes of Marshal Pétain's watchwords at Verdun in 1916.) A general commanding a division told a colleague: 'Everyone is holding on. Men are surrounded, but they hold on. . . . I am absolutely convinced that the French Army will pull through.' These were only two examples among many. The Germans were shaken by this stern resistance, and even General Rommel's famous 7th Panzer Division found itself struggling to break through on the Somme. But the recovery came too late, and the odds were too heavy. A French *chasseur* officer wrote despairingly that 'when we mowed down twenty, another forty sprang up in their place'. On 12 June General Weygand told the French Cabinet, meeting at the château de Cangé, near Tours (having left Paris on the 10th), that coordinated defence of the country had come to an end, and he therefore recommended that the government should ask for an armistice.

For the next four days the Cabinet debated whether or not to follow this advice, which was supported by Marshal Pétain, whom Reynaud had appointed to his government to raise morale and who carried immense prestige; or to continue the war from Algiers, which was at that time legally part of France. The government moved in disorderly fashion to Bordeaux, where its agonised discussions came to a head on 16 June. That evening Reynaud felt he could no longer keep his Cabinet together, and resigned. He was at once replaced by Pétain, who on the 17th asked the Germans for an armistice. The terms proved far-reaching. Two-thirds of France (including Paris and the Channel and Atlantic coasts) were to be occupied; the army was to be reduced to 100,000 men (the figure set for the German army by the Treaty of Versailles in 1919); the fleet was to be disarmed under German or Italian supervision; France was to meet the costs of its own occupation; and all prisoners of war were to remain in captivity until peace was concluded. These terms were severe, but not fatal. A French government was to remain in control of the unoccupied zone, and the Germans made no demands on the French Empire. The French government accepted these terms, and the armistice came into force at 12.35 a.m. on 25 June. The authority of Pétain's name and prestige ensured that the French colonies across the world took the same course.

All in all, these were astonishing events. The Germans had accomplished in six weeks in May and June 1940 what they had failed to achieve in four years of hard struggle from 1914 to 1918. They had defeated the French and British armies and dictated terms to the French government. The causes of this victory were not exactly what they seemed on the surface. The picture conjured up in most minds in the summer of 1940 was one of overwhelming German materiel superiority in tanks and aircraft. In fact, the Allies had more tanks than the Germans when the battle opened on 10 May – 3,250 French plus 640 British tanks as against 2,440 German. The best French types (the Somua medium tank and the heavy Type B) were of good quality, and in some respects superior to the German armour; though the Type B had only a small fuel tank that limited its range. French tanks were also handicapped because they had few radios, leaving them isolated when in action. As for aircraft, the French and British together outnumbered the Germans in total numbers of bombers and fighters on the 10th, by about 4,250 to 3,600; but on the main battlefront the Germans deployed 2,600 against 1,350 – a 2-to-1 superiority where it mattered most. Later on, the French assembled large numbers of aircraft in depots, but failed to get them into action.

In manpower, the two sides were roughly equal at the start of the battle, with the German armies totalling 135 divisions, and the French, British, Belgians and Dutch together 152 divisions – though the Dutch and Belgians were not in action for long. Nor was there a great difference in the degree of mechanisation. The German Panzer and mechanised divisions, which wrought such havoc in the opening stages of the campaign, were only the steel tip of a force that still relied heavily on horses for its transport – at the start of the war the German Army mobilised some 600,000 horses.

All in all, the balance of strength between the two sides was close enough to give the Allies a chance of success. What secured the German victory was a combination of bold strategic thinking (the assault through the supposedly impassable Ardennes); daring attacks (the Panzer Commander Heinz Guderian's dash to the Channel, which was on his own initiative and unauthorised by the high command); and sheer speed of movement (the French moved at the tempo of 1914–18, whereas the Germans had moved up a couple of gears). On the Allied side, the French failed to use their tanks effectively, and could not cope with the surprise and pace of the German assault. When eventually they had got the measure of the German tactics and learned how to cope with them, it proved too late.

The military defeat of France was at once followed by a political upheaval. Pétain's government moved from Bordeaux to the spa town of Vichy, which was well provided with hotels to house ministers, officials and hangers-on. The National Assembly (Chamber of Deputies and Senate) was summoned to meet there on 9–10 July. In the shock of defeat, and responding to a widespread sentiment that the Third Republic as well as the Army had failed, the Assembly voted itself out of existence by 569 votes to 80, granting Pétain full powers to change the constitution. The new regime took the name of the French State (*Etat Français* – no longer the French Republic). A new motto of *Travail, Famille, Patrie* replaced the Republican trinity of *Liberté, Egalité, Fraternité*, and the government announced its intention of embarking on a national revolution, as yet undefined but certain to be authoritarian in character. Military defeat was thus accompanied by the fall of the Third Republic and the destruction of French democracy.

France - democracy → authoritarian

The impact of these events was profound. Far away in Rumania, the novelist Olivia Manning felt that 'the fall of France was the fall of civilisation'. Throughout Europe there was a sense that the old order was finished, giving way to the new. Pétain's suppression of 'Liberty, Equality, Fraternity' had a symbolic significance that reached far beyond France. For everyone with a sense of history, it seemed that the age which began with the French Revolution had come to an end. The shock was felt all over Europe and well beyond, in the Americas, the Far East and Pacific.

In France, the whole population suffered a vast upheaval. About 1,800,000 prisoners of war were held in German camps, removing men in the prime of life from their families and their work. During the German invasion, something like six million refugees left their homes and sought refuge across France, often aiming vaguely to get somewhere south of the Loire. They left behind half-deserted towns and villages. One man described what had happened to his own town:

> . . . in twenty-four hours the unhappy town has emptied like a burst water bottle. What a panic! I am sure that three-quarters of the population has left already. A few grocers, a few foodshops are still open, and two or three cafes. All the rest is shut up. No more cinemas, no more newspapers – I find the gates closed at the swimming pool.

It is this small, inconsequential detail that is the most telling – why did the writer go to the swimming pool, of all places? Over time, the deeper consequences struck home. In 1975 a French soldier-turned-historian wrote:

> The disaster of 1940 made a profound impression on our national consciousness. Never throughout our long history had our army been so swiftly and decisively defeated, our territory so comprehensively invaded, our economic potential taken over so absolutely by the enemy, our independence so completely destroyed.

[margin note: significance of battle]

In practical terms the French had to do something to cope with the disaster. Most refugees made their way home, and people settled into a new form of normality, rubbing along with the occupying troops, who on the whole behaved well. At Vichy, Pétain's government assumed that Germany had won the war, that Britain would not last long, and that France must therefore work out her future within a new Europe under German domination. The word 'collaboration' rapidly came into use, and Marshal Pétain gave it his blessing when he met Hitler at Montoire on 24 October 1940 and accepted the principle of collaboration with Germany – though without defining its precise meaning.

This was the common-sense reaction – to accept the fact of defeat and get on with life, whether at home or in the conduct of foreign policy. Yet a totally different course was open to those who dared to take it. General de Gaulle, who had been a junior minister in Reynaud's government for a brief ten days (6–16 June), and had flown to London on 17 June, chose to reject the defeat that Pétain had accepted, and continue the war that Pétain thought was over. Broadcasting from London on the 18th, de Gaulle declared that: 'This war is not confined to the unhappy territory of our country. This war has not been decided by the Battle of France. This war is a world-wide war.' France still possessed her own Empire, and could unite with the British Empire that was continuing the struggle. Both could make use of the vast industries of the United States.

There could be no clearer demonstration of the importance of individual choice in the course of history. The defeat of France in 1940 was beyond doubt a decisive event in French history. But that event opened the way to two roads, not one: to end the war and accept German domination, or to fight on. De Gaulle took the harder – indeed, the apparently impossible – route, from which he emerged successfully, and eventually became President of France. Pétain took what seemed to be the sensible –

[margin note: Importance of independent choice]

indeed, the inevitable – route. He also became head of the French State for a time, but ended his days in prison.

Britain faced the same choice – to come to terms with Germany or to continue the war – but by a strange turn of events actually came to a decision earlier than France. As early as 16 May, Churchill made his first visit to Paris as Prime Minister, and was dismayed to find that defeat was in the air. Officials at the Foreign Ministry were trying to burn their archives – though on one occasion they only managed to set fire to the chimney, and the fire brigade turned up to put it out. Paul Reynaud, the Premier, was already talking (though not to Churchill) of fighting on the Loire or even shifting the government to Algeria. When Churchill returned to London on the 17th he at once asked Neville Chamberlain, the former Prime Minister, to take the chair of a committee to consider the general consequences of the defeat of France, and requested the Chiefs of Staff to examine the military aspects of the same question. Chamberlain, efficient as ever, reported to the War Cabinet the very next day, to the effect that Britain should continue the war alone until the United States came to her aid, setting up 'a form of government which would approach the totalitarian', with the government taking almost unlimited powers over all aspects of national life. A day later, on 19 May, the Chiefs of Staff had before them a draft report on 'British Strategy in a Certain Eventuality', a form of words that avoided a straightforward reference to the defeat of France. The main thrust of this draft was that, even if France collapsed, Britain could still hold out against a German attack as long as air superiority was maintained; though the Chiefs of Staff could offer no realistic idea of how the war was actually to be *won*. The final version of this report, a long and detailed document, was submitted to the War Cabinet on 27 May.

In the meantime, the War Cabinet had unexpectedly confronted the deepest issues of war and peace. On 26 May Reynaud visited London, and asked the British to consider trying to keep Italy out of the war by offering Mussolini territorial concessions, and also – though more vaguely – suggested using Mussolini to open peace talks with Hitler. For three days (26, 27 and 28 May) the War Cabinet held tense discussions on this absolutely crucial question. Lord Halifax, the Foreign Secretary, was in favour of finding out what the German terms would be and ascertaining whether they would endanger British independence – which he insisted he would not accept. At one point Churchill said that he would not join the French if they asked for terms, but 'if he were told what the terms were, he would be prepared to consider them'. But he went no further, and in the main he refused to embark on 'the slippery slope' of negotiations, from which there could be no turning back. Clement Attlee and Arthur Greenwood, the Labour members of the War Cabinet, supported him, and so, after some hesitation, did Chamberlain, leaving Halifax isolated. This resolve was strengthened by the formal Chiefs of Staff report on 27 May, which gave sound reasons for thinking that Britain could survive a German attack, as long as the RAF remained in action. Churchill also took the precaution of assessing the views of ministers who were of Cabinet rank but outside the small War Cabinet, finding them to a man determined to continue the war. By the evening of the 28th the question of making an approach to Germany was settled, not by a formal resolution, but simply by being dropped.

This was without any doubt a turning point in the history of Britain and of the Second World War. If the War Cabinet had agreed to get in touch with Mussolini to ascertain German peace terms, they could never have gone back. Once the door to negotiations had been opened, it could not have been closed, because the morale and will of government and people would have been undermined. There would have been no Battle of Britain, because it would have been lost in advance. In the event, this decision to continue the war was reached on 28 May, a full three weeks before France actually asked for an armistice. By the time France dropped out of the war, the principal British decision had already been taken, and the matter was not reopened.

So it happened that, of the three main belligerent powers, France was knocked out of the war by the end of June, except for the symbolic resistance of de Gaulle, while Britain was determined to fight on. That left Germany. What was Hitler to do with his victory? Nobody knew. The speed of the victory took everyone by surprise – the military high command, government ministries, even Hitler himself. There was no plan ready to be put into operation. For some days, Hitler behaved like a tourist, visiting the old Western Front in Flanders to seek out the places where he had served as a soldier in the First World War. On 28 June he went to Paris, arriving at 5.30 in the morning, touring the main sights and leaving by mid-morning. On 6 July he returned to Berlin by train, to be greeted by enormous crowds.

But amid the euphoria he was not sure what to do. He was baffled by Britain's refusal to sue for peace. Three times he put off delivering a speech to the Reichstag to make a peace offer to the British, and when he finally got round to it on 19 July the offer proved no more than a brief passage at the end of a long speech. He vaguely threatened to destroy Britain, and

3 After a brief visit to a defeated France, Hitler returns to Berlin on 6 July 1940. Vast crowds greeted him with a hero's welcome.

then made an equally vague 'appeal to reason', with no specific content at all. Churchill briefly wondered whether to reject Hitler's offer by resolutions in both Houses of Parliament, but decided that this would give his speech a dignity which it did not deserve. Instead, Halifax dismissed it in a broadcast that sounded rather like a sermon – he mentioned God no fewer than 17 times in a short talk. Only then did the Germans belatedly begin seriously planning for the invasion of England, Operation SEALION.

[margin note: Hitler's uncertainty wit Britain]

For a time, Hitler's uncertainty as to how to deal with Britain did not seem important. After all, Germany had already conquered a large part of Europe, and exercised a powerful influence over most of the rest. The country began to improvise plans for the economic reorganisation of the continent. In June 1940 the German Foreign Ministry sketched out an idea for a tight sphere of control in western and northern Europe, with a looser association with the Danubian states, Sweden and Finland. Goering (who was Economics Minister as well as head of the Luftwaffe) rejected these proposals, because they impinged on his own sphere of economic control, but the Economics Ministry only produced ideas for inner and outer rings of German dominance, which looked very much the same. Hitler himself referred from time to time to the economic reorganisation of Europe, on the basic theme of specialisation in the service of the German economy. Rumania, for example, was to give up its own industries and concentrate on producing oil and cereals for export to Germany; Norway would supply hydroelectric power. Sweden would provide Germany with iron ore at prices agreeable to the Germans. Occupied countries were compelled to make a profit for Germany. The French were to pay the Germans to occupy their own country, to the tune of 20 million marks per day. All occupied countries had to provide labour for Germany, at cheap rates or without pay at all.

At the same time, a new political order for Europe took shape. Germany itself now included Austria, the Sudeten areas of the former Czechoslovakia, a large part of Poland, and Alsace-Lorraine; while the Germans exercised direct or indirect rule in Bohemia-Moravia, Slovakia and the Government-General of Poland. The 'New Order' was primarily imposed by force, but it was also based on the powerful ideological appeal of Nazism, which to all appearances was now the wave of the present, and even more of the future.

All over Europe, one country after another had to confront the consequences of German military victories and the advance of Nazism. In Italy, Benito Mussolini had been a formal ally of Germany since the so-called Pact of Steel in 1939, and he now made a deliberate choice to enter the war.

[margin note: Mussolini enters war]

In September 1939 he had been forced to recognise that Italy, even after 17 years of fascist rule, was not ready to wage war. By the turn of the year little had changed, and in January 1940 Marshal Badoglio, the Chief of the General Staff, told Mussolini that Italy would not be ready for war before the end of the year, and even then would have to remain on the defensive. This would not do for Mussolini, who refused to stand by with folded arms while others made history. On 13 May 1940, only three days after the opening of the German offensive in the west, he told Count Galeazzo Ciano, his foreign minister and son-in-law, that the Allies had lost the war. Italy had already suffered enough dishonour, and he would declare war within a month. He stated that he needed a few thousand Italian casualties to secure him a place at the peace conference which he could already foresee. Ciano urged caution; generals and admirals were pessimistic; but Mussolini recklessly brushed them all aside. He simply could not afford to wait. Italy declared war on France and Britain on 10 June.

This had the immediate effect of extending the war to the Mediterranean and North Africa, thus opening a whole new theatre of operations. But in the long run, this opportunity that Mussolini was so eager to seize turned into a disaster for himself and for Italy. He thought the war was over, but it was not. He was sure he was joining the winning side, but in fact he picked the loser, and took the path to his own destruction.

Another right-wing dictator, General Francisco Franco in Spain, was more cautious. Franco welcomed the German victory in France, and appears to have been certain that the Axis powers were going to win the war. He was willing, even anxious, to join in on the German side, but he wanted to make sure of his price, which he named in September 1940 as the whole of French Morocco, part of Algeria, the French Cameroons, and some minor gains on the Pyrenean frontier with France. When Hitler went in person to meet Franco at Hendaye on the north coast of Spain on 23 October, the Spanish dictator presented a long list of the supplies and military equipment that he needed in order to enter the war, amounting to more than the Germans would or could provide. Franco wanted to join the winning side, but not yet. Meanwhile, he provided limited assistance to the Axis, and left it at that.

[margin note, handwritten: Franco more hesitant to enter war]

At the other end of Europe another dictator watched the German victories with dismay. In August 1939 Joseph Stalin had negotiated a non-aggression pact with Germany, followed by a treaty of friendship and an economic agreement. He partitioned Poland with the Germans, and provided Germany with vast quantities of oil, raw materials and foodstuffs; though always at a price, for example in ensuring Russian access to German technology and equipment. His calculation was that Germany and the western Allies would fight a long war, while he stood on the sidelines and built up the strength of the Soviet Union. He was completely taken by surprise when France was defeated and the British were driven back across the Channel, and he was left virtually alone to face a victorious Germany. Nikita Khruschev later remembered: 'He let fly with some

Stalin took whatever he could get

choice Russian curses and said Hitler was now sure to beat our brains in.' Stalin took what precautions he could. In July 1940 he annexed the Baltic republics of Estonia, Latvia and Lithuania in the north, and the Rumanian provinces of Bessarabia and Northern Bukovina in the south. As for the Germans, all Stalin could do was to play for time, to keep up the supplies to Germany, and observe the courtesies – he was prompt to congratulate Hitler on his triumphs. Germany was to be treated as a sleeping dog, and left to lie as long as possible. But the fall of France was an unexpected, and potentially disastrous, blow to the Soviet Union.

Elsewhere, various smaller European states that had so far been spared from involvement in the war had to adjust to the German victory as best they could. One case in particular was very striking, though often forgotten: that of Switzerland, a quintessential neutral and the oldest continuous democracy in Europe. On 25 June 1940, the very day the French armistice came into force, the President of the Swiss Confederation, Marcel Pilet-Golaz, addressed the nation by radio, warning the Swiss people that they must adjust themselves to the new realities. He mentioned the army only once, not to say that it would defend the country, but that it would be gradually demobilised. The whole broadcast was widely interpreted as indicating Swiss acceptance of the new authoritarian Europe. But on 18 July General Guisan, the commander of the Swiss Army, called all the officers of the rank of battalion commander or above (some 650 in all) to meet on the Rütli meadow, above Lake Lucerne, where the Swiss Confederation had been founded in 1291, and told them that they must be ready to defend the independence and liberties of their country. If attacked, Switzerland would defend itself, falling back on a National Redoubt in the mountainous southern half of the country. An order of the day to that effect was handed to every officer present, for distribution to the whole army. The message was clear. Despite the German victory over France, the war was not over, and the Swiss would defend themselves if need be. British resistance was having its effect.

Far away across the Atlantic the United States faced a much less immediate threat. The *Wehrmacht* might well have marched into Berne or Geneva, but it was not going to land at the mouth of the Potomac and advance on Washington. Even so, the defeat of France was still ominous for the Americans. If the Germans were to take control of French colonies in West Africa, it was then no great distance to Brazil and other parts of Latin America. Closer at hand, Martinique and Guadeloupe were French islands in the Caribbean which might well be open to German influence

British resistance → Swiss involvement

or even occupation. The United States took quiet precautions against this by sending an admiral to visit the French authorities on Martinique, and stationing a destroyer squadron to keep an eye on the French islands. There was another danger: what was to happen to the French fleet? The German armistice terms provided that French warships were to be disarmed at their peace-time stations, which were mostly ports under German occupation. The perilous, if distant, prospect arose of the German Navy, reinforced by French warships with German crews, disputing the control of the Atlantic. The American government was much relieved when the British partially removed this danger on 3 July by bombarding a French squadron at Mers-el-Kébir in North Africa and seizing a number of French warships in British ports.

These were comparatively limited dangers. In a wider perspective, what President Roosevelt and his military advisers had to face after the defeat of France was the possible, or even likely, defeat of Britain. They might meet this danger by direct help to Britain, but this would only end in throwing good resources away if Britain was invaded or made peace. To let Britain go, and settle for the defence of 'fortress America', trusting in the protection of the Atlantic, might be the safer course; but this would give the Germans a dangerously free hand in Europe and Africa. Indeed, even the Atlantic might not be broad enough for complete safety – if German bombers were based in the Azores they could reach the east coast of the United States, and the aircraft firm of Messerschmitt had begun work on an *Amerika-bomber* in 1939. The fall of France brought the perils of war very close to the United States.

What was a danger for the Americans was an opportunity for Japan. South-East Asia was largely made up of European colonies: the Dutch East Indies, with their resources of oil, tin and bauxite, and French Indo-China, with its important strategic position south of China, were suddenly cut off from their European bases, now under German occupation. The British colonies in Malaya, Singapore and Hong Kong were in a better position, in that Britain remained undefeated; but the British were threatened with invasion at home and could not send a strong fleet (or perhaps any fleet at all) to the Far East. All these territories therefore lay open to Japanese pressure or attack. The Japanese Army Minister at the time, Hata Shunroku, told his officials on 25 June 1940 (the day when the French armistice came into force): 'Seize this golden opportunity! Don't let anything stand in the way.' The naval staff was less confident, aware of the risks of a war with the United States, and at that stage Japan remained cautious. Militarily, Japanese forces took the limited step of occupying the northern part of French Indo-China in September 1940. Diplomatically, the Japanese concluded the Tripartite Pact with Germany and Italy (27 September), in the hope that this powerful combination would deter the United States from going to war, either against Germany on the Atlantic front or against Japan in the Pacific. Even so, the sense of a historic opportunity opened up by the crises of the European colonial powers remained strong, and was to exercise its influence over Japanese policy for many months to come.

The defeat of France by Germany in May and June 1940 marked not so much one turning point in the war as several. The torpor of the phoney war changed overnight into lightning movement. All the previous expectations that the Second World War would be, at any rate in western Europe, a replay of the First were swept away. France had lost its army, its Republican regime and its role as a great power in two months. Germany had conquered half of Europe, and Hitler had attained the peak of his career as a political wonder-worker and military genius. Britain was holding on by its fingertips, and was waiting to see whether it could survive a German assault. Countries across Europe, from Spain to the Soviet Union and from Norway to Italy, faced the consequences of the German victory and coped with the new situation as best they could. The United States awoke to the prospect that the Atlantic Ocean was not quite so broad as it had always seemed, and that Hitler's Germany was a dangerous neighbour even 3,000 miles away. In the Pacific and Far East, Japan was presented with an opportunity for expansion that eventually proved irresistible. The war was utterly changed from the limited, half-hearted conflict that began in September 1939, and the world itself was changed in ways that proved impossible to foresee.

CHAPTER TWO

'FINEST HOUR'

THE BATTLE OF BRITAIN, JULY–SEPTEMBER 1940

'The outcome of the war had already been decided. . . . Britain, however, was still not aware of it.'
(Hitler, speaking at a conference with service chiefs, 21 July 1940)

On 18 June 1940, the day after the French government under Marshal Pétain had asked for an armistice, Churchill told the House of Commons: 'What General Weygand called the Battle of France is over. I expect that the Battle of Britain is about to begin.' It appeared that the Germans thought the same. When the Franco-German armistice was signed at Compiègne on 21 June, German radio ended its description of the event with a male choir singing *'Wir fahren gegen Engelland'* ('We march against England'). The British had been warned.

The Battle of France was over, but its effects were not. The Germans had won a notable victory in the air over France, but they had paid a heavy price. During the campaign of May–June 1940 the Luftwaffe lost 1,401 aircraft – about a quarter of its total strength at the beginning of May. Moreover, the German aircrews who had fought in the Battle of France went into action again over England, often with a break of only two or three weeks, so that many of them were in almost continuous action from May to September, and some were nearing exhaustion. The RAF too suffered badly in the Battle of France. Their losses over Dunkirk alone (26 May–3 June) were 77 aircraft destroyed or damaged. Moreover, in their desperate efforts to cover the evacuation of the BEF, fighter pilots often flew four missions in a day, and they too came near exhaustion.

However, on balance, the British emerged surprisingly well from the Battle of France. The crushing military defeat in Flanders was somehow redeemed by the miracle of Dunkirk – an unexpected deliverance. Moreover, when France surrendered, and Britain lost her great continental ally, British morale remained higher than could possibly have been expected. At least in part this was because the British did not yet realise what they were up against. A wounded fighter pilot, flying back across the Channel one day in mid-June, looked down on the peaceful Dorset countryside, with a cricket match in progress in the sunshine. 'I was seized', he wrote, 'with utter disgust at the smug insular contentedness England enjoyed behind the sea barrier.' This was a harsh judgement, made in anger, but there was probably some truth in it. If so, the contentedness was about to come to an end. Dorset was soon to be in the firing-line of the air war, and its coastline figured in the German plans for the invasion of England.

As it happened, in mid-June 1940 those plans were as yet conspicuous by their absence. As long ago as November 1939 Admiral Raeder, the Commander of the German Navy, had asked his staff to examine the possibility of an invasion of England, not in any expectation that it would actually happen, but to cover himself in case Hitler raised the question. The naval staff were not enthusiastic about the idea; nor were the army and the Luftwaffe when they were consulted. At that stage nothing further was done, and it was not until 21 May 1940, with the German attack on France going well, that Raeder told Hitler for the first time about these discussions. The Führer showed no interest – he had, after all, more urgent things to think about at the time.

So it came about that at the very time when the Germans had the best chance of mounting an invasion of Britain they had made no preparations for such an operation. In early June, immediately after the evacuation from Dunkirk, Britain was almost defenceless against a landing. Some 224,000 men of the BEF had been saved, but they were tired and disorganised, and had lost almost all their equipment. Other troops were still in training and unready for battle. Even a little later, at the beginning of July, General Brooke, Commander-in-Chief, Southern Command, and so in the front line against invasion, wrote in the privacy of his diary: 'The more I see the nakedness of our defences the more appalled I am! Untrained men, no arms, no transport and no equipment.' He wondered in despair what the country had been doing in the ten months since war began. If the Germans had got across the Channel, even with a fairly small force, victory would surely have been within their grasp. But to get across the Channel needed a plan and some basic preparations – ships, barges and troops with at least a rudimentary training in amphibious warfare. But there were neither plans nor preparations, and the opportunity slipped by. A turning point in the Battle of Britain passed before the battle had really begun, and it could not be recaptured.

In the next few weeks, British land forces achieved some sort of readiness to resist an invasion. In the air, the situation was transformed. On 4 June, the last day of the Dunkirk evacuation, Fighter Command of the RAF had only 331 Hurricanes and Spitfires ready for service, with immediate reserves of 36. Just over two months later, on 11 August, there were 620 Hurricanes and Spitfires ready for service, with 289 immediate reserves – a great improvement. The British made the most of these two months; and the Germans later paid the price.

The delay arose from an uncharacteristic hesitation on Hitler's part. Even when he eventually issued a directive (Directive No. 16, 16 July 1940) for invasion, code-named SEALION, it was in curiously indecisive terms. '... I have decided to begin to prepare for, and if necessary to carry out, an invasion of England.' This lacked, as Peter Fleming observed, 'the crisp, compulsive, off-with-his-head ring' of Hitler's usual style on such occasions. The truth was that Hitler did not really think an invasion would be necessary. He expected the British to make peace. He thought that even Churchill would see sense and realise that the war was over; and if not he hoped that a 'peace tendency' would make headway – the names of Halifax, Samuel Hoare, Lloyd George and the Duke of Windsor were mentioned from time to time. Moreover, Hitler was reluctant to destroy the British Empire, which he preferred to keep intact as a stabilising factor in world affairs in readiness for his ultimate turn to the east against Russia. He envisaged invasion only as a last resort, perhaps as the death blow to a tottering structure. It was surely symptomatic that at no time did he go to the Channel coast to have a look. Napoleon had taken more trouble than that, though he still failed to grasp the full problems posed by winds and tides.

Uncertainty also plagued the military and naval staffs who had to prepare for Operation SEALION. Early plans envisaged a broad front for the landings, from Weymouth (Dorset) in the west to Margate (Kent) in the east (about 150 miles), but the German Navy quickly declared this to be impossible. The final plan, prepared between 13 and 20 August, proposed a narrower front, with seaborne landings between Worthing in West Sussex and Folkestone in Kent (about 65 miles), accompanied by an airborne attack near Ramsgate, also in Kent, by way of a diversion. The plan was for six divisions to cross the Channel in the first six days, with six more to follow in another ten days. For these landings, the naval staff

Hitler's HESITATION

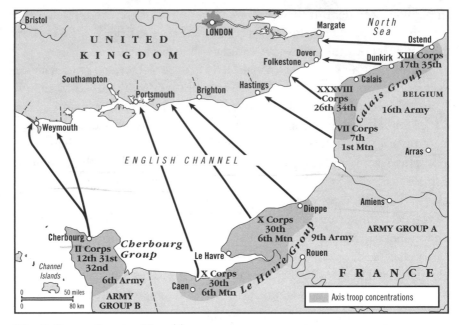

Map 2 German Invasion Plans (1).

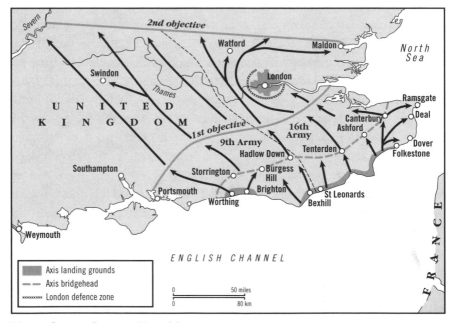

Map 3 German Invasion Plans (2).

reckoned that they would need 1,722 barges gathered from rivers or canals, with 471 tugs. Most of these vessels could make no more than 5 knots, which would mean a crossing time of about 15 hours in good conditions. The German surface fleet, which had suffered heavy losses during the Norwegian campaign (9 April–10 June 1940), was far too small to provide enough escorts for this clumsy armada. The invading force would therefore have to rely, for protection against naval attack, on mine-fields to cover its flanks, coastal artillery to provide covering fire, and above all air support. Repeatedly the staffs declared that the key to the operation was air superiority, or preferably total supremacy, to prevent any British attacks on the slow-moving barges.

Germany lacked naval fleet @ time of battle

It was an unpromising prospect, but the German Army did its best to prepare for it. Many officers used the analogy of a river crossing, which they understood, but of course the Channel was not a river. It was a tidal sea, and to make a landing on the opposite coast, the state of the tides was crucial. The Navy knew this perfectly well, and Admiral Raeder explained to his fellow service chiefs that the tides would only be favourable on 20–26 August or 19–26 September; after that the autumn weather would rule out the operation altogether. But not everyone grasped these simple facts. Mountain troops from Bavaria and Austria, included in the invasion force in order to scale the coastal cliffs, were amazed that the sea was in a different place each day when they turned out to take swimming lessons. This was only one example – minor but symptomatic – among a host of detailed maritime problems that the Germans had too little time to resolve. It is not surprising that Raeder concluded as early as 31 July 'the best time for the operation, all things considered, would be *May 1941*' (my italics). But no one could accept such utter pessimism, and preparations continued while Hitler made his mind up – or rather failed to do so.

running out of seasonal time for invasion

Since the Germans agreed that air superiority was vital to the success of an invasion, all eyes turned to the Luftwaffe and its plans. On 30 June, General Jodl, Chief of the Operations Staff of the German high command, outlined three methods for a direct attack on England: (1) air and sea attacks on British shipping and industry, and especially the aircraft industry, which would cut off the production of planes for the RAF; (2) air attacks to strike terror into the population; and (3) an invasion. Jodl believed that a combination of the first two methods would break the British will to fight, so that an invasion would be the death blow to end resistance. On the same day, Goering himself, the head of the Luftwaffe, signed a directive for the air war against England, laying down that the German Air Force would attack the RAF, its ground support systems and the aircraft industry. This in turn would create the conditions for an attack on British imports, on which the country's population depended.

In principle, these ideas were sound enough, but in practice they proved sadly defective. Goering was far too optimistic in his reckoning of how long it would take to defeat the RAF. In an order to one of his Luftwaffe Air Fleets, he assumed that it would take only four days to destroy the fighter defence of southern England, and then another four weeks to defeat the rest of the RAF. This optimism doubtless sprang in large part from the sheer confidence generated by two months of unbroken success; but it also arose from poor intelligence. For the crucial months of July, August and September, the Luftwaffe estimated the total British aircraft production to be 940, whereas the actual figure was 1,439. In October, when the daylight air battles were over, General von Waldau, the head of the Luftwaffe Operations Department, admitted that the German Air Force had underestimated British fighter strength by 100 per cent. They were also mistaken as to the quality of their opponents and the efficacy of their defensive system. A Luftwaffe intelligence paper of 16 July rated the performance of the Hurricane and Spitfire fighters far too low, and did not mention radar at all, referring lightly to 'the inadequate air defence system of the island'. Even a month later, when the Germans came to understand something of the British radar system, they did not grasp its full workings.

Buoyed up by their over-optimism, the Germans tried to do too much. On 30 June a Luftwaffe high-command directive produced a catalogue of different targets – the RAF in general, aircraft factories, ports and shipping. Over three weeks later, on 24 July, one of the Air Fleets involved in the attack on Britain set out four missions: to attain air superiority by attacks on the RAF and aircraft factories; to support a cross-Channel invasion by attacks on British warships and bomber stations; to attack ports and destroy imports; and to attack major cities to terrify the population – though at that stage terror attacks were against official German policy. Then Goering's 'Eagle Attack' directive on 2 August included attacks on airfields, ports and factories. Concentration on any one of these various objectives might well have produced results, as nearly happened at the end of August, when the Germans systematically attacked the RAF's airfields. But instead they dispersed their efforts and failed to carry anything through to a conclusion.

Against the threat of German invasion, the main line of British defence was, as it had been for centuries, the Royal Navy. When Napoleon had threatened to invade England in 1804–05, Lord St. Vincent is said to have declared: 'I do not say they cannot come. I only say they cannot come by sea.' In 1940 this remained basically true, despite the added danger of airborne landings – which was less serious than the British feared, because German airborne troops were as yet few in number. The Admiralty's plan to defeat an invasion by sea was to attack the Germans – at their points of departure, at their points of arrival, or (what was described as a 'happy possibility') while they were at sea. For this purpose, four destroyer flotillas (36 destroyers in all) were based at the Humber, Harwich, Sheerness and Portsmouth or Dover. These flotillas had cruisers in close support – as Admiral Drax, commanding at the Nore at the mouth of the Thames Estuary, put it, 'to destroy an invading force we need gunfire and plenty of it'. To these forces were added about a thousand small craft, of which two or three hundred were constantly at sea. To the north, at Rosyth in Scotland and Scapa Flow in the Orkneys, the battleships of the Home Fleet could be called on in case of need.

Such a heavy concentration of forces left the British weak elsewhere, and the Atlantic convoys suffered heavily through lack of escorts while the destroyer flotillas stood guard against invasion. But sea power did its work so well that it never had to be called on. On 31 October, when the autumn weather had brought the immediate danger to an end, Churchill formally asked Admiral Forbes, commanding the Home Fleet, for his views on an invasion, and Forbes replied: 'while we are predominant at sea and until Germany has defeated our fighter force invasion by sea is not a practical operation of war.' Admiral Raeder would have heartily agreed.

too late
for
Germany
to
invade
by sea

The safeguard of the sea was still Britain's main defence against invasion. But Forbes's proviso ('until Germany has defeated our fighter force'), which itself echoed the Chiefs of Staff's insistence that 'The crux of the matter is air superiority', hung over all British calculations. For the Navy to defeat an invasion in the face of total German mastery of the air would certainly have been very costly, and might well have proved impossible. So the ultimate key to defence against invasion lay in air power. Could the RAF prevent the Germans from securing air mastery?

The numerical odds were unfavourable for the RAF. About the middle of July 1940 the Germans had nearly 1,600 bombers and 1,100 fighters available, whereas RAF Fighter Command could muster only some 700 Hurricanes and Spitfires. It was true that the German bombers could not operate without escorts, so that the crucial battle was between the Germans' 1,100 fighters and the RAF's 700, which shortened the odds considerably. Even so, the German advantage in numbers was formidable.

The RAF's sober history of the Battle of Britain concluded that: 'On virtually every occasion that the Germans operated in force they grossly
outnumbered the defending squadrons. There were not sufficient forces
available for a reserve of fighters . . . to be kept back and used only when
the direction and strength of the enemy's attack were known.' Churchill
was right when, in the middle of the battle, he honoured 'the few': 'Never
in the field of human conflict was so much owed by so many to so few.'
(Incidentally, it is possible to put a number on 'the few'. The total of
Fighter Command aircrew who qualified for the Battle of Britain clasp on
their campaign medals was precisely 2,917.)

The odds were unfavourable, but the RAF's chances were much improved
by a double revolution in air defence in the four years before the Battle of
Britain was fought. First, Fighter Command was equipped with the Spitfire
and the Hurricane, two fast monoplane fighters, armed with eight machine
guns and powered by Rolls-Royce Merlin engines. The Spitfire proved superior in speed and performance to the best German fighter, the single-
engined Me109; the Hurricane was slower, but was sturdy, manoeuvrable,
and more numerous than the Spitfire. Both types were more than a match
for the twin-engined Me110 fighter, which often needed a fighter escort.
Second, a remarkable scientific team developed what was first called Radio
Direction Finding, but became better known as radar – a means of detecting
the approach of enemy aircraft from a distance of up to 100 miles. These
developments came only just in time, and it was particularly fortunate that
the head of Fighter Command from 1936 to 1940 was Sir Hugh Dowding,
who had gained vital experience as the head of Research and Development
at the Air Ministry. Dowding was a prosaic figure, 'careful, thorough and
thoughtful' rather than charismatic. His nickname was 'Stuffy Dowding'.
No matter – he understood perfectly how to use the new fighters and the
radar stations with which the Battle of Britain was fought. He set up a well-
organised defence system, in which radar enabled Fighter Command to
anticipate German attacks and get its squadrons into the air at the right time
and place. At a crucial point in the war, he was the unspectacular leader of a
dashing and heroic band of fighter pilots – a winning combination.

The RAF had another advantage in Ultra, the decrypts of German signals
traffic available from the code-breakers at Bletchley Park, Milton Keynes in
Buckinghamshire. This was not yet the large-scale, and sometimes decisive,
intelligence source that it became later in the war, but even so it provided a
picture of the Luftwaffe's organisation, order of battle and equipment which
was superior to the knowledge the Germans had about the RAF.

RAF = British

4 Sir Hugh Dowding, head of Fighter Command, here in civilian suit with rolled umbrella. He was the unspectacular leader of a dashing band of pilots.

These various advantages did much to make up for German numerical superiority. Even so, the air battle was to prove a close-run thing. If the balance had tilted the other way, and a victorious Luftwaffe had been able to protect a German invading army, Britain would have been left with its third line of defence – the Army. The military weakness that was so grievous in June and July was slowly made good, and in September General Brooke (by then Commander-in-Chief, Home Forces) thought there was at least a chance of success in a land battle. If so, it would have been the first victory over the German Army since the war began, and the prospect still seemed unlikely.

chance of success in Brit's land army

So both sides came back to the battle for air superiority – the Battle of Britain which Churchill had foretold. Oddly enough, it is hard to put precise dates to this famous and decisive battle. There is no clear-cut equivalent to 21 October 1805 for Trafalgar, or 18 June 1815 for Waterloo. The dates of 10 July to 31 October 1940, selected by the British Air Ministry after the war (mainly as a means of deciding who was entitled to be awarded a Battle of Britain clasp to add to their medals) were arbitrary, and corresponded to little or nothing in the course of the struggle. The most authoritative German history places the start of the battle sometime in July 1940, and fixes its close as late as 10 May 1941, shortly before the German attack on the Soviet Union.

In fact, the dates of the battle are less important in describing it than its character, which was twofold. First, the Battle of Britain was a public drama, played out in the skies over southern England, and watched by innumerable spectators on the ground. One eyewitness may stand for many. On 15 August a commuter from London was going home when his train was stopped by an air raid:

Going out on to the platform I joined a small group gazing into the sky. A diamond-shaped cluster of enemy bombers and fighters was sliding away almost overhead towards the south-east. The sky was blue and almost cloudless. There were the puffs of bursting shells, the rattle of machine guns and the tiny shapes of our own interceptor fighters darting into the swarm . . .

Second, and much more seriously, it was a hidden war of attrition, defined by aircraft losses and production, and by pilots lost and replaced – or not. This secret aspect of the struggle was hidden from the public, but was watched with acute anxiety by the British high command.

After a spell of probing and reconnaissance, the main battle began on 13 August 1940, which Goering grandly called 'Eagle Day'. His order to Air Fleets 2, 3 and 5 proclaimed: 'Operation Eagle. Within a short period you will wipe the British Air Force from the sky. Heil Hitler.' Unfortunately for the Luftwaffe, Goering was not content to issue an order of the day, but also intervened personally to postpone the morning attack at a moment when the first German planes were already in the air. Confusion ensued. One bomber force flew on while its fighter escort turned back, and suffered heavily at the hands of the RAF in consequence. In another case the bombers turned back but the fighters flew on, only to find when they reached the rendezvous that they had no one to protect. The afternoon attacks went much better, and the Germans scored a notable success in bombing the RAF airfield at Detling, near Maidstone in Kent. This was virtually undefended, and made 'a dive-bomber's dream target'. One of the ground crew wrote: 'We had been caught stone cold, airfield defences were antique and minimal. . . . The enemy carried out the entire attack undisturbed and the bombing was lethally accurate.' The station was wrecked and its commander killed, without the Germans losing a single aircraft. Fortunately for the RAF, Detling was a Coastal Command airfield, not Fighter Command as the Germans believed, but the damage showed what the Germans could achieve when they were effectively unopposed. Wiping out Fighter Command might well be feasible.

There followed a period of three and a half weeks, ending on 6 September, which witnessed the crux of the battle. The Germans began by suffering a bad defeat on 15 August, when they despatched the immense total of 1,790 aircraft (about one-third of them bombers) against Britain, flying across the North Sea from Norway and Denmark as well as across the Channel. Air Fleet 5, flying from Scandinavia, exceeded the range of Me109 fighter escorts and suffered losses so heavy that the attempt was never repeated in daylight. Air Fleets 2 and 3 mounted four vast assaults, but their formations were broken up by RAF fighters and achieved little success in their bombing attacks. In the course of the day the RAF lost 34 aircraft destroyed, but the Germans 76. That evening, the British High Command claimed 182 German planes certainly shot down, with another 53 probables – a result greeted with great enthusiasm by the British people. This wide discrepancy between claims and actuality was doubtless inevitable. No one could keep track of events in a vast and hectic air battle, and three or four RAF fighters might well have fired at a German bomber before it finally crashed. Both sides overestimated their successes, the Germans a good deal more than the British. When the true figures for German losses came to light after the war, they caused dismay and disappointment in Britain, but at the time the figures for 'kills', running sometimes into very high figures (as they did on 15 August), had a heartening psychological effect, among the RAF aircrews as well as the civilian population.

In fact, the RAF needed all the encouragement it could get. Losses of pilots and aircraft, and the sheer wear and tear of continuous action, were taking a heavy toll. Between 8 and 18 August, Fighter Command lost 154 pilots, killed, missing or badly wounded, while the training units produced barely more than one-third of that number. In the nature of things, the casualties were particularly high among the experienced pilots, including a high proportion of squadron and flight commanders, who were

[margin annotation: Claims of German loss vs actual loss]

replaced by beginners – a dangerous state of affairs. Air Vice Marshal Keith Park, the commander of 11 Group, which was in the forefront of the battle, wrote later that: 'I was worried daily from July to September by a chronic shortage of trained fighter pilots.' What this could mean in an individual case was vividly illustrated when an officer introduced a newcomer to his airfield: 'Come on in and meet 145 squadron – great chaps, both of them' – words that were deadpan at the time, and chilling in retrospect.

The crisis of men was accompanied by a crisis of machines. Again, between 8 and 18 August, Fighter Command lost 231 fighters, 30 of them destroyed on the ground. In the same few days, only 150 Hurricanes and Spitfires were produced. Fighter Command was living on its reserves. Even though, day by day, Luftwaffe losses exceeded those of the RAF, the cumulative arithmetic showed a dangerous, and potentially fatal, trend for the British.

The situation was made worse for the RAF when the Germans attacked radar stations, the eyes of the defence. On 12 August the Luftwaffe bombed five radar stations, rendered conspicuous by their tall and fragile masts, and were confident that they had all been put out of action. In fact by the next day all except one were operating again; the exception, at Ventnor on the Isle of Wight, was out of action for a full eleven days. Goering himself grew doubtful about the success of such attacks, and only two more were made.

Instead, the Germans switched their attacks to targets even more dangerous for the RAF: the Fighter Command Sector Stations. In the RAF's defensive system, fighter squadrons were ordered into the air by Group Headquarters, and then they were guided into action by Sector Stations, using radio-telephones, which the Germans could overhear. The Germans thus grasped the importance of the Sector Stations, and between 18 and 24 August they made heavy attacks on seven of the stations operated by 11 Group, which was in the front line covering the whole of southeast England. All seven were damaged, and the stations at Biggin Hill in Kent and Kenley in south London suffered very heavily. At Kenley on 18 August all the aircraft hangars except one were destroyed, and the airfield was reduced to operating two instead of three squadrons. Worse still, the Sector Operations Room was put out of action for 50 hours.

For a few days at the end of August the Germans came closer to success than at any other stage of the battle. On 31 August Fighter Command lost 39 aircraft, the highest total for any day in the battle. In a fortnight, at the end of August and beginning of September, the RAF lost 277 aircraft and the Luftwaffe 378 – the best proportional figures the Germans ever achieved. In his official despatch submitted after the war, Dowding recorded that the losses of pilots were so severe that even fresh squadrons were becoming exhausted before others were ready to take their places. At the time (on 5 September) a young Spitfire pilot wrote to his parents: 'Dear Mum and Dad. . . . For the last three days we have been at it pretty hard, and I for one am getting a wee bit tired.' In the understated language of the day, this was the clearest possible testimony to weariness. Looking back in 1991, the authors of the official German military history of the war estimated that the Luftwaffe came 'close to achieving air supremacy over Sussex and Kent'– a cautious and significant claim. Fighter Command was coming close to defeat.

But the strain was not one-way traffic. The Germans, too, were suffering the wear and tear of battle. In August the Luftwaffe lost 229 of its best fighters, the Me109s; and losses in pilots were 57 killed, 3 known to be captured and 84 missing. Goering was so worried by the casualties among officers that he ordered that bomber crews should include no more than one commissioned officer on any single sortie. After 18 August, the Germans had to withdraw the Ju87 Stuka dive-bombers from all operations over England because their losses were so high – they could achieve great success when they were unopposed, as in the attack on Kenley, but were slow and fatally vulnerable when intercepted by fighters.

At the end of August and beginning of September, the hidden battle of attrition was becoming a close-run thing. Then suddenly the picture changed, almost literally overnight. On 7 September the Luftwaffe changed its tactics and launched a tremendous daylight bombing attack on London. Nearly 350 bombers, with over 600 fighters as escorts, began to drop their bombs at 5 o'clock on a warm Saturday afternoon, causing heavy damage to the docks and starting intense fires all along the river. That evening, just after 8 p.m., another 300 bombers began a second assault, which lasted with little respite until 4.30 the next morning, causing the most tremendous fires seen in the city since the Great Fire of London in 1666. Over 400 people were killed and thousands injured. It was the beginning of what the British were to call 'the Blitz' – a misleading name, because *Blitzkrieg* meant 'lightning war', whereas what London and other cities endured in the following months was a long and grinding battle of attrition.

The day of 7 September 1940 was a tremendous one for the German Air Force. Goering and his staff turned out to have a picnic at Cap Gris Nez on the Channel coast, gazing out towards Kent and watching the

5 Goering's day out. The head of the Luftwaffe and his staff looking across the Channel, watching the vast German air assault on 7 September 1940 – the first heavy attack on London.

planes go over. The scale of the attack was enormous. Even an experienced Fighter Command pilot was astonished: 'As we broke through the haze, you could hardly believe it. As far as you could see, there was nothing but German aircraft coming in, wave after wave.' The defence was over-stretched, and German losses were only 41 in the whole day. Yet for the RAF the immediate reaction was one of relief. The assault on London meant that the battered Sector Stations were reprieved. The pressure on Fighter Command airfields slackened, and the hard-worked ground staff were spared from constant attack. As the raids on London continued, the British fighters gained an advantage from the increased distances the German planes had to fly when compared with attacks on Kent or Sussex. It became clear that the German switch to the bombing of London instead of the Fighter Command airfields was a profound mistake. Why did the Germans do it?

The most obvious reason lay in RAF bombing attacks on Berlin, which provoked Hitler into retaliation against London. It so happened that on the night of 24–25 August a few German aircraft bombed central London by mistake when they were looking for factories on the outskirts of the city. Churchill at once ordered a retaliatory attack on Berlin, which the RAF carried out the very next night. It was not much of a success. A total of 81 aircraft took part, and barely half of them found their target, causing little damage. Attacks were resumed on later nights, when weather permitted. The material results were negligible, but the psychological effects were dramatic. Goering had claimed from time to time, with Hitler's backing, that no enemy bombs would fall on Berlin; and when they did, Hitler felt bound to retaliate. In a speech on 4 September, to a cheering audience, Hitler promised reprisals; and on 7 September they came, on a devastating scale.

But this was only part of the story. At a meeting on 3 September between Goering, Albert Kesselring and Hugo Sperrle (the commanders of Air Fleets 2 and 3 respectively), Sperrle opposed the switch to London, arguing that the RAF fighters had not yet been sufficiently worn down to justify a change of strategy. Kesselring and Goering, on the contrary, maintained that Fighter Command had already been fatally weakened, and that an assault on London would bring it into the air for a final battle in which its last forces would be destroyed. (This was also the view of the Luftwaffe's Intelligence Department, which consistently underestimated the strength of Fighter Command.) Kesselring and Goering also believed that bombing attacks on London would bring about a breakdown in civil administration and strike such terror into the population so that surrender would become inevitable. As it turned out, Sperrle was right: Fighter Command, though depleted and strained, was not yet exhausted; but Goering and Kesselring made a strong strategic case to add to Hitler's instinctive desire for retaliation. The switch to London was by no means irrational.

Even so, the immediate effect of the German change in tactics was to give Fighter Command a breathing space at a crucial point in the battle. As events turned out, the breathing space amounted to a British victory. The Germans were at any rate right in one of their predictions. Fighter Command rose to the defence of London in a final battle. The trouble from the German point of view was that the battle went the wrong way. The decisive day proved to be 15 September, when the Germans launched two heavy daylight raids on London. At noon some 200 bombers, with escorting fighters, crossed the English coast and headed for London. They were met first by 21 fighter squadrons from 11 Group, which got into the air early and were ready to attack; and then by Douglas Bader's Duxford Wing, flying from the north. The German attack broke up in disorder, and achieved little. In the afternoon another 150–200 bombers, with a large fighter escort, made a second assault. They were met first by over 150 Spitfires and Hurricanes of 11 Group, and then again by the Duxford Wing with 60 Spitfires, which arrived just as the Me109s of the fighter escort were having to turn for home as their fuel ran low.

In the day's fighting, the RAF lost 26 fighters, and claimed 183 planes shot down. The true figure was only 60, but as things turned out the exaggerated claims did not matter. The true RAF victory was psychological. The Germans had hoped, and had perhaps been half convinced, that Fighter Command was all but finished. They discovered that it was not, but instead was able to mount a massed defence which broke both the formations and the spirit of the attackers. Only two days later, on 17 September, Hitler ordered the indefinite postponement of Operation SEALION. The threat of invasion was over, though the British did not yet know it. As both sides had recognised, the crux of the matter lay in air superiority; and by the 15th that superiority, at any rate in daylight, had been secured by the RAF. German daylight raids continued for a time, but in diminishing force. On the 30th, the Germans lost 48 aircraft against the RAF's 20, with very little damage to show for their efforts. Thereafter they withdrew their bombers from daylight operations. This simple fact makes 30 September as good a date as any – and better than most – to conclude that the Battle of Britain was over.

Within the battle there had been two turning points. The first was the German switch to bombing London, and the end of the attacks on Fighter Command's Sector Stations and airfields, which if continued *might* have won the battle. We must say only 'might', because it would have been open to Dowding to give up his Kentish airfields either partly or completely, and continue the fight from north of the Thames, which would have been difficult and clumsy but not impossible. The second turning point was Fighter Command's victory over London on 15 September, when the German errors about British fighter strength were finally exposed. At that point, the Germans knew they had lost, and the British knew they had won.

The battle itself was a turning point in the war. On 20 August 1940 Churchill spoke of the Battle of Britain in words that at the time were an act of faith rather than a statement of fact:

> The gratitude of every home in our Island, in our Empire, and indeed throughout the world, except in the abodes of the guilty, goes out to the

British airmen who . . . are turning the tide of the World War by their prowess and devotion. Never in the field of human conflict was so much owed by so many to so few.

It is the last sentence that has lived in popular memory, but it is the phrase about 'turning the tide of the World War' that engages our attention here. Churchill could not see the end of the story, but events were to vindicate his faith. When Richard Hough and Denis Richards came to write a history of the Battle of Britain fifty years later, they concluded that:

the passing years have only confirmed, what was hoped and thought at the time, that the Battle was one of the great turning points in World War II – a defensive victory which saved the island base and so, once Russia and the United States became involved, made future victories possible.

This was surely true. The Battle of Britain was the first defeat suffered by Germany since the war began. This went largely unobserved by the Germans themselves, because the battle did not last long, and was fought only by the Luftwaffe, with only slight casualties in terms of numbers killed. It made little impression on the German population, and by the following year was almost forgotten in the tide of greater events. But it was indeed a defeat, and was seen as such all across Europe outside Germany. The war was not over. In Spain, Franco remained strongly pro-Axis but found it safer to wait and see rather than to join in the war. Other neutrals – Portugal, Switzerland, Sweden and Turkey – were encouraged to resist German pressure. In France, crushed by defeat in June and July, resistance to German occupation began, however tentatively, to take shape. These were as yet small rocks in the broad field of German-dominated Europe, but they counted for something. It counted for rather more that the Soviet Union, badly shaken by the sudden defeat of France, was heartened by the survival of Britain. Vyacheslav Molotov, the Soviet Foreign Minister, remarked in a speech on 1 August that the end of the war was not yet in sight, and the war between the Axis powers and Britain, supported by the USA, seemed likely to intensify. The struggle between the imperialist camps, on which Stalin had been counting, was still going on, offering the chance that the Soviet Union could still gain time.

More important still was the effect of the British victory in the United States. In the short term, the Battle of Britain strengthened those who favoured American intervention in the war, and changed the minds of some of those who thought that helping Britain was a waste of effort, because the British would only lose anyway – the vivid broadcasts of the American Ed Murrow and other radio correspondents had a marked effect on public opinion. Without victory in the Battle of Britain, the confidence in British survival that led to Lend-Lease assistance in 1941 would not have been built up. In the long term, if the USA were to join in the war, for whatever reason, British survival kept open a base from which the Americans could fight Germany. To wage a war across some 4,000 miles of ocean would surely have been beyond even American ingenuity. As events in 1944 were to prove, it was just about feasible to invade France across the Channel, but to send a force across the Atlantic to land on a hostile coast would surely have been impossible.

Above and beyond all this, the Battle of Britain was a turning point for the British themselves. The RAF had won a victory over the previously all-conquering Luftwaffe in the skies over south-east England, in full public view. The results had been broadcast on the radio and published in the newspapers almost like cricket scores. A country that had not been successfully invaded since 1066 had been shaken by the German threat, but emerged convinced that it was indeed invincible. To victory in the air was later added the survival of London under continuous bombing attack. In both cases a veneer of legend was soon added to the solid core of truth. The struggle behind the scenes in the Battle of Britain, which no one could see, had been a closer-run thing than the conflict in the skies before everyone's eyes. The nerve and steadfastness of Londoners sometimes came near to breaking, especially under the very first shock of heavy bombing in the night of 7–8 September. But the legends of an invincible Fighter Command and the steadfastness of Londoners were based on fact, and established a self-belief that upheld the British people for the whole of the rest of the war, and played no small part in winning it.

There was another part of this story. The Battle of Britain was a battle of many nations. The list of Fighter Command aircrew not of British nationality comprises 13 different countries. Many were already familiar in those days – Australians, New Zealanders, Canadians, South Africans, Rhodesians; others became familiar – Poles, Czechs, Belgians, French; others were perhaps unexpected – Irish, American, Jamaican. It is often said that Britain stood alone in 1940, but in fact the British stood amidst a fellowship of nations, united against an enemy who threatened them all. This fellowship lasted throughout the war, and its creation was another turning point, moral rather than material, which helped to decide the outcome of the conflict.

The year 1940 was a time of might-have-beens. One was the possibility of a British surrender. Hitler hoped for a surrender without an invasion, and speculated on potential leaders of a peace party – Lloyd George, the Duke of Windsor, Halifax. Of these, Halifax was a non-starter – he could not bear the thought of German boots marching across his native Yorkshire. The Duke of Windsor was at the centre of much intrigue during his stay in Lisbon in August 1940. The Germans wanted him to move to Madrid, to be more under their influence. Churchill wanted to get him out of Europe and across the Atlantic, out of harm's way, and succeeded in sending him to be Governor of the Bahamas. Lloyd George was the most serious possibility as a British Pétain, and there is some evidence that the man who had won the war in 1918 was holding himself in readiness to become the man to save something from defeat in 1940. Twice Churchill tried to include Lloyd George in his government, perhaps to bind him to the policy of no surrender, but it was probably fortunate that these attempts came to nothing. In any case, victory in the Battle of Britain settled the matter. The post of a British Pétain was no longer open.

Still, there might have been at some stage a successful German invasion, and in one respect at any rate the Germans were ready. In May 1940, even before France was defeated, the Gestapo had prepared a Black Book of 2,820 names of those to be arrested when Britain was occupied. It was an oddly miscellaneous list, in which Noël Coward found a place along with Winston Churchill under the letter C. The Germans had also drawn up a 'White Book', listing people in Britain thought to be sympathetic to their cause. For their part, the British government also had a list (with only 82 names on it) of potential traitors or defeatists who were to be arrested in the event of a German invasion. As it happened, none of these lists, German or British, had to be activated.

It is natural to think of the 'might-have-been' of a German victory. But there is another possibility – that of a German defeat in an attempted invasion. The German barges might have been caught by the Navy in the open sea, and been subjected to Admiral Drax's 'gunfire and plenty of it', with disastrous results. Or perhaps German troops might have got ashore, but seen their communications cut behind them. In these ways the British might have been in the position of not suffering a defeat but inflicting one, which would have been more obvious and resounding than their actual victory in the skies above Kent. The possibility of a British triumph over the German Army on British soil is a 'might-have-been' worth speculating about. But the fact is worth more than speculation. The Germans *might* have defeated Britain in 1940, and so won the war, but they did not. Instead, Britain survived, to become the cornerstone of the coalition that eventually destroyed Nazi Germany.

CHAPTER THREE

OPERATION BARBAROSSA

THE GERMAN ATTACK ON THE SOVIET UNION, 1941

'In my view one of the basic rules of war is: don't march on Moscow.'
(Field Marshal Viscount Montgomery of Alamein, 1968)

Hitler silently abandoned his plans for the invasion of Britain on 17 September 1940, by the indirect means of postponing the date for fixing a date for the operation. Yet several weeks before this the German high command had begun to turn away from Operation SEALION and look eastward towards the Soviet Union. As early as 3 July 1940 General Halder, the Chief of the Army General Staff, began work on a plan for an attack on the Baltic states and the Ukraine. On 31 July Hitler himself told a meeting of senior commanders that he intended to smash the Soviet Union with one blow in spring 1941. Operational planning for this attack began in September, and Halder presented a complete plan to Hitler on 5 December. The Führer signed Directive No. 21 for Operation BARBAROSSA on 18 December, opening with the following sentence: 'The German Armed Forces must be prepared to crush Soviet Russia in a quick campaign even before the end of the war against England.' He thus deliberately took the risk of embarking on a war on two fronts, something which German military leaders had long sought to avoid, presumably calculating that Britain, even if undefeated, would be unable to interfere with his plans. Preparations for the invasion of the Soviet Union were then pressed forward with great speed; though in April and May 1941 there was a brief diversion of effort when Germany crushed Yugoslavia and Greece, delaying the invasion date for some time.

So it came about that in the early hours of 22 June 1941, German forces invaded the Soviet Union in one of the biggest operations in the

6 Operation BARBAROSSA. German tanks drive into Russia. Hitler gambled on a rapid advance and quick victory.

history of warfare. The attacking armies included 3,100,000 German troops, accompanied by 650,000 allies. They were equipped with 4,000 tanks, which proved to be too few; and much of their transport was provided by 750,000 horses, which proved to be too many. (Only a part of the German Army was mechanised, and in fact the Germans covered the ground to Smolensk and later almost to Moscow more slowly than Napoleon's army had done in 1812.) Hitler had no doubt that in this assault he was launching an operation which would be a decisive turning point of the war, and indeed in the history of Germany, Europe and perhaps the world. He expected a rapid and decisive success, ending in a victory parade through Moscow in August and the establishment of a German predominance over the whole of Europe which would last for generations – the Thousand-Year Reich was doubtless a figure of speech, but it represented a real intention.

The German code name for the invasion was chosen by Hitler in person: Operation BARBAROSSA, after the red-bearded twelfth-century Holy Roman Emperor Frederick I. If Hitler had been a more careful student of history, he might have reconsidered this choice. Frederick's long dispute with Pope Alexander III had ended in humiliation when he knelt to swear fealty to his opponent – three pieces of red marble were actually set in the cathedral at Venice to record the spot for posterity. Moreover, the Emperor had died during the crossing of an icy stream in Cilicia while on a crusade against Saladin. BARBAROSSA might well have been thought an ill-omened code name.

Hitler expected Operation BARBAROSSA to be a turning point, and so it proved, but not in the way he intended. The German invasion of the Soviet Union certainly changed the whole scale and nature of the war, and did much to decide its outcome. But instead of bringing about a quick and decisive German victory, it began an immense struggle on the Eastern Front which lasted for four years, from June 1941 to May 1945, and ended in the total defeat of Germany. Moreover, the war in the east opened the way for an Anglo-American invasion of western Europe which would surely have been impossible if the Red Army had not engaged the bulk of the German forces. By his attack on the Soviet Union, Hitler brought ultimate destruction upon himself and upon his country.

In some moods even Hitler seemed to fear the outcome of his enterprise. He had a premonition of misfortune in the night before the attack: 'I feel as if I am pushing open the door in a dark room never seen before, without knowing what lies behind the door.' He was well aware of the precedent of Napoleon's disaster in 1812; but even so he went ahead, leaving us still wondering why he chose to invade Russia while Britain remained undefeated.

Why did he do it? After all, he had an alternative policy ready to hand, and working well. In August 1939 Hitler and Stalin had concluded the German-Soviet Pact, which under the guise of a non-aggression treaty provided for the partition of Poland and divided other parts of eastern Europe into spheres of influence. This agreement opened the way for Hitler to attack Poland; and indeed Stalin took part in the invasion and divided Poland with the Germans. Later, in May and June 1940, Hitler was able to attack France without fear of Soviet intervention, so that he was free to concentrate almost all his forces in western Europe, leaving no more than a screen in the east. In February 1940 and April 1941 Germany and the Soviet Union concluded far-reaching economic agreements which operated very much to Germany's advantage, providing imports of foodstuffs, oil and raw materials on favourable terms. Moreover, the Soviet Union agreed to make purchases in other countries on Germany's behalf and to transport goods from the Far East by way of Vladivostok and the Trans-Siberian railway – supplies of rubber by this route were particularly valuable to the Germans. So Hitler had in place an arrangement with the Soviet Union that on any reasonable calculation worked to Germany's material advantage.

But Hitler's motives went well beyond what was reasonable or rational. He was driven largely by his ideology and beliefs. In 1952 Alan Bullock concluded in his early biography of Hitler that: 'Hitler invaded Russia for the simple but sufficient reason that he had always meant to establish the foundation of his thousand-year Reich by the annexation of the territory between the Vistula and the Urals.' Forty years later, a German historian, using the vast quantities of evidence that had come to hand in the meantime, reached essentially the same conclusion. 'Operation Barbarossa was not a campaign like those that had preceded it, but a carefully prepared war of annihilation', whose origins lay in Hitler's world view and political aims – living space, German racial superiority, economic autarky and world power. This mindset stands out in Hitler's *Mein Kampf*, in his Second Book (unpublished in his lifetime), and in his talks to Nazi and military leaders in the 1930s. The invasion of the Soviet Union drew together all the threads of his thought and inner convictions. Germany would conquer and colonise living space in the east, and at the same time destroy the Jewish-Bolshevik system. The SS were to liquidate the Jewish-Bolshevik intelligentsia, and the 'commissar order' of 6 June 1941 laid down that the political commissars attached to Soviet military units were to be shot out of hand when captured. For Hitler, BARBAROSSA was more than just another military operation. It was what the war was all about.

Hitler's insistence on putting Nazi racial doctrine into practice threw away a political weapon of potentially vital importance. As the Germans advanced in the summer of 1941 they were often welcomed by the non-Russian nationalities and by others who had suffered under Stalin's oppression. This was especially true in the Ukraine, where nationalists set up a provisional government in Lwow at the end of June 1941. One German soldier wrote with amazement: 'In every village we're showered with bouquets of flowers, even more beautiful than we got when we entered Vienna. Really it's true!' During the war of 1914–18 the Germans had made successful use of anti-Russian sentiment, and had encouraged the establishment of a Ukrainian government. But in 1941 they came as a master race. The provisional Ukrainian government was at once suppressed, and the people were condemned to be mere labourers, or often left to die of starvation. This may well have been fatal to the German cause. In Robert Service's judgement, 'If it had not been for Hitler's fanatical racism, the USSR would not have won the struggle on the eastern front. Stalin's repressiveness towards his own citizens would have cost him the war against Nazi Germany, and the post-war history of the Soviet

Union and the world would have been fundamentally different.' Indeed the Germans threw away the welcome their troops had received, and instead reaped an intense hatred.

Ideology was foremost among Hitler's motives for the invasion, but it was not alone. In the summer of 1940 he repeatedly emphasised the strategic argument that it was necessary to attack the Soviet Union in order to defeat Britain. He told a meeting of senior commanders on 31 July 1940: 'England's hope is Russia and America. If hope in Russia is eliminated, America is also eliminated. . . . Russia is the factor on which England is mainly betting. . . . Should Russia, however, be smashed, then England's last hope is extinguished.' Hitler returned to this argument repeatedly, in one form or another, in the following months, notably in a speech to some 200 generals on 30 March 1941, and in private conversation with Walter Hewel (one of his lesser-known but devoted followers) on the eve of the assault on 21 June 1941 – 'The Führer expects a lot from the Russian campaign. . . . He thinks that England will have to give in.' His arguments did not always carry conviction, and even Halder wrote in his diary on 28 January 1941: 'Barbarossa: purpose not clear. We do not hit the British that way.' Even so, it is likely that Hitler believed his own assertions, and seriously thought that Britain could be defeated in Russia.

In the background to these arguments lay another question – that of an alternative policy to an invasion of the Soviet Union. It was a truth so obvious as to be often missed that the alternative to marching on Moscow was '*not* to march on Moscow'. In that case, where were the Germans to go? There was not the slightest chance that Hitler would be content to stand still, digest the gains he had made in 1940, and consolidate Germany's position as the dominant power in Europe. He was a man in a hurry. He was afraid of an early death, either by disease or assassination, and he was convinced that only he could lead Germany to victory. He sensed that his opportunity would be fleeting, and that as time passed his enemies and potential enemies would grow stronger.

For a time Hitler considered strategies other than an invasion of Russia. He contemplated a Mediterranean campaign, drawing Spain into the war and closing the straits of Gibraltar in the west while reinforcing the Italians for an attack on the Suez Canal in the east. He thought of bringing together a vast global coalition, based on the Axis powers and drawing together Spain, Vichy France, the Soviet Union and Japan, to form a combination so formidable that it would force Britain to surrender without further fighting. He pursued these projects in the autumn and

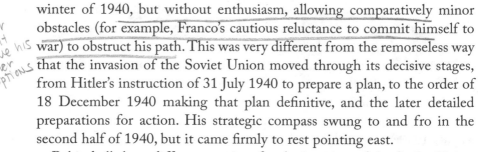

winter of 1940, but without enthusiasm, allowing comparatively minor obstacles (for example, Franco's cautious reluctance to commit himself to war) to obstruct his path. This was very different from the remorseless way that the invasion of the Soviet Union moved through its decisive stages, from Hitler's instruction of 31 July 1940 to prepare a plan, to the order of 18 December 1940 making that plan definitive, and the later detailed preparations for action. His strategic compass swung to and fro in the second half of 1940, but it came firmly to rest pointing east.

Behind all these different motives for the invasion of the Soviet Union lay a crucial assumption: that Germany could pull off a speedy victory. This was by no means unreasonable. After all, well within living memory the German Army had knocked Russia out of the war of 1914–18, and in March 1918 had imposed on the Bolsheviks the humiliating Treaty of Brest-Litovsk, which had pushed Russia back to its frontiers before the reign of Catherine the Great. The Germans had beaten Russia once, and they could do it again. This encouraging reading of recent history was reinforced by Hitler's racial and ideological assumptions. He was convinced that the Russians were an inferior race, ruled by incompetent Jews and Bolsheviks, whereas the Germans had the solid advantages of a well-educated population and a well-trained army. Hitler therefore had some plausible reasons for thinking that he could pull off his most daring stroke to date.

Hitler was confident. So was Stalin, the other player in the deadly game of German-Soviet relations. He too believed that he had done well out of the German-Soviet Pact of 23 August 1939. He told his companions at dinner that night that he had tricked Hitler, because the pact would allow the Soviet Union to build up its strength while Germany fought a long war in the west. He did not believe that war with Germany could be avoided altogether. He had read *Mein Kampf*, underlining the passages that revealed Hitler's obsession with living space in the east; so he knew what was coming. But he believed that he could delay a war with Germany by a policy of appeasement on the one hand and rearmament on the other. This cautious and apparently sensible policy was dangerously undermined by the defeat of France in June 1940. Instead of being entangled in a long war in western Europe, Hitler was left with a free hand to act as he wished.

Moreover, Stalin failed to take full advantage of the two gains he had made through the German-Soviet Pact: territory and time. The territory occupied by the Soviets in eastern Poland, the Baltic states and Rumania in late 1939 and 1940 proved of little value, and in some respects weakened the Soviet position rather than strengthened it. The fortifications along the old frontiers were abandoned, but defences along the new borders were still incomplete by the spring and summer of 1941. Similarly, the time gained was largely wasted by a double reorganisation of the Red Army. In 1939, adopting what were assumed to be the lessons of the Spanish Civil War, the Soviet high command broke up its existing mechanised corps and dispersed their tanks to support the infantry. Then, following the German victories in France in 1940, the Red Army changed its mind again and set out to restore its mechanised corps, a task that was still under way when the German blow fell in June 1941. If Stalin had tricked Hitler in August 1939, he had failed to exploit his gains by 1941.

[margin note: Stalin hadn't taken advantage of time + territory gained]

Yet Stalin could not bring himself to accept that he had failed. Above all, he failed – or rather he refused – to read the signs that he faced an imminent invasion by Germany. In the first half of 1941 reports of a coming German attack accumulated ominously. Some of these reports, it is true, came from British and American sources, and could be discounted on the ground that their purpose was to provoke hostility between the Soviet Union and Germany. But many were from unimpeachable sources among well-placed Soviet agents and reliable communist supporters. They even included, on 21 June, a warning from the Chinese communist leader Mao Tse-tung that the attack would come that very day. In addition to all these reports there was the evidence of the plain facts, on the ground and in the air. A force of three million men could not gather on the frontiers of the Soviet Union without being observed. Deserters from the German forces managed to cross the borders, bringing their news at the risk of their lives. In the air, German flights over Soviet territory could not be missed – Soviet observers reported over 2,000 between January and 10 June 1941. But to all this information Stalin turned a blind eye. He appears to have been 'completely in denial'. He knew best, and no one was likely to contradict him. The head of Soviet Military Intelligence in 1941, General Filip Golikov, knew only too well that three of his predecessors had been shot. We may safely assume that he did not wish to suffer the same fate.

[margin note: Soviets did have an idea of German attack]

Even when the invasion began, Stalin at first refused to accept the facts. At 3.30 in the morning of 22 June, General Zhukov, the Army Chief of Staff, telephoned Stalin and told him of the German assault. Stalin called a meeting of the Politburo and told his ministers that 'Hitler surely does not know'. They must get in touch with Berlin and put things right. It remains astounding that this man, who was so suspicious by nature and who had survived by trusting no one, trusted Hitler to the verge of self-destruction. He left the task of addressing the people to Molotov, who denounced the German attack as 'an act of treachery unprecedented in the history of civilised nations' – words similar to those later used by Roosevelt after Pearl Harbor in December 1941. So it came about that Stalin, in his resolute blindness to all warnings, almost delivered his country over to its enemies, and came near to presenting Hitler with the victory that he expected.

The Germans began their invasion of the Soviet Union with a three-pronged attack. Army Group North, commanded by General von Leeb and supported by the Finns, was to capture Leningrad. Army Group Centre, under General von Bock, was to advance on Moscow by way of Smolensk – the route taken by Napoleon in 1812. Army Group South, led by General von Rundstedt and including forces from Hungary and Rumania, was to invade the Ukraine and capture Kiev. It was an ambitious plan, relying on the impact of surprise and speed to bring about the collapse of the Soviet forces and the Soviet state. In fact it was a gamble, and Hitler was uneasy in his less confident moments. So was Joseph Goebbels, who confided a curious mixture of feelings to his diary. On 22 June he wrote: 'A glorious, wonderful hour has struck, when a new empire is born. Our nation is making her way up into the light.' But on the 23rd: 'We shall win. We must win, and quickly. The public mood is one of slight depression. The nation wants peace, though not at the price of defeat, but every new theatre of operations brings worry and concern.'

At the start of the battle it seemed that the Germans might well win quickly. The Luftwaffe achieved complete mastery of the air. Most of the Soviet air force was caught on the ground – one of the results of Stalin's refusal to see what was coming. In the first week the Germans destroyed some 1,800 Soviet planes, at the cost of only 330 of their own. Soviet troops on the ground suffered from 'aeroplane panic', in much the same way as some of the French had suffered from 'tank panic' in May 1940. On 3 September the head of the Belorussian Communist Party reported to Stalin that: 'The retreat has caused blind panic. . . . The soldiers are tired to death, even sleeping under artillery fire. . . . At the first bombardment, the formations collapse, many just run away to the woods, the whole area of woodland in the front-line region is full of refugees like this. Many throw away their weapons and go home.' Indeed, the German armies won immense battles of encirclement, surrounding Russian forces by sheer speed and power of manoeuvre. They took something like 750,000

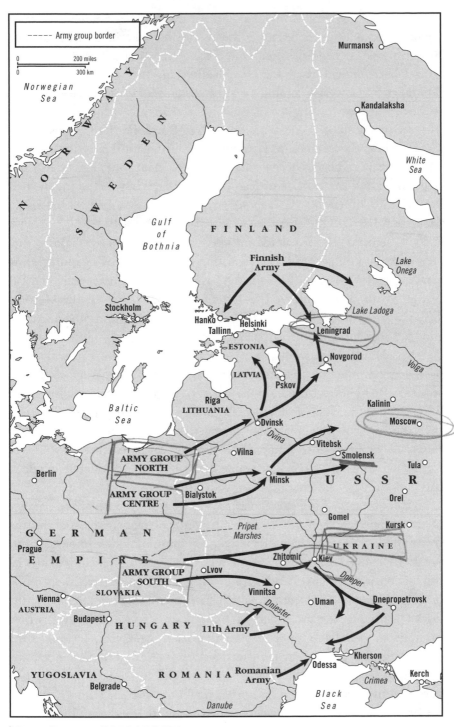

Map 4 Operation BARBAROSSA.

prisoners on the central front by the end of the battle of Smolensk in mid-August, and another 660,000 in the battle for Kiev in mid-September. Soviet losses in men killed amounted to about 2,000,000 by the end of September. Army Group Centre, heading towards Moscow, advanced 440 miles in six weeks, coming to within 220 miles of the capital.

At the end of July Hitler insisted on a change of plan, checking the advance on Moscow, and moving one of von Bock's Panzer Groups northwards to help the advance on Leningrad, diverting another to the south to capture Kiev. The drive on Moscow was not resumed until mid-September, and this change of plan may well have lost the Germans their best chance of taking the capital – one of the 'might-have-beens' of Operation BARBAROSSA.

What is certain is that while the Germans won immense victories and captured vast numbers of prisoners (often the fatal sign of a disintegrating army), the Russians still held on. The Red Army did not break, and the Soviet government continued to function. General Halder, the German Chief of Staff, was at first carried away by the exhilaration of victory, and thought on 3 July that the campaign had been won in the first two weeks. But by 11 August he thought otherwise. He began to realise that the Germans had underestimated the Russian reserves of manpower. It was true that Russian infantry divisions were not as good as German divisions. 'But they are there', wrote Halder. 'And if we knock out a dozen of them, then the Russian puts up another dozen.' At the same time the Germans too were suffering losses, and some Panzer divisions in Army Group Centre were down to ten serviceable tanks. As one officer remarked: 'If this goes on we shall win ourselves to death.'

The endurance of the Russian armies arose from the desperate courage of the troops themselves, backed up by ferocious discipline. Behind the front line lay the sheer size of the country and its hidden resources. The Germans had failed to grasp the scale of the manpower and industrial production available in the Urals and Siberia. These resources had to be organised and brought into action, which was the achievement of the Soviet central government and of Stalin himself, on whom the whole machinery depended. This was by no means a foregone conclusion. At the end of June it appears that Stalin suffered an acute crisis of morale. On the 29th he retreated to his dacha at Kuntsovo and isolated himself for two days. On the 30th Molotov and other members of the Politburo went to see him, and he was afraid that they had come to arrest him. In fact they had come to encourage him and stiffen his resolve. What exactly happened is not clear, but the upshot was a restoration of Stalin's nerve, which never seriously wavered again.

The first public sign of this change was seen in Stalin's broadcast to the people on 3 July. He opened with an appeal to 'Comrades! Citizens! Brothers and Sisters!' He stressed the importance of having friends and allies such as Britain and the United States – a departure from the communist line that all capitalist states were enemies of the Soviet Union; and in moving words, he spoke of 'a patriotic war of all the people'. John Lukacs has summed up the effects: 'Russians and other peoples of the Soviet Union responded to what seemed a patriotic call issued by their leader, his first clear and strong encouragement since the war had started, more than ten days before.'

Under this new impulse from the top the resources of the country were mobilised. Some five million reservists were called up, and nearly 200 new divisions were formed – the divisions that surprised and dismayed Halder. On the central front, Volunteer Divisions were raised to defend Moscow: poorly trained and ill-equipped, they died in tens of thousands, but they slowed the German advance and bought time.

The German high command had gambled on speed, and had counted on winning the war in six to eight weeks. But by the end of August ten weeks had passed; the Germans had won immense victories, but the Russians had held on, fighting with a tenacity that could not be overcome. The Germans had reckoned that the war in the east would be decided in a few weeks. It was, but it was decided against them. This was the first turning point of the campaign. The hope for a short war had come to nothing.

The Germans had failed to win a short war, but they still hoped to win a longer one. They again concentrated their main forces on the central front, and resumed their advance on Moscow. On 16 September 1941 von Bock, commanding Army Group Centre, issued a directive for the capture of Moscow, Operation TYPHOON. He mustered two million men and three Panzer Groups for this assault, which began on 1 October. By the 13th they had reached the 1812 battlefield of Borodino, where the Russians defended the old Shevardno redoubt with great courage. The first snow fell on 7 October, earlier than in 1812, and it then melted, producing a particularly glutinous mud. There were few metalled roads, and the dirt tracks that carried the German supplies became almost impassable. The Luftwaffe was forced to operate from advanced airfields that were mere strips of mud. Yet despite these difficulties the Germans still struggled on towards Moscow.

On the other side, Stalin was at one stage so anxious that on 13 September he appealed to Churchill to send 25 or 30 British divisions

7 Snow fell early in the winter of 1941, then melted into heavy clogging mud. German horse-drawn transport struggles to get through.

to help on the Russian front, either by way of Archangel in the north or across Persia in the south – an admission of weakness so dire that it can only have arisen from a sense of desperation. Yet Churchill could only refuse. The appeal simply could not be met. The British had neither the troops nor the ships to transport them The Russians had to shift for themselves, and in mid-October they almost broke.

On 15 October Stalin held a high-level meeting, which decided that large parts of the Soviet government, and all foreign embassies, were to leave Moscow at once for Kuibyshev, on the Volga. Officials began to burn papers. Lenin's mummified body was removed from the Kremlin and sent to safety in a school well to the east of Moscow. The next morning, the 16th, the people of Moscow woke up to find that there were no buses, trams or metro trains running. There were no newspapers; factories and bread shops were closed; and there were no police on the streets. In this eerie emptiness, panic broke out and thousands of people fled from the city as best they could. Stalin saw the crisis and responded quickly. He ordered martial law to be imposed in Moscow, and stationed NKVD troops around the city, to defend it against the Germans from the outside and if necessary against defeatists within. He also decreed that the following day transport had to be restored and the bread shops reopened; to make doubly sure, he ordered the Army to set up field bakeries in the city.

Moscow cleared out

The panic passed, and was little known outside Moscow itself. But the Germans still closed in on Moscow, and within a few days the question arose as to what to do about the ceremonies that usually marked the anniversary of the Bolshevik Revolution. Stalin insisted they should not be cancelled, and on 6 November the formal commemoration was held, though it took place underground at the Gorky Street Metro Station. Stalin declared that they were fighting a war of defence and liberation, and in a remarkable passage claimed the Soviet Union was not alone but was supported by Britain and the United States, countries that were capitalist but also democratic. This meant victory was certain, because the three countries together could out-produce Germany – a prophecy that was eventually fulfilled. Next day, again at Stalin's insistence, the traditional military parade was held in Red Square, despite the danger of German air attack. The Red Army found 28,000 men and two tank battalions for the march-past, and in a gesture of defiance they were ordered to go straight from Red Square to the front. It was a striking piece of theatre and prop-aganda, and there could have been no better antidote to the panic only three weeks earlier.

The parade was magnificent, but it could not of itself remove the German threat to Moscow. On 15 November the Germans began a fresh offensive – the last throw of Operation BARBAROSSA – and their forward units actually came within sight of Moscow. At first they were helped by the severe cold, which froze the ground and allowed their tanks and vehicles to move again. But soon the frost and renewed snowfalls took a disastrous toll. A German Army chaplain wrote in his diary: 'Everything round about is clad in white and all the time you are haunted by the thought that a snowstorm may bury every trace of a road. It is this that makes the Russian winter so horrible.' Engines and weapons froze and became useless. Only a few of the troops had been issued with adequate winter clothing, and most had to improvise as best they could. Von Bock, commanding Army Group Centre, concluded that the time had come to abandon the attack and prepare defensive positions for the winter. Von Rundstedt, commanding in the south, agreed. But on 1 December Hitler intervened in person to stop what he held to be defeatism. He dismissed

8 An act of defiance. The military parade marking the anniversary of the Bolshevik Revolution was held as usual on 7 November 1941. Afterwards these troops marched straight off to the battle-front.

von Rundstedt at once, and von Bock shortly afterwards; and prepared for a battle of wills.

But hidden from German view the tide was about to turn. For some time, and in complete secrecy, the Soviet high command had been preparing a counter-offensive, which began on 5 December and was extended on the 6th. The Germans, who did not think that their opponents had any substantial forces in reserve, were taken by surprise and were driven back, in some places as far as 30 miles. Even Hitler had to change his mind, and on the 8th issued a directive to go on to the defensive on a more tenable front. It is true that later that month he ordered fanatical resistance to prevent any further retreat, with a surprising degree of success. Even so, the Soviet counter-offensive on the 5th and Hitler's directive on the 8th marked the end of the great German invasion of the Soviet Union. BARBAROSSA had been tried, and had failed. The Germans were to attack again in 1942, but only on one front, in the south. They could not repeat the all-embracing assault of 1941; and in the meantime their enemies had grown stronger.

The significance of these events between June and December 1941 cannot be overstated. The German achievement had been immense, but not enough. They won one victory after another. They took 3,300,000 prisoners in the six months between 22 June and the end of the year. The Soviet armies lost about three million dead, and the Germans only 302,000. Even so, the German figure amounted to one-tenth of the forces they had committed at the start of the campaign; and when the wounded, prisoners and missing were added, the total reached over 900,000, or nearly one-third of the troops involved. In cold blood, and in terms of sheer numbers, the Russians were better able to absorb their losses than the Germans. German reserves were fewer, and above all they could never replace the quality of the army they had launched into Russia in June 1941. By contrast, in the last stages of the campaign, from October to early December 1941, the Red Army was able to commit no fewer than 99 fresh divisions in the Moscow area; and at the same time they brought new tanks and guns into action. It is true that they proved unable to drive the Germans out of Russia in 1942, as Stalin briefly hoped at the turn of the year. But the Soviet armies had survived, and their survival decided the future pattern of the war. The failure of BARBAROSSA was the crucial military turning point of the whole of the Second World War.

That was not all. The political impact of BARBAROSSA was immense. It was felt almost instantaneously in London, when the Prime Minister Winston Churchill broadcast on the radio after the nine-o'clock news on 22 June. Churchill was well-known as an opponent of communism, and he refused to unsay anything he had said in the past about the communist regime in Russia. But he declared:

> We have but one aim and one single, irrevocable purpose. We are resolved to destroy Hitler and every vestige of the Nazi regime. From this nothing will turn us – nothing. . . . Any man or state who fights on against Nazism will have our aid. Any man or state who marches with Hitler is our foe. . . . It follows therefore that we shall give whatever help we can to Russia and the Russian people. We shall appeal to all our friends and allies in every part of the world to take the same course . . .

For some time the promised aid to Russia amounted to little. Britain had little war material to spare, and the routes to Russia were long, and, in

[handwritten margin note: Russians could absob losses greater than Germans]

the case of the Arctic convoys, extremely hazardous. Even so, Churchill's instant declaration of support for Russia marked a turning point – in British policy, for the Soviet Union, and in the war itself. From that point onwards, the war against Germany was waged by a powerful alliance – dogged by difficulties and suspicions, it is true, but in the long run steadfast.

The position of the United States in what eventually became the 'Grand Alliance' was particularly difficult in 1941. Until December that year the United States remained neutral. Inside the country anti-communist sentiment was strong, and there were substantial religious and national groups (notably the Polish-Americans) who were bitterly hostile to the Soviet Union. In these troubled circumstances, and also through an ingrained political caution, President Roosevelt reacted more slowly and carefully than Churchill had done. He waited for four months, until 7 November 1941, before he declared the Soviet Union eligible for Lend-Lease aid; and even then the actual despatch of material began slowly. Despite this caution, the outline of what was to become the three-power alliance between Britain, the United States and the Soviet Union appeared within a few months of the German invasion of the USSR. For his part, Stalin acknowledged, in his speeches on 3 July and 6 November, the value of having allies and friends like the British and Americans. A crucial element in the shape and conduct of the war thus emerged, and went on to play a vital part in the defeat of Nazi Germany.

Another political transformation took place in the position of the Communist Parties, especially in Europe. At the end of August 1939 the conclusion of the German-Soviet Pact had shaken party members, who for the past few years had thrown themselves into the struggle against fascism and Nazism. After a period of uncertainty, discipline and loyalty had prevailed, and most communists had accepted the fact of cooperation between the USSR and Nazi Germany; and some had even on occasion agreed to collaborate with the Germans. This uneasy state of affairs was transformed by the German attack on the Soviet Union. Almost overnight the Communist Parties became the leaders of resistance to Nazi Germany. Their discipline, ruthlessness and experience in clandestine organisation equipped them admirably for resistance activity in occupied countries. In France, Yugoslavia and Italy the communists emerged as resistance forces on a large scale; and everywhere the Communist Parties, even when weak in numbers, enjoyed the reflected glory of the Soviet Union's struggle against Germany. It was after all the *Red* Army that won victories on the

Eastern Front, and the communist regime that could claim credit for leading the people and creating a vast war machine. Moreover, as the war went on, Stalin increasingly became a hero and a figurehead in the whole Allied war effort. By 1945 the communists had acquired a prestige that was in some respects to last for many years to come, and to exercise a powerful influence on post-war European politics.

Operation BARBAROSSA also transformed the whole nature of the Second World War in ways that only became clear with the passage of time. Hitler had declared he would wage a war of annihilation in the East, and it became apparent that this annihilation was to be carried out against prisoners of war and against the Jews.

From June to December 1941 the Germans took 3.3 million Soviet prisoners of war. Most were dead by the spring of 1942. During the whole war on the Eastern Front, the Germans captured some 5.7 million prisoners, of whom no fewer than 3.3 million, or 58 per cent, died in captivity – some were killed deliberately, while others died of starvation, neglect or ill-treatment. Some were simply kept in barbed-wire enclosures and left to fend for themselves, with fatal results. (The treatment of British and American prisoners of war was completely different, and only 3.6 per cent died in German captivity.) On the other side, the Soviets treated their German prisoners just as badly. On the Eastern Front, the rules for the treatment of prisoners of war established by the Geneva Convention of 1928 (which in any case the Soviet Union had never ratified) were largely disregarded. This return to barbarism marked a turning point of a particularly grim kind in the history of the Second World War, and in the history of war itself.

Another act of extreme ferocity was the massacre of Jews in the Soviet Union during the second half of 1941. In the history of the Holocaust, so much attention has been concentrated on the Wannsee Conference in January 1942 and the order for the Final Solution that it is often forgotten, or simply not known, that numbers of Jews estimated at somewhere between half a million and a million were killed in the Soviet Union before the Wannsee Conference even met. These events included two particularly horrifying massacres at Babi Yar in Kiev in September and at Odessa in October 1941. The slaughter was mainly carried out by the SS, organised in special task forces (*Einsatzgruppen*) which followed the German armies, but also sometimes by the Army itself and by allied forces – Rumanian troops took part in the Odessa massacre. Thus the war on the Eastern Front set in motion the destruction of European Jews, which was later pursued systematically and ruthlessly in the death camps. This was another, almost inconceivable, turning point in the history of the Second World War.

Hitler intended Operation BARBAROSSA to be a decisive turning point in the war through a rapid and total military victory over the Soviet Union. Instead, the campaign produced three military turning points, all contrary to Hitler's intentions. First, the Germans failed to secure a quick victory – by the end of August 1941 they had scored immense successes, but the Russians still held on. Second, between September and November the Germans made a great attempt to reach Moscow, but fell just short of their objective. Third, in December the Russians themselves launched an offensive which took the Germans by surprise and marked a new stage in the war on the Eastern Front – for the first time the Red Army took the initiative and drove their enemies back. These military turning points were accompanied by a political turning point of the highest significance: the emergence of the Grand Alliance between the USSR, Britain and the USA, which was eventually to win the war. The contrast between June and December 1941 was complete.

The BARBAROSSA campaign ended with a remarkable coincidence of dates. The Russian offensive to drive the Germans back from Moscow began on 5 December 1941. On the 7th the Japanese attacked the Americans at Pearl Harbor, heralding another turning point and change in the scale and scope of the war.

CHAPTER FOUR

PEARL HARBOR, DECEMBER 1941
THE WAR BECOMES A WORLD WAR

On 9 December 1941 Vere Hodgson, living in London and keeping a diary for Mass-Observation, recorded the events of the previous day with a modest degree of emphasis. 'We are now at war with Japan – and the Whole World is in it', she wrote. 'Listened to the Midnight News on Sunday, after they told us at 9 p.m. that American bases in the Pacific had been bombed. Studied the map of the area, found Hawaii, and it looked so far from Japan – but we had forgotten Aircraft Carriers.' The commander of the Japanese aircraft that had taken off from those very carriers to attack the American base at Pearl Harbor on 7 December was almost equally matter-of-fact in his account of events:

I continued to watch the sky over the harbour and activities on the ground. None but Japanese planes were in the air, and there were no indications of air combat. Ships in the harbour still appeared to be asleep, and the Honolulu radio broadcast continued normally. I felt that surprise was now assured, and that my men would succeed in their mission.

In Washington a State Department official, Breckinridge Long, was more deeply stirred:

Sick at heart. I am so damned mad at the Navy for being asleep at the switch at Honolulu. It is the worst day in American history. They spent their lives in preparation for a supreme moment – and then were asleep when it came. At the Defense Communications Board this morning I learned of the extent of our losses – and it is staggering.

These very different diarists seized on crucial points about Pearl Harbor: the role of aircraft carriers; Japanese efficiency; and American anger. All contributed to the making of what was undoubtedly a turning point in the war and indeed in world history. How did events of such far-reaching importance come about?

In 1931, ten years before the dramatic events at Pearl Harbor, Japanese forces had occupied Manchuria, a northern province of China, and organised it as a puppet state under the name of Manchukuo, exploiting its resources of coal and rice. In the next few years, Japanese troops had pushed southwards towards Peking, sometimes clashing with Chinese forces. One such incident occurred on 7 July 1937, near the Marco Polo Bridge outside Peking. It was a minor affair – shots were fired but no one was hurt, and the local Japanese and Chinese commanders quickly agreed on a ceasefire. The episode might easily have been forgotten, along with others like it; but in fact it escalated into a major conflict. The Chinese Nationalist leader, Chiang Kai-shek, seized on the incident as an opportunity to show his firmness by taking a stand against the Japanese; while the Japanese forces in Manchuria (the Kwantung Army), were equally determined to assert their own authority. The Japanese government in Tokyo was by no means eager to become involved in an adventure in China, which would be easy to get into but hard to get out of; but they had no effective control over the Kwantung Army, which took matters into its own hands. By December 1937 the Japanese had captured Nanking, then acting as the capital of China, committing atrocities against the civilian population which were widely reported in the foreign press.

Despite its reluctance to become involved in China, the Japanese government did nothing to stop these attacks, and instead took the lead in a grandiose declaration of Japanese aims. On 3 November 1937 the Prime Minister, Fumimaro Konoe, proclaimed the establishment of a New Order in East Asia, in which Japan, Manchukuo and China would together form a political, economic and cultural bloc. A few days later Japan renounced the principle of the 'open door' policy (that is, equal access to markets and trade), much favoured by the Americans, and put in its place a new policy of economic self-sufficiency for Japan and its sphere of influence. In January 1938 Konoe announced that Japan would no longer deal with Chiang Kai-shek's government and would instead wait for a new Chinese authority to take its place; but by March the Japanese had lost patience and set up their own provisional government of China. Chiang for his part remained defiant, setting up a new capital in Chungking, deep in the interior, and refusing either to resign or come to terms with the Japanese.

In the next two years, by the end of 1939, the Japanese occupied the whole north-eastern quarter of China, together with all the major ports. But they could not clinch their victory, and instead found themselves bogged down in a war that sometimes absorbed up to a million troops, but which they could neither win by force nor end by negotiation.

This Japanese invasion of China was not seriously opposed by other powers. The Americans were at the height of their commitment to isolation and neutrality. In May 1937 Congress passed a permanent Neutrality Act, embodying in law a widespread and popular resolve not to become involved in any future war. With regard to China, the American government adopted a lofty pose of refusing to recognise any territorial changes brought about by force, but in practice did very little to oppose such changes by deeds. In July 1939 President Roosevelt took a step toward the imposition of trade sanctions against Japan, by giving notice that the USA would not renew the 1911 trade treaty between the two countries; but this amounted to only a distant and uncertain threat. Among the European powers with Far Eastern interests, Britain and France were heavily preoccupied with the growth of German power, and were not anxious to court further trouble in the Far East. The Soviet Union was in the grip of Stalin's great purges and not disposed to take unnecessary risks; though when the Japanese ventured into the Soviet sphere of influence in Outer Mongolia, the Russians drove them back in a series of battles around Nomonhan (July–September 1939). But this was an exceptional event; and for the most part the outside powers stood by while Japan occupied large parts of China.

The upshot of all this was that by the end of 1939 Japan was heavily committed to the war in China, but had failed to win it. For both sides, Japanese and Chinese, the conflict was a matter of prestige as much as material interest, and all the more difficult to deal with for that.

Then in the summer of 1940 Japan was suddenly presented with a new opportunity. Far away in western Europe, the Germans defeated the Netherlands and France, and to all appearances were on the verge of invading Britain. These countries possessed extensive colonies in the Far East (the Netherlands East Indies, French Indo-China, and British territories in Hong Kong, Malaya, Singapore and Burma), all of which were now open to Japanese pressure and ill-defended against Japanese attack.

The Japanese seized on this new situation to try to finish the war in China by cutting off Chiang Kai-shek's government from all foreign assistance. On

Map 5 Japanese Occuption of Parts of China.

19 June 1940 Japan presented the British with a demand to close the Burma Road, which carried supplies across Burma into China. The British asked the USA whether they could count on American military support if they refused the Japanese demand, and were told that they could not. Britain therefore agreed to close the Burma Road, though only for a three-month period from 17 July. The Japanese then moved to close off communications into China through French Indo-China. On 11 September they required Admiral Decoux, the French Governor-General, under what amounted to a threat of war, to allow Japanese troops to occupy the northern part of the colony, and the Japanese air force to use air bases there. The French had little choice but to accept, and the Japanese moved in.

A few days later, on 27 September, Japan formally threw its lot in with the Axis powers by signing the Tripartite Pact with Germany and Italy, promising mutual aid if any of the signatories was attacked by a power not yet involved in the European war or the 'China Incident' – which in effect meant the USA. In the event, the British and Americans were not intimidated by the new diplomatic line-up. Buoyed up by their victory over the Luftwaffe in September 1940, the British government announced on 8 October that the Burma Road would reopen on 18 October, three months to the day after it had been closed. At the same time, the United States replied to the Japanese occupation of northern Indo-China by forbidding the export to Japan of all scrap metal, and of petroleum suitable for use as aviation fuel, an embargo that was more serious than might appear at first sight, because scrap metal was an important source of supply for the Japanese steel industry.

There for a time matters rested. The next Japanese move was a diplomatic one, to improve their relations with the Soviet Union. On 13 April 1941 the two countries concluded a treaty, with Japan undertaking that the country would remain neutral if the USSR became involved in a war with Germany. Japan also undertook to respect the territorial integrity of Outer Mongolia, and in return the Soviet Union accepted the Japanese occupation of Manchuria. This was a useful agreement for the Japanese, taking another step towards the diplomatic isolation of China and covering their rear if they chose to expand to the south.

But everything was suddenly plunged into uncertainty when Germany attacked the Soviet Union on 22 June 1941, taking Japan by surprise. The Japanese government and high command hastily took stock of their options. One was to denounce their recent treaty of neutrality with the USSR and join Germany in attacking the Russians. Another was to maintain the treaty, and move southward to secure the resources of the Dutch

East Indies and Malaya. Finally, they might take a completely different line and try for peace with China and an agreement with the United States; though this ran so counter to basic Japanese thinking that it was surprising that it was even considered.

At this time, a body called the Liaison Conference, made up of members of the Inner Cabinet and of the military and naval staffs, had become the principal forum for the discussion of Japanese foreign policy, making recommendations to the Imperial Conference, which was sometimes attended by Emperor Hirohito in person, and which took final decisions. The military and naval staffs were well represented at the Imperial Conference, and usually carried more weight than the Foreign Ministry. It was a meeting of the Imperial Conference on 2 July 1941 that reached a crucial decision on the next step after the German attack on the Soviet Union. The Foreign Minister, Yosuke Matsuoka, proposed to join the Germans in their assault on Russia, but gained no support; and Stalin was thus saved from what might have been a fatal blow. Instead, the Imperial Conference decided to move southward, towards the oil of the Dutch East Indies; and to that end they began by occupying southern Indo-China. On 14 July 1941 the Japanese demanded permission from the Vichy government in France to occupy the southern part of Indo-China – they had already occupied the north since 1940. The French, in face of superior force, had little choice but to comply. The first Japanese troops landed unopposed on 28 July.

The American response was surprisingly swift and severe. On 25 July, even before the Japanese went ashore, the United States announced the freezing of all Japanese assets in the country, to take effect the following day. It is not absolutely clear how Roosevelt intended to apply this measure, which stopped short of a complete embargo on all oil sales to Japan, as advocated by Henry Stimson, the Secretary for War. In principle, the Japanese were still free to apply to the USA for an export licence for oil, and then apply for another licence to unfreeze dollars to pay the bill – a cumbersome and humiliating procedure which they were unlikely to use. In the event, the United States Economic Defence Board took matters into its own hands, and imposed a total ban on the export of oil to Japan, of which it appears that Roosevelt remained ignorant until September, when it was too late to change tack. The final upshot, however arrived at, was an embargo on the export of oil to Japan. Britain and the Netherlands rapidly imposed a similar embargo, leaving Japan with nowhere to buy oil, and dependent solely upon its stocks.

This was a remarkable change of policy by the United States. For some four years the Americans had for all practical purposes accepted Japanese expansion, first into large parts of China, and then in 1940 into northern Indo-China. The American government had complained about Japanese atrocities and waxed indignant when the Japanese had attacked an American gunboat on the Yangtse River; and in 1940 Roosevelt had imposed limited economic sanctions on Japan. But now, suddenly, the United States had imposed a potentially ruinous economic sanction, under which Japan would simply run out of oil in two years or less. What had happened?

One answer was that in late September 1940 American cryptanalysts had broken the principal Japanese diplomatic code by a method so remarkable that Roosevelt himself gave it the code name MAGIC. Those few American leaders who had access to the secret could now read all important Japanese diplomatic telegrams, which shone a sharp but restricted beam of light on Japanese policy. The decrypts tended to reveal only decisions, and not the process of argument and discussion that had preceded them, and therefore conveyed an impression of a single-minded Japanese policy, without disclosing the frequent disagreements which lay in the background. This impression had a strong influence on the severe American reaction to the occupation of Indo-China.

But this was not the whole story. Secret intelligence, however high its quality, is always fitted into a wider picture, made up of existing ideas, prejudices and instincts – maps in the mind, which are every bit as important as those in the atlas. By mid-1941 the maps in the minds of American leaders showed a Japan that had been expanding for a long time, and was in alliance with the aggressive power of Nazi Germany. The very fact that the United States had reacted only cautiously and mildly to Japanese conquests in China between 1937 and 1940 became in itself a reason to respond firmly when the Japanese moved into southern Indo-China in July 1941. Indo-China was America's anti-appeasement moment, the time to draw a line and call 'enough'. The work of the code-breakers reinforced this mood, but did not create it.

In this growing rivalry between Japan and the United States, each underrated the other. The Japanese never believed that the Americans had the ability to crack their diplomatic code. The Americans for their part did not believe that the Japanese had the capacity to carry out more than one large-scale naval operation at once. In Britain, the Foreign Secretary Anthony Eden referred to Japan in September 1941 as 'this probably over-valued military power'. Alas, within six months this 'over-valued military power' was accepting the British surrender at Singapore. The British Ambassador in Tokyo, Sir Robert Craigie, warned his government that to underestimate Japanese strength and resolution was 'about the worst mistake that we and the Americans can make'. But they made it.

In August 1941 Japan and the USA were still willing, at least in principle, to pursue negotiations in search of an agreement. The Japanese suggested a personal meeting between Konoe and Roosevelt, and a rendezvous in Hawaii. Roosevelt replied encouragingly, and proposed Jumeau, in Alaska, as the meeting place. Eventually nothing came of this idea of a summit meeting, and instead negotiations were carried on through the Japanese Embassy in Washington, in conversations between the Ambassador (Admiral Nomura) and the Secretary of State, Cordell Hull.

The negotiators had a difficult task, because their basic positions were far apart, and neither side had the will to bridge the gap. On 6 September 1941 the Imperial Conference set out Japan's minimum terms, which had been under discussion since mid-August. These were: (1) the USA and Britain must stop aiding Chiang Kai-shek in his war against Japan; (2) the USA and Britain were not to establish military bases in China, Thailand or the Dutch East Indies; and (3) the Americans and British must restore trade relations with Japan. In return, Japan would agree to undertake no further military expansion, and to withdraw its troops from Indo-China when a just peace in Asia had been established – whatever that might mean. To this already formidable list of demands, the Army Chief of Staff, General Sugiyama, insisted on the maintenance of three further principles: the Japanese alliance with the Axis powers; the securing of the Greater East Asia Co-prosperity Sphere; and the maintenance of Japanese troops in China.

On the American side, Cordell Hull had laid down as early as April 1941 four fundamental principles: (1) respect for the territorial integrity and sovereignty of all nations; (2) non-interference in the internal affairs of other countries; (3) equal commercial opportunity for all states; and (4) respect for the territorial status quo, unless changed by peaceful means. Hull adhered to these principles in his conversations with Nomura, and on 26 November added for good measure a final 'Ten Points', requiring Japan (among other things) to: withdraw all troops from China; renounce all concessions gained from China since 1900; and accept Chiang's regime as the sole government of China. These conditions would have nullified all that the Japanese had gained in China since the turn of the century, and were completely unacceptable. As early as 16 October Konoe had resigned as Prime Minister, recognising that the negotiations were making no headway. He was replaced by General Tojo, who advocated going to war with the Americans in order to resume negotiations from a position of strength.

At a Liaison Conference in Tokyo on 1 November 1941, Tojo set out three possible courses for Japan to take. The first was to come to terms with the United States, accepting the material costs and loss of prestige that this would involve. The second was to decide immediately upon war, and act accordingly. The third was to decide on war, but allow military preparations and diplomatic negotiations to continue together for a limited period. In the ensuing discussion only the Foreign Minister, Shinegori Togo, supported the first option; and eventually the third course was adopted, but setting a very short timescale. It was agreed that Japan would go to war with the USA, Britain and the Netherlands unless negotiations with the Americans reached a favourable outcome by 1 December. This decision was formally confirmed at an Imperial Conference on 5 November, which left a mere 26 days to conclude negotiations to Japanese satisfaction. This was a sheer impossibility. The Imperial Conference had in fact decided on war, with only a thin and temporary veil of negotiations to conceal that fateful choice for a few more days.

The Japanese government had chosen war, not in some general sense, but in the form of a specific operation. The Japanese Navy stood ready to carry out one of the most daring feats in the history of war. Admiral Isoroku Yamamoto, the Commander-in-Chief of the Japanese Combined Fleet in 1941, had been among the first Japanese naval officers to envisage a new role for aircraft carriers, not just as providing a defensive umbrella for the fleet, but as forming an independent striking force. The Navy adopted this new strategic concept in 1938, and began to build big new carriers to put it into execution. By the end of 1941 the Japanese Navy included ten aircraft carriers. The Americans had five, of which only three were in the Pacific. The target for the Japanese carrier force was nothing less than the main American naval base in the Pacific, at Pearl Harbor in the Hawaiian Islands. Yamamoto had proposed this daring idea in May 1941, and tried it out in a war game in September. It was accepted by the Chief of the Naval Staff on 20 October, and embodied in an Operation Order on 1 November – the date of the Liaison Conference which resolved upon war.

This attack on Pearl Harbor was to be only a part of a vast offensive, including assaults on the Philippine Islands, Malaya and the Dutch East Indies, aimed at seizing control of the whole of South-East Asia. In this grand scheme, the immediate purpose of attacking Pearl Harbor was to put the American Pacific Fleet out of action, and so cover the flank of the massive move southwards; but there was more to it than that. Yamamoto understood very well the weight of industrial resources that the United States could bring to bear in the long run, and he was pessimistic about Japan's chances of success in a long war. He had told Konoe as early as September that: 'If I am told to fight regardless of the consequences, I shall run wild for the first six months or a year, but I have utterly no confidence for the second or third year.' He therefore hoped that the destruction of the Pacific Fleet at the very outset of the war would strike such a blow at American morale that it would never recover. American industrial power would thus be nullified by breaking the American will to fight, and the fate of the war might be decided on the very first day. It was an extraordinary gamble.

The plan for a carrier-borne attack on Pearl Harbor was fraught with risks and difficulties. The distance involved was enormous – 3,400 miles from Japan to Hawaii. The fleet might be spotted at sea, destroying the vital element of surprise. To diminish this risk, the Japanese embarked on a northerly approach to Hawaii; but this took the fleet through stormy waters, increasing the hazards of refuelling at sea, on which the whole operation depended. If the dangers of the voyage were safely passed, there remained the problems of the assault itself. High-level bombing was known to be inaccurate. Dive-bombing against strong defences was dangerous and uncertain in its results. Torpedo-bombing seemed to offer the best chance of success, and the Japanese had noted the achievements of British torpedo-bombers against Italian battleships at Taranto in November 1940; but they were not sure how well their torpedoes would work in the shallow waters of the American harbour, and they did not know whether the heavy ships would be protected by anti-torpedo nets. (As it turned out, they were not.)

The Japanese took great trouble to foresee these difficulties, and to deal with them by intensive training and exercises. Lieutenant-Commander Fuchida, who was designated to command the attacking force in action, also supervised the training of the aircrews. Submarines (including some new midget submarines) were added to the attacking forces, to intercept American warships if they put to sea to escape the air attacks. To prepare for the assault, Japanese Naval Intelligence asked the Consulate in Hawaii to prepare a grid of the waters at Pearl Harbor, with the normal positions of warships marked on it. American intelligence officers intercepted this request, made on 24 September; but astonishingly did not grasp its significance, and did not pass it on to the naval and military commanders. The Japanese made meticulous preparations. They were also lucky.

The Americans for their part put a good deal of effort into assessing Japanese intentions. On 31 March 1941 two senior intelligence officers, Major-General Martin and Rear Admiral Bellenger, prepared a report predicting that a declaration of war by Japan might be *preceded* (the word is worth noting) by surprise submarine or carrier-borne air attacks on Pearl Harbor. They proposed guarding against such attacks by mounting long-range air patrols all around the island base, but they had to conclude rather lamely that there were not enough aircraft available to provide such intensive cover. In August another officer, Colonel Farthing, again recommended all around patrols by long-range aircraft, and again acknowledged that the necessary planes (he put the figure at 180) were not available.

Even more important than lack of resources was the fixed belief among Americans that the Japanese were simply unable to carry out an air attack on Pearl Harbor. Farthing himself later declared with commendable frankness: 'I didn't think they could do it. I didn't think they had that ability.' Astonishingly, this refusal to believe that the Japanese were up to the job persisted while the attack was actually going on. An American lieutenant watching a Japanese plane shooting up an airfield said to the men with him: 'He must be a German.' When General MacArthur, the American Commander-in-Chief in the Philippines, heard of the attack on Pearl Harbor, he at once assumed that the pilots must be white mercenaries. At the centre of government in Washington, Admiral Stark, the Chief of Naval Operations, asked whether a submarine reported sunk at Pearl Harbor was German. The mistake of underestimating the Japanese, largely on racial grounds, was widespread. It almost proved fatal.

By the end of November 1941 the American high command understood that a Japanese attack was imminent, but they did not appreciate its scale and geographical range. On 25 November they had accurate information that a large Japanese force had left Shanghai heading southwards towards the Philippines, Malaya or the Dutch East Indies. On the 27th Admiral Stark began a signal to Admiral Kimmel, the commander of the Pacific Fleet at Pearl Harbor, with the words: 'This despatch is to be considered a war warning.' He went on to say that an aggressive move by Japan was expected within a few days, and went on to name the likely targets as the Philippines, the Kra Peninsula in Thailand, or possibly Borneo. There was no mention of Pearl Harbor, though the Japanese fleet due to make the attack was already at sea.

There was in fact a major gap in the American intelligence picture. They had lost track of the main force of Japanese aircraft carriers, Carrier

Divisions 1 and 2 – four carriers in all. On 2 December the chief intelligence officer for the Pacific Fleet, Lieutenant-Commander Layton, drew up for Kimmel a report on the whereabouts of all the major Japanese warships. He omitted Carrier Divisions 1 and 2 because he simply did not know where they were – he thought they were probably in home waters, using only low-power radio transmissions that could not be picked up, but he did not know. By a striking coincidence, the Japanese had a similar gap in their information about the American fleet. The Americans had three aircraft carriers in the Pacific, and the Japanese did not know where any of them were – only that none of them were at Pearl Harbor. So each side approached the coming battle in ignorance of the location of key vessels in the other's fleet.

In fact the Japanese task force for the Pearl Harbor operation had gathered in late November at the island of Etorofu, one of the Kurile Islands to the north of Japan, where a fleet could be concentrated in complete secrecy. The fleet, under the command of Admiral Nagumo, put to sea at 6 a.m. local time on 26 November, taking a northerly route towards Hawaii. It comprised 6 aircraft carriers, 2 battleships, 13 cruisers and various smaller warships, accompanied by supply ships to ensure the refuelling at sea that was necessary for such a long voyage.

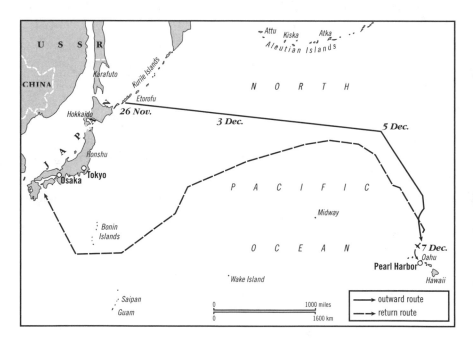

Map 6 Japanese Approach to Pearl Harbor.

The total air-striking force, packed aboard the 6 carriers, was made up of 450 aircraft. Of these, 40 were inoperative on the day of the attack, and 50 were held back to defend the fleet. The actual assault was delivered by 100 high-level bombers, 130 dive-bombers, 40 torpedo-bombers, and 90 fighters as an escort and to strafe targets on the ground. This mixed force comprised every available method of air attack, offering the best chance of success. A number of submarines approached Hawaii separately.

The Japanese attack began at 7.55 a.m. on Sunday morning, 7 December 1941. In the events that ensued, there was an almost uncanny contrast between the violence of the assault from the air and the humdrum routines being followed on the ground. The Japanese delivered three main attacks: first by torpedo and dive-bombers; next by high-level bombers; and finally by more dive-bombers. The Americans were taken completely by surprise. The calm of an early Sunday morning prevailed everywhere, with a few

9 Ready to attack Pearl Harbor. Japanese planes warm up on the flight deck of an aircraft carrier.

citizens and servicemen going to church for early service. Private Raymond McBriarty was on his way to church when he saw a lone aircraft come in from the sea and open fire on some tents. He thought the plane looked like an American trainer, and that the bullets were blanks, so he carried on and *went to church as usual*, with remarkable if misplaced sangfroid. Even those who grasped that they were under attack could do little about it. Only a few anti-aircraft guns, whether on ships or ashore, were manned; and most of the land-based gun-crews had no access to ammunition, which was carefully locked in stores for fear of sabotage. The same fear had led to many aircraft being lined up wing-to-wing in the open, where they were safe from saboteurs but wide open to air attack. At Wheeler Field airbase, for example, aircraft were lined up under armed guard. The commander of the base, Colonel William J. Flood, was quietly reading his morning newspaper when he saw Japanese planes strafing the American aircraft, and even the golf course. 'I could see some of the Japanese pilots lean out of their planes and smile as they zoomed by. . . . Hell, I could even see the gold in their teeth.' In the harbour, seven battleships were at their moorings, exactly as set out in the grid provided by the Japanese Consul, and unprotected by torpedo nets. Another battleship, the *Pennsylvania*, lay in dry dock. An American dive-bomber pilot, Lieutenant Dickinson, who was on shore at the time of the attack, watched the Japanese dive-bombers with a professional eye, noting how they systematically concentrated 18 to 20 planes against each battleship. He approved of what he saw, except that the Japanese dived at an angle of 50 degrees, whereas the Americans preferred 70 degrees, which he thought would be more effective – a point they were to prove at the Battle of Midway six months later.

The attacks scored a resounding success. Of the eight battleships in harbour, six were sunk or grounded, and two badly damaged. Notably, the *Arizona* blew up and the *Oklahoma* capsized, under the horrified gaze of onlookers. Eleven smaller warships were sunk or badly damaged. Ashore, 188 aircraft were destroyed on the ground, and many others damaged. Casualties amounted to 2,403 killed (including civilians) and nearly 1,200 wounded. Japanese losses were only 29 aircraft destroyed and 74 damaged. They also lost six submarines, including the midget submarines. One submarine was lost in the first action of the whole day, when the US destroyer *Ward* fired on an unknown submarine in the harbour at 6.40 a.m., and then sank the intruding vessel with depth charges. This incident, which took place an hour and a half before the first air strike, might (and indeed should) have alerted the shore defences that

10 After the Japanese air attack. The wreckage of American warships at Pearl Harbor.

something unusual was afoot; but in fact there was no reaction ashore until it was too late.

The Japanese made no further attacks on Pearl Harbor, though several officers, including Fuchida, who had led the whole air attack, strongly advocated finishing the job by bombing the shore installations, and above all the oil storage tanks, which as it happened contained all the oil reserves for the Pacific Fleet. But Admiral Nagumo judged that he had fulfilled his mission to put the American Pacific Fleet out of action for at least six months, and he did not wish to expose his own ships to the danger of attack. He therefore headed for home with his force intact, leaving the American oil tanks unharmed. It was an understandable decision, but was to prove a bad mistake.

At the time, this passed almost unnoticed. The Japanese success was overwhelming, and was only the first of a string of victories. In December 1941 the Japanese captured Hong Kong and Guam, and began their invasion of the Philippines. For good measure, they sank the British capital ships *Prince of Wales* and *Repulse*, which had been sent to the Far East to protect Malaya and Singapore. Early in 1942 the Japanese captured Singapore, receiving the surrender of a British army that outnumbered its assailants. They occupied the Dutch East Indies, and invaded Burma. On 1 March 1942 Japanese aircraft bombed Darwin, in Northern Australia, sinking ships in the harbour, setting buildings on fire, and starting a panic which almost emptied the town. In March and April Japanese carriers sailed into the Indian Ocean, attacking Ceylon and forcing the British Eastern Fleet to take refuge on the coast of Kenya. As it happened, this was the limit of the Japanese advance – they had no plans to invade Australia. It was indeed quite enough that in five months, from December 1941 to April 1942, the Japanese had conquered the whole of South-East Asia and much of the South Pacific. In these events Admiral Nagumo's carrier fleet had played a central part, sinking five battleships, one aircraft carrier, two cruisers and seven destroyers, as well as many merchant ships, without losing a single ship of its own. It was an astonishing achievement.

But there was good reason for the Japanese to fear that their success might be temporary. In the long run the Americans had the industrial power to outbuild Japan and win command of the sea. The Japanese therefore aimed, not to conquer more territory, but to set up a defensive cordon from the Kurile Islands north of Japan, through Wake Island and the Marshall Islands to the South Pacific, and then enclose New Guinea, the East Indies, Malaya, and so to Burma and the border of India. Within this vast area they had access to ample supplies of oil, raw materials and food; and they were confident that if the Americans attacked the cordon they could be repelled. If the Japanese could hold the line for 18 months or 2 years, they thought the Americans would weary of the struggle and be ready to make peace, leaving Japan in control of her conquests. Such was the strategy followed by the Japanese after Pearl Harbor. As it happened, they made the same mistake as the Americans had made earlier – they underestimated their opponents.

On the other side, Pearl Harbor left the Americans – high command, politicians and people alike – in a state of shock. Samuel Eliot Morison, the author of the semi-official American history of the US Navy in the war, wrote bluntly that the naval high command was 'unnerved' by the event. The harbour itself, a shambles of wrecked and shattered battleships, bore mute yet telling testimony to the defeat; but almost worse than the material disaster was the sense of humiliation. The defenders of Pearl Harbor had been caught napping, and their commanders had failed in their most elementary duty – to safeguard their ships and their base. With humiliation came anger, directed first against the Japanese, but then also against those who had been responsible for such a calamity.

Yet the shock passed, and it soon became clear that the disaster was appalling but not total. The battleships at Pearl Harbor had been sunk or damaged in shallow waters, which meant that most could be salvaged; and in fact all but two returned to service before the end of the war. Moreover, the three aircraft carriers of the Pacific Fleet had all been away from Pearl Harbor at the time of the Japanese attack. The *Lexington* and *Enterprise* were ferrying aircraft to Midway Island and Wake Island respectively, while the *Saratoga* was off the coast of California. The *Yorktown* was soon transferred from the Atlantic, bringing the carrier strength of the Pacific Fleet up to four – fewer than the Japanese, but a considerable force, and now obviously the key to naval warfare in the Pacific. So it became apparent that the Americans had lost a battle, but not the war. The new commander of the Pacific Fleet, Admiral King, prepared to stand on the defensive on a line from Hawaii to Midway Island, and then through the South Pacific to Australia. Like the Japanese, the Americans too had their defensive cordon, and in the next few months the line held.

The psychological effects of Pearl Harbor were more far-reaching than the strategic consequences, and more difficult to deal with. One historian has written without exaggeration that Pearl Harbor 'aroused the people of the United States as no other event in their history ever had', provoking surprise, grief, humiliation and 'bone-deep anger and hatred'. The key element in this mixture was the sense of *betrayal* caused by the Japanese themselves. It so happened that the Japanese Ambassador delivered to Cordell Hull a note breaking off their long-standing conversations at 2.20 p.m. Washington time, when the attack on Pearl Harbor was already in progress and the news had already reached the capital. Hull replied, in cold anger, that: 'In all my fifty years of public service I have never seen a document that was more crowded with infamous falsehoods and distortions . . . on a scale so huge that I never imagined until today that any Government on this planet was capable of uttering them.'

President Roosevelt put the matter more pithily when he addressed Congress. The day of Pearl Harbor, he said, was 'a date which will live in infamy'. This phrase took root in the American mind, but those that followed it were perhaps even more important. Roosevelt went on:

11 Avenge Pearl Harbor. An American poster catches a mood that lasted for the whole of the war.

The facts of yesterday and today speak for themselves. The people of the United States have already formed their opinions and will understand the implications to the very life and safety of our nation. . . . Hostilities exist. There is no blinking at the fact that our people, our territory, and our interests are in grave danger.

He therefore asked Congress, not to declare war, but to declare that 'since the unprovoked and dastardly attack by Japan on Sunday, December 7, 1941 a state of war has existed between the United States and the Japanese Empire'. The Senate was unanimous in its agreement. The House of Representatives voted in favour by 388 to 1. (Jeanette Rankin of Montana was against, as she had been in the vote for war in 1917 – a lady who knew her own mind.) This was a display of unity in the two Houses that would have been inconceivable a few days earlier, representing a mood shared by the American people as a whole. The sense of betrayal gave birth to a sense of unity.

Roosevelt, with his keen political instinct, was well aware that this unity could not be taken for granted, and might not last. There was indeed an immediate danger to his own policies, which might well split that unity. Months before, Roosevelt had agreed with the British that Germany was the principal enemy for them both, and must be dealt with first – 'Germany First', in a simple watchword. But the United States now found itself at war with the Japanese, in circumstances that demanded concentration on the Pacific, and *not* at war with Germany. We do not know how Roosevelt would have dealt with this problem, because Hitler saved him the trouble by declaring war on the United States. On 11 December 1941 Joachim von Ribbentrop, the German Foreign Minister, read a formal declaration of war to the American representative in Berlin, and Hitler later announced the event to the Reichstag.

This has often seemed a freakish and irrational decision, but there were reasons that seemed powerful at the time. Only recently, the Japanese had specifically asked Germany for an assurance that, if they attacked the United States, Germany would herself declare war on the USA; and von Ribbentrop had formally given this assurance on 21 November. Now it is true that Nazi Germany was not always punctilious in keeping its diplomatic promises, but this one was unusually plain and very recent, and surely had to be kept. Moreover it seemed advantageous to do so. The German Army was at that very time in danger of defeat outside Moscow, and Germany was anxious to make a show of solidarity with Japan, and perhaps even to receive some material assistance. Hitler was also well aware that for some months Germany had faced an undeclared war in the Atlantic, where the US Navy was escorting British convoys as far as Iceland, and American warships had been ordered to attack German U-boats on sight. There was some advantage to the Germans in bringing this hidden war into the open; and indeed in the first part of 1942 the U-boats enjoyed a 'happy time' off the east coast of America, sinking merchant ships almost at will. In addition, von Ribbentrop took a perverse pride in the German decision: a great power, he said, does not wait to be declared war upon – it declares war itself. And all this must be seen against the dark background of Hitler's erratic thinking about the United States, which veered from claims that the Americans were a decadent people who could not face a war to a far-sighted understanding that the United States was destined in the long run to be a new world power. On this occasion he took the Americans too lightly.

Whatever the German reasons, their declaration of war rescued Roosevelt from a difficult, perhaps even insuperable, political problem. In principle and in the long term, he could adhere to the strategy of 'Germany First', because the Germans had brought war upon their own heads. But in practice and in the short term, the Americans deployed more forces in the Pacific than in the Atlantic, and public anger against Japan was to some degree satisfied by a daring carrier-borne air attack on Tokyo and other cities on 18 April 1942. The 'Doolittle Raid' (taken from the name of its commander, Colonel Doolittle) did little material damage, but it lifted American morale and had an important effect on Japanese strategy (see below, p. 83). So enough was done in the Pacific to satisfy American public opinion, and meanwhile the build-up of forces to use against Germany went ahead. This double policy would have been extremely difficult, if not impossible, without the German declaration of war.

Pearl Harbor was a turning point. Even among all the disputes and controversies in the history of the Second World War, it would be hard to find anyone to deny that. But what sort of a turning point was it? We may start with the main belligerent powers – Japan, the USA and the British Empire.

For Japan, Pearl Harbor marked a crucial move from a war against China, which had been going on since 1937, to a wider conflict in the Pacific and South-East Asia against the United States, Britain and the Dutch – or rather, it added the second war to the first, because large

Japanese forces were still engaged in China. In this extended war, Pearl Harbor started a run of victories that lasted for six months, but ended after four years in complete disaster and destruction. The attack on Pearl Harbor transformed first the type of war waged by Japan, and then the history of Japan itself.

For the United States, the attack on Pearl Harbor marked a similar – perhaps even greater – transformation. First the country was catapulted in a very few days from neutrality to playing a leading role in a world war. Then in the next four years the United States became, by its industrial, military and political efforts, the greatest power in the world. The national character of the country was thus altered beyond recall.

For Britain, Pearl Harbor meant both triumph and disaster. Churchill wrote in his memoirs, '. . . now at this very moment [when he heard of the attack] I knew the United States was in the war, up to the neck and in to the death. So we had won after all.' In the long run this was true. But in the next few weeks Britain suffered the loss of the battleship *Prince of Wales* and battle cruiser *Repulse*, the humiliating surrender at Singapore, and a disastrous defeat in Burma. The British Empire in Asia never recovered from these blows, and the British position in the world was weakened. These changes followed from Pearl Harbor as surely as the war's final victory, which Churchill foresaw.

In the Second World War as a whole, Pearl Harbor marked a decisive turning point, transforming what had been essentially a European war into a world war. The United States fought in two oceans and on three continents. British land and air forces fought in Europe, North Africa, the Middle East and Asia, and the Navy in the Atlantic, the Mediterranean, the Indian Ocean and the Pacific. The Soviet Union's campaigns were mainly in Europe, but finally in Asia also. Germany and Japan, on the other hand, fought almost entirely separate wars, out of a combination of geographical necessity and political choice. In 1942 there seemed a chance that the two powers might link up directly, as the Germans pressed southwards in the Caucasus and the Japanese advanced towards India; but the distances were too great and the momentum could not be kept up. The best opportunity of direct cooperation lay with Japan, and was not used. The Japanese had the geographical position and the naval power to blockade the Soviet Far Eastern port of Vladivostok, but they did not do so. From 1941 to 1945 ships sailed past Japan to Vladivostok, bearing American Lend-Lease supplies and other cargoes, while the Japanese stood by and watched. They preferred not to add the Soviet Union to their already formidable list of enemies, and their best means of helping their German ally lay unused. Even so, from December 1941 onwards the war was truly worldwide in its scale and in its interactions between continents. By comparison, the First World War scarcely deserves its name.

Pearl Harbor also brought home a change in the nature of naval warfare and sea power. The long era in which the battleship had been the main weapon of sea power came to an end, and the aircraft carrier took its place. This change had been coming for some time, as naval staffs and theorists debated the possibilities of air power at sea. The successful British torpedo-bomber attack at Taranto in Italy in November 1940 had shown what could be achieved, and the Japanese had learned from it. But it had been a small-scale action, using only 21 Swordfish biplanes. At Pearl Harbor the Japanese used 360 modern aircraft, and achieved decisive results by the sheer scale of their assault. This time the lesson was inescapable, and the later events of the war in the Pacific confirmed the change.

There remains another dimension to the story. Pearl Harbor and its immediate aftermath were no less than a turning point in world history. The Japanese victories in the five months from December 1941 to April 1942 brought an end to the European empires in East Asia. The tale is worth retelling. Even before Pearl Harbor the French had yielded to Japanese pressure and handed over their authority in Indo-China, retaining only a shadow of their colonial rule. The fatal blows came later. At Singapore in February 1942 some 70,000 British, Australian and Indian troops surrendered to a mere 35,000 Japanese. The surrender of Dutch forces in the East Indies followed in March. The British lost Burma, and their hold on India was shaken though not broken. Moreover, it became starkly clear that Britain could not defend Australia and New Zealand, which became dependent on the protection of the United States. It was the end of an era for the British Empire and its most distant members.

At the end of the war the imperial powers returned to their possessions and tried to restore the status quo. But their authority in these territories had long depended as much on prestige and custom as on force. In early 1942 Humpty Dumpty fell from the wall. Prestige and custom were broken, and they could not be put together again. It was the end of a story going back for two centuries or more. The world would never be the same again.

CHAPTER FIVE

THE BATTLE OF MIDWAY, 4 JUNE 1942

The Japanese attack on Pearl Harbor on 7 December 1941 marked the beginning of a series of disasters for the United States and its allies in the Pacific and South-East Asia. Yet on 4 June 1942, six months later almost to the day, the Americans achieved a remarkable victory over the Japanese fleet, sinking four of the very same aircraft carriers that had carried out the assault on Pearl Harbor, and showing qualities of self-sacrifice that might have been thought to have been more intrinsic to the Japanese rather than the American national character. This was the battle of Midway, which outside the ranks of specialist historians may well not have received its full share of attention in Britain. Yet it was beyond doubt one of the turning points of the Second World War.

At first sight, Midway Island seems an unlikely location for one of the decisive battles of history. It is a tiny atoll where a barrier reef encloses two islands, Sand Island and the smaller Eastern Island, with a small harbour and a shallow lagoon. All told, the atoll measures no more than six miles across. It lies in the middle of the vast Pacific Ocean, about 1,150 miles north-west of Hawaii and 2,600 miles from Tokyo. It had been annexed by the United States in 1867 as a coaling station for the Pacific Mail Steamship Company, and was therefore American territory – a point of some political and psycho-logical importance. A cable station had been established, with a direct link to Hawaii, in 1903. In 1941, as tension developed in the Pacific, the United States established a station for flying-boats and seaplanes and an airstrip for land-based aircraft at Midway, guarded by a small garrison of marines. At the beginning of 1942, Midway was the westernmost American base in the central Pacific for the war against Japan, but in practice that did not amount to very much, since it housed only 32 long-range flying-boats and

12 Midway Island – a tiny atoll in the middle of the vast Pacific Ocean.

23 bombers, with some seaplanes and a few ageing fighters. To all appearances, there was little to attract the attention of Japanese strategists.

Yet as early as 1 November 1941, before the attack on Pearl Harbor, the Japanese Combined Fleet Operations Order No. 1 included, as one of its main points, the concept of an amphibious attack on Midway Island, mainly in order to draw the American Pacific Fleet into the defence of the island and so into battle with the Japanese fleet. This assumed that the Americans would fight a battle to defend Midway, and that the Japanese would win that battle. But not everyone was confident of victory. Admiral Yamamoto, the Commander-in-Chief of the Combined Fleet, was sure that he could engage the Americans on his own terms and defeat them; but some officers on the

Naval Staff were less certain, pointing out that Midway lay outside the range of Japanese land-based aircraft but within that of American Flying Fortresses based in Hawaii, and that a complete surprise like that at Pearl Harbor could not be achieved again. Even the commander of the Carrier Fleet and victor of Pearl Harbor, Admiral Nagumo, was doubtful of success.

This debate was brought to an end by the 'Doolittle Raid' of 18 April 1942, when the Americans flew 16 medium bombers from a carrier in the North Pacific to bomb Tokyo and other cities. This raid, commanded by Colonel Doolittle of the US Army Air Force, scored only a slight material success, damaging some buildings and killing about 50 people, and most of the aircraft were lost in crash-landings, because plans for them to fly on from Japan and land in China went wrong. But the side-effects were considerable. The very fact that the Americans had succeeded in bombing Tokyo shook the Japanese high command badly, not least because the personal safety of the Emperor might have been endangered. Yamamoto, who was responsible for the defence of the homeland, treated the raid as a personal defeat – almost an affront. The Japanese became determined to close the Midway Island gap in their defensive cordon; and opposition to an attack on Midway ceased. Shortly afterwards, the advocates of the operation were encouraged by reports of the Battle of the Coral Sea (7–8 May 1942), in which the Japanese believed that they had sunk two American aircraft carriers, the *Lexington* and *Yorktown*; whereas in fact both had been hit, but only one, the *Lexington*, was sunk. The Japanese therefore mistakenly assumed that the American Pacific Fleet was reduced to only two aircraft carriers. At the end of May, the Americans managed to magnify the effects of this error by deceptive wireless traffic, which led the Japanese to believe that both the surviving carriers were in the Coral Sea for the defence of Australia, and therefore far distant from Midway Island. In fact, the Americans had three aircraft carriers, not two; and all three were at Hawaii, not in the Coral Sea.

The Japanese prepared an elaborate plan for the attack on Midway, involving five different forces. The first was the Carrier Striking Force, made up of four large carriers, commanded by Admiral Nagumo, and a string of other actions. Next there was a force for the occupation of Midway Island itself, made up of transports for troops and supplies, with an escort of warships. Third came the Main Fleet, under Admiral Yamamoto, with seven battleships, including the massive *Yamato*, which at 62,000 tons was the biggest battleship in the world. Fourth was the Aleutian Force, made up of two light carriers, other warships, and transports, which was to attack the Aleutian Islands, far to the north off Alaska, a day in advance of the Midway

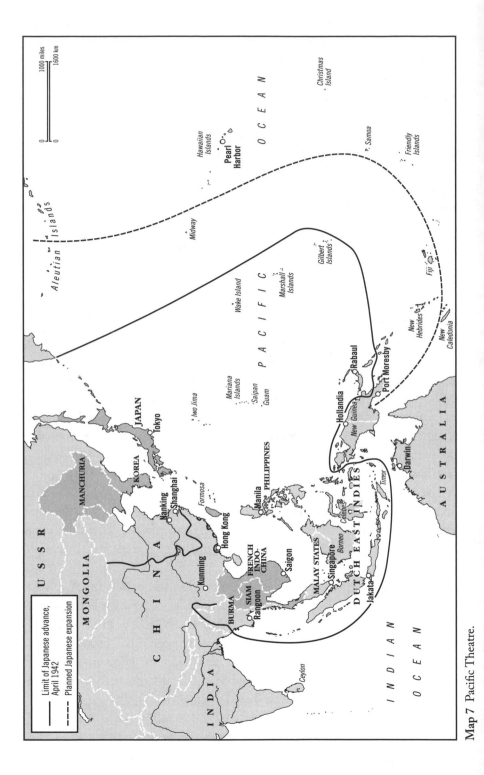

Map 7 Pacific Theatre.

operation, in the hope of diverting American forces from the main theatre. Finally, there were submarines, working ahead of the various fleets, as a combined reconnaissance and attack force. The total Japanese forces amounted to 4 large aircraft carriers and 2 light carriers, 7 battleships, 12 cruisers and 44 destroyers. This vast fleet far outnumbered its American opponents, made up of 3 carriers, 8 cruisers and 15 destroyers.

The orders for the Midway operation were issued on 5 May, setting out a complicated plan, requiring careful coordination between the different forces, difficult to achieve when the Commander-in-Chief was at sea with the Main Fleet and observing wireless silence. (By contrast, the American Commander, Admiral Nimitz, stayed ashore in Hawaii, where he could communicate with all his forces.) The plan placed a double responsibility on Nagumo's carrier force: to attack Midway Island, and to fight a battle against the US Pacific Fleet – two tasks that might well contradict one another, because aircraft being used to bomb Midway could not at the same time be available for a fleet action. The Japanese believed (mistakenly, as events proved) that they could deal with this problem by doing the two jobs in succession. The Commander-in-Chief, Yamamoto, confidently expected that the American main fleet would not leave its base at Pearl Harbor until *after* the attack on Midway had begun. Nagumo, the carrier commander, in an estimate prepared just before the attack, assumed that the enemy was not aware of the Japanese plans, and had no aircraft carriers in the vicinity. The Japanese admirals were wrong on all three counts. The American fleet left Pearl Harbor *before* the attack on Midway began; the Americans were well aware of the Japanese plans; and they had three aircraft carriers ready for action.

The main reason for these crucial American advantages lay in the successes of American signals interception and code-breaking. By May 1942 American cryptanalysts understood about one-third of the Japanese naval code, JN25, which meant that in some cases up to 90 per cent of a routine signal could be understood. As early as 21 May (16 days after the Japanese orders were issued on 5 May) Admiral Nimitz, the Commander-in-Chief of the Pacific Fleet, was aware that the Japanese intended to attack Midway. On 25 May the cryptanalysts in Hawaii, working with feverish intensity, were able to produce precise dates: 3 June for a diversionary attack on the Aleutian Islands, and 4 June for the main attack on Midway. They were also aware that their wireless deception plan, to convince the Japanese that there were two American carriers in the Coral Sea, had worked. There were limitations to the Americans' knowledge of Japanese dispositions; notably, they did not know where the main Japanese battleship divisions were stationed, which might have proved a dangerous gap in their information. But on the main lines of the Japanese plans, and notably on the crucial question of dates, Admiral Nimitz was fully informed, and could make his own dispositions accordingly.

He decided to disregard the diversionary attack on the Aleutian Islands, leaving the defence to the forces already stationed there. On 27 May he ordered two of his carriers, the *Enterprise* and *Hornet*, with an escort of cruisers and destroyers, to leave Pearl Harbor the next day, and take station north-east of Midway Island, away from Japanese submarines or reconnaissance aircraft. Also on 27 May the aircraft carrier *Yorktown*, severely damaged in the Battle of the Coral Sea, went into dry dock at Pearl Harbor for repairs which were expected to take 90 days to complete. In fact some 1,400 dockyard workers toiled round the clock to such effect that *Yorktown* put to sea ready for action at 9.00 a.m. on 30 May. This brought the American fleet up to three carriers, which were divided into two groups: *Enterprise* and *Hornet* under Admiral Spruance, and *Yorktown* under Admiral Fletcher. Nimitz ordered these two commanders 'to inflict maximum damage on enemy by employing strong attrition tactics', but he also insisted that the carriers themselves must not be risked – they were too precious, and if lost could not be replaced for some time. As events turned out, the crucial phase of the coming battle was to be more like lightning war than attrition.

Another element in the American preparations seemed at first sight of minor importance, but proved otherwise. Between Midway Island and Hawaii lay a group of tiny islets called French Frigate Shoals, which the Japanese intended to use as a base for seaplanes to reconnoitre the seas towards Hawaii; but the Americans forestalled them, sending two seaplane tenders to the Shoals on 26 May and landing a small force to guard the islands. This deprived the Japanese of an advanced reconnaissance base, and allowed the American fleet to move undetected towards Midway Island, so that Nagumo continued to believe that his enemy had no carrier force in the area.

The stage was now set. The Japanese diversionary attack on the Aleutian Islands, designed to draw Nimitz into weakening his main fleet by sending ships northward, achieved little. On 3 and 4 June, Japanese carrier-borne aircraft bombed the small port of Dutch Harbor, causing some damage and disturbance; and on the 7th Japanese troops landed on the islands of Attu and Kiska, which they proceeded to occupy. This was a blow to American pride, since the islands were part of the United States, but it did little material harm, and for the Japanese it proved a waste of effort.

The Battle of Midway itself was fought in the skies and oceans to the west of Midway Island, in operations that crossed the International Date Line as well as time zones. The Japanese used the East Longitude date and Tokyo time. The Americans used the West Longitude date; their main fleet used Zone plus 10 time, but the air forces based at Midway used Midway time, which was Zone plus 12. For example, the first Japanese aircraft to attack Midway Island took off from their carriers at 1.30 a.m. on 5 June by their time and date, which was equivalent to 4.30 a.m. on 4 June Midway time, and 6.30 a.m. on 4 June for the American fleet. The opposing forces therefore fought the battle on two different dates, while the American forces also used two different times. This has sometimes resulted in a certain confusion in accounts of the battle, which is best avoided by following the practice of Samuel Eliot Morison and Stephen Roskill in using the West Longitude date and Zone plus 12 time (Midway time). By this method of dating, the Battle of Midway was fought on 4 June 1942.

The opening moves in the battle took place on 3 June, when an American flying-boat from Midway Island discovered a large Japanese fleet (in fact the Midway Occupation Force) steering towards the Island. Flying Fortress heavy bombers from Midway bombed this fleet from a high level, and reported the sinking of two battleships or heavy cruisers and two transport vessels. They in fact hit nothing at all, so the opening skirmish amounted to very little.

The battle proper began in the morning of 4 June. At 4.30 a.m. Admiral Nagumo, commanding the Japanese Carrier Force, sent 108 aircraft (72 bombers and 36 escorting fighters) from his 4 carriers to attack the American base on Midway Island. This force was made up of half the complement of aircraft from each carrier, which later proved of vital importance. The Japanese bombing attack began at 6.30 a.m., causing serious damage, notably to oil tanks. American fighters which went up to meet the raiders suffered heavy losses – 17 out of the 26 engaged. The Japanese lost two aircraft destroyed, and some damaged. The Japanese attack scored a marked success, but the commander of the bomber force considered that a second strike would be needed to finish the job.

The Americans then launched their own attacks on the Japanese carrier fleet, using aircraft based on Midway Island, starting out at 7.10 a.m. on 4 June. These attacks lasted about an hour, without inflicting any damage on the Japanese ships. A flight of 15 heavy bombers (Flying Fortresses) claimed four hits, but made none. Torpedo bombers lost four out of six aircraft without scoring a single hit. Despite these failures, the attacks had an indirect effect by shaking Nagumo's confidence in the success of his own bombing raid on Midway, and confirming the view that another attack on the island was necessary. This was the start of a crucial chain of events.

As early as 7.15 a.m. that morning, when the American attacks had only just begun, Nagumo ordered that 93 strike planes still on his carriers should change the torpedoes with which they had been armed for bombs, in preparation for a second attack on Midway. But he then received reports from a reconnaissance plane that American warships were in the vicinity, without at that stage any definite news as to whether they included any carriers. At 7.45 a.m. Nagumo therefore countermanded his earlier order, and ordered his strike planes to change back to torpedoes, for an attack on warships. The result was a classic case of the military adage: order, counter-order, disorder. There was confusion below decks as the crews changed the weapons and often left bombs and torpedoes lying about. At the same time, the planes of the strike force against Midway were heading back to their carriers. For about an hour, from 8.20 a.m. onwards, the flight decks of all four Japanese carriers were busy receiving the returning aircraft, while below decks the second attack groups were still exchanging bombs for torpedoes. If Nagumo had flown his first strike force from only two carriers, he would have had another two with clear flight decks. But in fact he had used all four, and was committed to using all four to recover the returning aircraft. He therefore had no choice but to wait for this situation to be sorted out, and he ordered his carriers to complete their recovery operations before heading north to attack the American fleet – which by about 8.30 a.m. he knew included at least one carrier.

Meanwhile, the three American carriers were getting their planes into action. Admiral Spruance, commanding the carrier group made up of the *Enterprise* and *Hornet*, launched his whole striking force, consisting of 67 dive-bombers and 29 torpedo-bombers, starting about 7 a.m. They faced a flight of 175 miles to reach the Japanese fleet, which meant that some of them would certainly run out of fuel before completing the return trip. These aircraft flew off in different groups, and one group of 35 dive-bombers from the *Hornet* became separated from the main force, and never found the Japanese fleet at all. Meanwhile Admiral Fletcher, commanding the other American carrier, the *Yorktown*, waited until 8.30 a.m. before flying off a strike force, because he was uncertain where two of the Japanese carriers were located. He also cautiously kept some of his aircraft on board in case things went wrong.

The first American planes to reach their targets were torpedo-bombers, which were highly vulnerable to enemy fighters and anti-aircraft fire as they flew on a straight course into the attack. A total of 51 torpedo-bombers flew into action. Only seven survived to return to their carriers. Despite immense courage and determination, they scored no hits. One historian has called this the 'slaughter of the torpedo-bombers'; another the 'wasted sacrifice'. Slaughter it certainly was; but not entirely wasted. These attacks caused the Japanese warships to break their tight defensive formation, and they also drew in most of the Japanese fighter planes, which came right down to sea level to destroy the torpedo-bombers. This opened the way for the next, and decisive, phase in the battle.

At 10.20 a.m. on 4 June, Nagumo had 93 strike aircraft on board his four carriers, ready (or getting ready) to attack the American fleet. He gave the order to take off when ready, and at 10.25 the first planes were prepared to fly from the carrier *Nagaki* – in fact the first fighter had just taken off. But then, at 10.30, 54 Dauntless dive-bombers came down on the Japanese ships out of the sun, undetected by either gunners on the warships or fighters in the air. One of the dive-bomber pilots, Lieutenant Dickinson (who only six months earlier had watched the Japanese attack on Pearl Harbor), was astonished at being able to prepare his squadron of dive-bombers 'without a trace of fighter opposition. . . . The target was utterly satisfying. The squadron's dive was perfect.' The results were devastating. In some ten minutes three Japanese carriers were reduced to wrecks. The *Agaki* sustained two direct hits and a near miss from 1,000-lb bombs. One bomb penetrated to the lower deck and detonated a store of torpedoes. Another hit the flight deck, which was full of aircraft, some still refuelling, with petrol containers and pipes still littering the deck. The carrier *Kaga* was hit by four or five 500-lb bombs, which struck the flight deck and blew up bomb stores down below. Fierce fires killed everyone on the bridge. The carrier *Soryu* was hit by three bombs, causing explosions and fires. All those who survived from the three ships remembered above all that the vessels *burned* with a terrible fire which overwhelmed all safeguards. It was a tribute to the strength of their construction that none of the three aircraft carriers sank at once. The *Soryu* was sunk by an American submarine at 7.20 p.m. that evening (4 June). The *Kaga* stayed afloat until 7.25 p.m. The *Akagi* was scuttled at 5 a.m. the next day (5 June), it being judged impossible to tow her to safety. Taking careful precaution, the portrait of the Emperor that was carried aboard each vessel was shifted to another warship. The three aircraft carriers thus sank at different times and places,

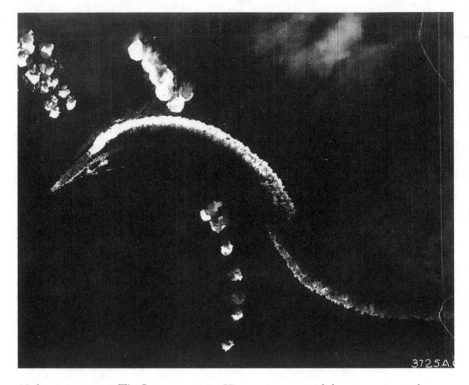

13 A moving target. The Japanese carrier *Hiryu* trying to avoid American air attack.

but they were all put out of action by no more than 10 or 11 hits scored by some 50 dive-bombers – an astonishing feat. Nagumo's famous carrier fleet, which had spread destruction from Pearl Harbor to the Indian Ocean, was almost wiped out.

Almost, but not quite. A fourth carrier, the *Hiryu*, was undamaged, with its planes still fit for action. At that point, it was open to the Japanese to pull the *Hiryu* out of the battle and fall back on the Main Fleet with its heavy battleships, as yet undetected by the Americans, and so live to fight another day. It seems that this was not even contemplated. *Hiryu* went straight into the attack, despatching two groups of aircraft against the American carrier *Yorktown* – dive-bombers flying off at 11 a.m. and torpedo-bombers at 1 p.m. The dive-bombers scored three hits, starting fires and causing heavy casualties; the torpedo-bombers then hit the carrier twice. The *Yorktown* began to list badly, and the crew abandoned ship; but she did not sink, and later she was re-manned and taken in tow. But finally, at 6 a.m. on 7 June, three days after the main battle, the *Yorktown* was sunk by a Japanese submarine.

14 The Japanese strike back. The American carrier *Yorktown* under attack.

It was some time before the other American carriers, *Enterprise* and *Hornet*, despatched aircraft to attack the *Hiryu*, which was only sighted by a reconnaissance plane at 2.45 p.m. on 4 June. At 3.15 p.m. *Enterprise* flew 25 dive-bombers off, followed by 20 more from *Hornet* just after 4 p.m. The *Enterprise* dive-bombers made their attack about 5 p.m., scoring four certain hits on the *Hiryu*, and perhaps two more. The sturdy carrier stayed afloat for 12 hours before the captain ordered the crew to abandon ship. At 5.10 a.m. on 5 June the portrait of the Emperor was removed, and a Japanese destroyer sank the carrier with torpedoes. The captain chose to go down with his ship.

That was the end of the main battle of Midway, but there was still some fighting to come. On 5 June four Japanese cruisers from the Midway Occupation Force (now unable to achieve its objective) were ordered to bombard Midway Island. Taking evasive action to avoid an American submarine, two of these cruisers (the *Mogami* and the *Mikuma*) collided, with damage to both ships. The next day (6 June) dive-bombers from the carriers *Enterprise* and *Hornet* attacked the crippled cruisers. The *Mikuma* was sunk, but the *Mogami* survived, and with great resilience made her way to the Japanese base on the island of Truk.

The commanders on the two sides still had decisions to make. Yamamoto, commanding the Japanese Main Fleet, still had his strong force of battleships. During the night of 4–5 June, when he had heard of the loss of three carriers but not the fourth, he sailed at high speed through thick fog in the hope of attacking the Americans. But early on the 5th he heard of the sinking of the *Hiryu*, and he abandoned this intention. His fleet was reinforced by the arrival of two light carriers from the Aleutian task force, and on 5 and 6 June he waited, hoping to draw the Americans into a battle, or at least bring them within range of Japanese bombers based on Wake Island. But Spruance, the American commander, had no intention of risking his two remaining carriers, *Enterprise* and *Hornet*. He had won a victory that would surely have satisfied even Horatio Nelson; and he had also sustained heavy casualties in aircraft and men, as well as the loss of the *Yorktown*. Spruance declined to be drawn into Yamamoto's trap. On 7 June the Japanese commander had to turn westward to a refuelling rendezvous, and on the 8th he gave up all hope and returned to base. The Battle of Midway was not to be resumed.

As wartime goes, the Battle of Midway was not exceedingly costly in lives. The Japanese lost perhaps 3,000 dead, the Americans under 1,000. But the Japanese casualties included at least 90 highly trained and experienced pilots, who were hard to replace. Both sides' aircrews showed remarkable courage, many of whom took off from their carriers in the sure and certain knowledge that they did not have enough fuel to get back.

But it was the losses in aircraft carriers that were truly decisive. The Japanese lost all of the four fleet carriers that made up Admiral Nagumo's famous Carrier Fleet. The Americans lost only one' and kept two intact. In the coming years, the Japanese built three new carriers in 1943 and another four in 1944. In the same two years the Americans built *ninety* – many of them light escort carriers, but including nearly 30 fleet carriers.

In retrospect the Japanese fully acknowledged the significance of the battle. The Navy Minister, Mitsumasa Yonai, said after the war: 'After Midway I was certain there was no chance of success.' Naval officers interrogated by the Americans after the war repeatedly described Midway as 'the decisive turning point'. These comments naturally owed something to hindsight, but even at the time there was a sense the defeat had been so great that its extent must be concealed. The Japanese wounded, when they returned to base, were kept separate from others in hospital, to prevent them talking about the battle. A newsreel cameraman who filmed parts of the battle had his film confiscated, and was kept as far as possible in isolation. Even the Liaison Conference, the principal body that directed Japanese policy and strategy, was given only incomplete information about Japanese losses at Midway.

On the other side, the importance of the American victory may best be grasped by looking at the likely consequences if they had lost the battle. If the Japanese had won at Midway and continued to dominate the Pacific Ocean, they might well have forced Roosevelt to give up his strategy of 'Germany First', with far-reaching consequences for the whole war. But instead victory at Midway gained the Americans the initiative in the Pacific war, which they never lost again. Rather strangely, the Americans wasted some of the psychological advantages of their victory, and the consequent effects on morale, by mishandling their public relations. The government story put out to the press and radio gave the impression that the battle had been won by land-based heavy bombers, notably the Flying Fortresses, which in fact hit nothing at all. This caused acute resentment among the naval airmen who had achieved so much and lost so heavily, and who found themselves disregarded when they got back to Hawaii. The misapprehensions thus begun persisted for many years, and were still going strong when Samuel Eliot Morison wrote his account of the battle in the late 1940s. Another aspect of this distortion was that the Dauntless dive-bombers were 'airbrushed from history' (or at any rate from popular history) when the story was told for large audiences by television and films, so that the aircraft which struck the crucial blows in the battle did not receive full public acknowledgement.

Despite these oddities in propaganda and presentation, there was (and is) no doubt of the central result of the Battle of Midway. The Japanese domination of the Pacific had lasted six months, and was overthrown in a few hours – indeed, with only a modicum of exaggeration, it had been destroyed by ten bombs in ten minutes. It is hard to think of a turning point that was achieved so quickly and so decisively. Churchill struck a true note in his war memoirs. 'This memorable American victory was of cardinal importance, not only to the United States, but to the whole Allied cause. The moral effect was tremendous and instantaneous. At one stroke the dominant position of Japan in the Pacific was reversed.' Moreover, he went out of his way to emphasise the courage and devotion of the American airmen, which showed the Japanese that they faced 'a will-power

15 The victorious American planes – Dauntless dive-bombers.

and passion' equal to their own – an achievement in its way as great as the sinking of four aircraft carriers.

For the Americans, the disaster of Pearl Harbor had been reversed by a resounding victory, achieved by a remarkable combination of circumstances. Their code-breaking had secured a vital success at a crucial moment, revealing the precise dates for the Japanese attack on Midway two weeks ahead. They had used this intelligence to produce a simple and flexible plan, in contrast to the elaborate nature of the Japanese operations. The American aircrews displayed great determination and courage throughout the battle. They also benefited from a tremendous slice of good luck – that vital element in all military affairs – when their dive-bombers went into the attack just minutes before the Japanese were able to fly their own aircraft from their carriers. Yet in Britain, Midway has been to some degree a forgotten victory. Churchill said in the House of Commons in July 1942 that the American achievements at Midway had not fully received the attention they deserved in Britain. This may well still be the case in Britain, though not in the United States where the story of the battle has often been told and much debated. But in any case the tale is still well worth the telling.

CHAPTER SIX

THE BATTLE OF STALINGRAD, JULY 1942–FEBRUARY 1943

'. . . here, on the very edge where the real Europe fades into the Asiatic wastes, a few grand Guards Divisions and local Home Guard who had become the strong bleeding heart of all the Russias saved Continental civilisation, and with it, perhaps, our England too'. So proclaimed a despatch from Stalingrad in the *Daily Telegraph*, that sound Conservative newspaper, on 18 January 1943. Three weeks later the equally sound Labour paper, the *Daily Herald*, carried an article predicting that 'Children all over the world will learn for centuries to come about Stalingrad . . .'. At almost exactly the same time the Turkish Consul in Moscow was moved to prophesy that 'the lands which the Germans have destined for their living space will become their dying space'.

The words were dramatic and the mood almost apocalyptic. There was a sense that something of immense significance had happened at Stalingrad. Posterity has endorsed that belief. It may well be that other battles on the Eastern Front – at Moscow in 1941, for example, or at Kursk in 1943 – were equally decisive, but none has achieved the same resonance in the public mind as Stalingrad. If children still learn about these events, it is Stalingrad that takes pride of place. Even though Stalin's reputation has suffered in the intervening years, and the name of his city has been changed to Volgograd, the fame of the battle waged there remains intact. Before Stalingrad, the Germans won one victory after another, with only a limited setback in the winter of 1941–42. After Stalingrad, they won no more victories, even in the summer. The contemporary impressions of the battle of Stalingrad still ring true.

Yet at the start of the summer campaign in 1942 there was no sign that Stalingrad would assume such crucial importance. It was a city of about

450,000 people, recently developed as a centre for arms production in what
had been assumed to be a 'safe' area; and in the early part of 1942 it was one
of the main manufacturing centres for the T-34, the standard tank used by
the Red Army. Geographically, the city stood at a great bend on the River
Volga, which was one of the main supply routes from the Caucasus and
Persia to the centre of Russia. In recent history, it had played a significant
role in the Russian Civil War in 1918–19, when Stalin had been jointly in
command of its defence against Cossack forces. Its name had been changed
in 1925 from Tsaritsyn to Stalingrad, and a personal link between Stalin
and the city had thus been publicly established. But at the beginning of
1942 it was nowhere near the centre of Russian operations and planning.

random area for a battle

When the German high command planned its offensive operations for
summer 1942, the principal objective was to capture the oilfields of the
Caucasus. At a conference on 1 June, Hitler confirmed this as the main
purpose of the summer campaign. An attack on Stalingrad appeared in the
planning only as a secondary operation, to divert Soviet forces from the
Caucasus, to attack the city's arms factories, and to cut the supply route
along the River Volga.

Hitler's goal and plan

The Soviets for their part misread the Germans' intentions, assuming
that they would resume the drive towards Moscow which had been halted
in December 1941. Stalin and the General Staff therefore prepared to
defend the capital, and also planned a counter-attack to encircle the
German forces when they advanced on Moscow. Their main attention was
thus concentrated on the central sector of the long front line, and there
seemed no reason for Stalingrad to loom large in their thoughts.

The Germans opened their summer offensive on 28 June 1942, along
the line of the River Don from Voronezh in the north to Rostov in the
south. They achieved complete surprise, and captured Rostov on 23 July,
cutting the pipeline that carried the main supply of oil from the Caucasus
to central Russia. At that stage, the Germans might conceivably have
attained their main objective, the capture of the Caucasian oilfields,
though the distances were great and the passage through the Caucasus
Mountains would be difficult. But instead Hitler chose to divide his forces,
and pursued two objectives at once. Army Group A, under Field Marshal
List, was to move south-eastwards into the Caucasus, to capture the
oilfields; while Army Group B, under Field Marshal von Bock, was to drive
eastward towards Stalingrad and the River Volga.

MISTAKE

Hitler shouldn't have tried to pursue 2 objectives @ once

This pursuit of two major objectives proved disastrous, and is widely
recognised as one of several occasions during the war when Hitler imposed

a faulty strategy upon his generals. The further the two Army Groups advanced, the further they moved away from one another, and the longer grew their lines of communication. In the south, Army Group A reached the line of the Caucasus Mountains, and a party of mountain troops actually climbed Mount Elbrus, the highest peak in Europe. But at a more practical level the Germans failed to cross the mountain barrier, and came to a halt without reaching Grozny, and a full 350 miles from Baku, their key objective. Meanwhile, Army Group B made rapid progress across the steppe, and reached the Volga just north of Stalingrad on 23 August. Their guns could then command the river, hindering if not completely preventing the passage of barges, and forcing the Russians to rely on a newly built railway line from Astrakhan to Saratov as their main supply line from the Caucasus and Persia to the north.

With that success, the German advance on Stalingrad had achieved its strategic objective. The invaders needed to do no more than consolidate their position on the Volga, shoot up any barges that tried to pass up the river, and bombard the factories in Stalingrad. But instead, during the next few weeks, the battle changed its character completely. The city itself assumed a crucial *symbolic* importance, and its possession became the focus of political and personal obsessions. With this change, the battle for Stalingrad began to attain the status of a turning point in the 1942 campaign – though at that time no one knew how events would turn out.

Colonel Groscurth, Chief of Staff of the German XI Corps on the Stalingrad front, grasped this change at the beginning of October, writing in his diary that 'It [the battle] has become a matter of prestige between Hitler and Stalin'. On Hitler's part the process began early in September, when he realised that the offensive in the Caucasus had stalled, and he resolved to capture Stalingrad to make up for this failure. To achieve this he first had to impose his will on the German General Staff. Halder, the Chief of Staff, was afraid that the army at Stalingrad was dangerously exposed at the end of a long supply line; but Hitler insisted that warfare was a matter of willpower rather than practical matters of supply and transport. On 24 September he dismissed Halder, replacing him with General Zeitzler, who fell in more readily with the Führer's ideas.

With this change, Hitler's concentration on capturing Stalingrad grew more intense, and also more public. On 30 September he gave a speech in the Berlin *Sportpalast*, broadcast on the radio for the country and the world to hear, declaring that the city which bore Stalin's name would be captured and never lost – 'You can be sure that nobody will get us away from this place again.' In fact the German Sixth Army had already announced publicly that the German flag had been hoisted over the Communist Party headquarters in Stalingrad; and a camera team was kept near the front line to film the formal raising of the flag over the last part of the city to be conquered. On 9 November Hitler visited Munich for the anniversary of the failed Nazi *putsch* in 1923, and proclaimed that Stalingrad was already virtually captured. 'I wanted to take it and, you know, we are modest: we have it.'

The German commitment to the capture of Stalingrad thus became public property, and a matter of psychology and prestige rather than strategy. The military price for this commitment was heavy. The Germans lost all the advantages that they had held in open, mobile warfare, when their tanks had rolled across the steppe. Their commander, General Paulus, a staff officer who had never commanded even a division in battle, proved ill-fitted to conduct the type of street fighting in which his men now became engaged as they fought their way into Stalingrad, street by street, house by house, and ruin by ruin.

Stalingrad itself stretched for about 30 miles along the west bank of the River Volga, and the Soviet forces clung to a narrow strip only a mile or two-and-a-half miles wide. In late July 1942 the city was put on a war footing, and some 180,000 civilians were put to work to dig trenches, build fortifications and barricade streets. At the same time, industrial equipment, stores and livestock were removed to the east bank of the river. But at the end of August Stalin ordered that the city must be held at all costs, and the evacuation of industry was stopped, because it would imply that Stalingrad might be lost. As John Erickson commented, with that decision 'Stalin had committed himself, the Red Army and the Russians at large to one of the most terrible battles in the whole history of war.' The ferocity of the German attack was matched by the tenacity of the defence. A giant grain elevator was held at one stage by Soviet marines, one of whom wrote an account: 'In the elevator the grain was on fire, the water in the machine-guns evaporated, the wounded were thirsty, but there was no water near by. This was how we defended ourselves twenty-four hours a day for three days.' In all, the grain elevator held out for eight weeks against constant attack. In another part of the city the main railway station changed hands from one side to the other no fewer than 16 times in four days. General Vasily Chuikov, who was appointed to command the defence of the city in September, described what he found: 'The streets of the city are dead. There is not a single green twig on the trees: everything has perished in the flames. All that is left of the wooden houses is a pile of ashes and stove chimneys sticking out of them. The many stone houses are burned out . . .'

As the German troops crept forward in Stalingrad, their position grew more precarious, at the end of a long salient whose northern flank stretched for some 250 miles along the River Don. This flank was held, not by Germans, but by their allies – Rumanians, Hungarians and Italians – *reliance on allies* who were not up to German standards in either equipment or morale. The situation of the German Sixth Army at Stalingrad was more vulnerable than its commanders realised.

On the other side, Stalin too became personally committed to the battle of Stalingrad. The city bore his name, and had been written into his version of Bolshevik history, and he was determined that it should not fall to the Germans. At the end of August he showed the importance he attached to the battle by putting Georgy Zhukov (his most trusted as well as most distinguished general) in command of the whole front around Stalingrad. On 12 September Stalin ordered that at least some part of the city must be held, whatever the cost, and sent reinforcements to the defenders. It was not entirely strange that rumours circulated that Stalin himself had been seen in the city, walking calmly in the forward defences, and visiting his old headquarters where he had worked in 1918. Antony Beevor assures us that these stories 'had absolutely no foundation in truth';

16 Stalingrad – battle among the ruins. Soviet troops in the wreckage of a factory.

but they were mentioned in *Pravda* in January 1943, which gave them official sanction. There was a curious parallel on the German side, where one diarist wrote on 1 December: 'The Führer is amongst us. This stiffens our backs and we find the pluck to carry on.'

So the two dictators faced one another in an intense, though long-range, personal duel. But while Hitler's obsession forced the German army at Stalingrad into a position of desperate danger, Stalin's helped to prepare a trap. The troops on both sides suffered heavily, but to very different purposes. German lives were simply thrown away. The Russians, however, were sacrificed, not just to hold the city, but to fix German attention while a whole new Soviet force was formed to the north of Stalingrad, with the Germans completely unaware of its existence.

By mid-November 1942 what may be called the first battle of Stalingrad drew to an end. The last German offensive to capture the remaining scraps of territory and ruined buildings came to a halt through sheer exhaustion, and the weary German troops prepared as best they could to spend a winter in their cellars and dug-outs. It was not yet clear what had happened. The Germans had not won the battle of Stalingrad, but equally they had not yet lost it. They had dug for themselves a dangerously deep hole, but it was not yet certain that it would become a death-trap. The Soviets for their part had won a limited victory, holding on, at terrible cost, to a narrow strip of a ruined city; but it was by no means certain that they could convert this into a triumph. The first battle of Stalingrad was grim and hard-fought, but not a turning point for either the Germans or the Russians. It was the second battle of Stalingrad that proved decisive for both sides.

On the Soviet side, the key to the new scale and nature of the operation lay in the plan conceived by Generals Zhukov and Vasilevsky for an offensive that would not simply drive the Germans back, but achieve a deep, large-scale encirclement from both north and south, which would cut off the whole German Sixth Army at Stalingrad. The Soviet attack from the north (Operation URANUS) began on 19 November in an area where Rumanian divisions held a line near the River Don, about a hundred miles away from Stalingrad itself. The assault came as a complete surprise – German Army intelligence had been convinced that the Red Army simply did not have the strength to launch such an offensive. A smaller attack, some 30 miles to the south of Stalingrad, opened on 20 November, and the two Soviet forces met near the town of Kalach, on the Don, on the 23rd. This meeting was re-enacted for the newsreel cameras a few days later, to be shown in cinemas across the world – the Soviets fully understood that they were winning a propaganda victory as well as a military one.

The scope of the Soviet encirclement now became clear. The German Sixth Army was cut off around Stalingrad, not by a narrow corridor, but by a tract of territory that left it 75 miles from the nearest German forces. The trap was well and truly sprung. The Soviets had won surprise; and they had also achieved material superiority, in tanks, guns and aircraft. In 1942 Soviet tank production far exceeded anything expected by the Germans. Halder, while still Chief of the General Staff, had warned Hitler that the Russians were producing 1,200 tanks a month, but Hitler refused to believe that they could make so many. They were both wrong: the true figure was 2,200 per month, including large numbers of the formidable T-34s. The Soviet forces also massed some 3,500 guns and mortars for their opening bombardment. Moreover, the whole operation was directed with a completely new degree of flexibility. In earlier campaigns the Germans had counted on defeating superior Soviet numbers by speed of movement and manoeuvrability, but they could do so no longer. They were now out-thought as well as out-fought.

The Germans around Stalingrad were in a desperate plight. One soldier wrote in his diary: 'We are surrounded. From the 21st of November to this day [1 December] has been the most frightful period of my life. All that time we were out in the open fighting as we retreated. Always only a hair's breadth removal from captivity or death. Both of my big toes are frostbitten.' Another found himself at the end of the world:

> It was probably the saddest and most desolate place I had laid eyes on in the east. A bare, naked steppe landscape with not a bush or tree, not a village for miles around. . . . Occasionally an ice-grey mist from the Volga drifted over this desolate piece of ground and the wind, which cut through everything with its biting edge, blew unmercifully over the boundless snowy waste.

The best hope (though a slender one) for the beleaguered army was to break out from its encirclement. As early as 22 November, just before the ring was finally closed, Paulus and his chief of staff, General Schmidt, began to make plans for a break-out to the south-west, towards the nearest part of the German line. Other generals at Hitler's headquarters had the same idea, but Hitler would not hear of it. Instead, on 24 November, he ordered that 'Fortress Stalingrad' was to be held, whatever the cost and whatever the circumstances. He was convinced that if the Germans left the Volga they would never return; and therefore they must not leave. It was the final expression of his obsession with Stalingrad.

If the Sixth Army was not to break out of its encirclement, then it would have to be supplied by air until a relief operation could be mounted. The army's own estimate of its needs was 700 tons per day – food, munitions and all the other necessities of daily life. Goering, who undertook to carry out the operation, scaled this down, and instructed his transport commanders that they must fly in 500 tons per day, but they told him that they could manage no more than 350 tons per day, and that not for very long. In fact, in the first *week* – not day – of the airlift (23–30 November), the Luftwaffe delivered only 350 tons. This improved in the second week to 512 tons, but this was still far short of the army's needs. A German corporal wrote in his diary: 'Snow, snow and nothing but. The food is horrible and we are hungry all the time. . . . One loaf must do for seven men. We shall now have to tackle the horses.' He found horse-meat not so bad, but killing horses left the troops short of draught animals if they were ever to move. The Ju-52 transport aircraft, flying in appalling weather, suffered heavy losses. Despite heroic efforts on the ground and in the air, the Luftwaffe could not sustain the Sixth Army.

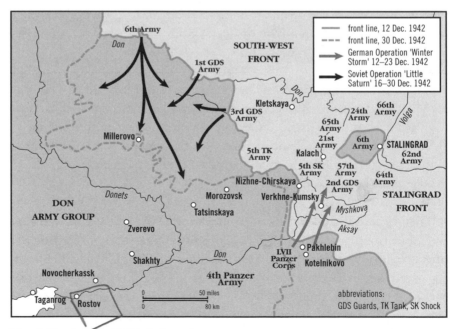

Map 8 Russian Attack 'Little Saturn'.

Meanwhile, the Germans prepared an offensive to break through to Stalingrad; yet still, at Hitler's insistence, the object was not to get the Sixth Army *out* of Stalingrad, but to enable it to *stay* there. A newly formed Army Group, commanded by General Manstein, one of the ablest German generals of the whole war, was assembled, including a full-strength Panzer division newly arrived from Brittany; but its success was short-lived. The Germans opened their attack, code-named WINTER STORM, on 12 December, from an area around Kotelnikovo, about 100 miles from the nearest German lines at Stalingrad. It was spear-headed by the Fourth Panzer Army, under General Hoth, which advanced at one point to within 40 miles of the German lines at Stalingrad. The gunfire of the relief army was heard in Stalingrad, raising hopes that rescue was at hand – indeed, it seems that the soldiers of the Sixth Army still believed Hitler would not abandon them. But the Russians too had prepared an offensive (code-named LITTLE SATURN), to be launched from the north, striking at the left flank of Manstein's army and threatening to encircle it. The assault opened on 16 December, only four days after the Germans' own attack had begun, and achieved a rapid success. The Russians advanced so quickly that Manstein feared at one stage they were going to reach Rostov, at the mouth of the Don, and cut off his army completely. So on 23 December, only eleven days into its attempt to relieve the Sixth Army, Hoth's Panzer Army was ordered to retreat. That was the end for the Germans at Stalingrad. Paulus's army could not be saved.

In fact it was worse than a defeat; it was a disaster, though it was remarkably slow in coming. At the beginning of January 1943 the Germans held a roughly circular pocket, or cauldron, with the city of Stalingrad at one edge. The Russian assault to finish off the encircled army, called simply Operation RING, began on 10 January. The Russians used masses of guns and rockets, and attacked in enormous numbers, regardless of casualties. But the Germans resisted with dogged determination. The airlift continued, using two remaining airfields, sometimes taking in as much as 120 tons of supplies a day, and taking out as many of the wounded as possible. The fighting was so severe that General Rokossovsky, commanding the Soviet forces, had to call a temporary halt on 17 January. The attacks resumed on the 21st, when the Germans lost their last airfield. On the 22nd Paulus suggested to Hitler that he should surrender, but Hitler refused. On the 30th Hitler promoted Paulus to Field Marshal, hoping that this would inspire him to hold on to the end and then commit suicide.

In fact Paulus received his promotion on 30 January and surrendered on the 31st, along with the troops in the small patch of ground where he still held the command. Another small pocket of resistance held out until 2 February. In all, about 91,000 men surrendered – many of them to face certain death as prisoners. The number of those killed since the Sixth Army was cut off in November 1942 was somewhere between 60,000 and 100,000. At the time of the surrender, a war correspondent wrote in the *Daily Herald* that 'it was the biggest defeat the German Army has ever suffered in its history'. Some 60 years later the historian Evan Mawdsley judged that 'The disaster was unprecedented in the history of the German Army.' Journalists and historians do not always see so closely eye to eye, so these virtually identical judgements are remarkably impressive.

This crushing defeat made a profound impact in Germany. The casualties in the two battles of Stalingrad, from August 1942 to the beginning of February 1943, amounted to about half a million killed, Germans and their

17 After the battle. German prisoners trudge through the snow to captivity. Many would not survive.

allies together. The scale of these losses could not be concealed, even by Goebbels's propaganda machine. Nor could the stories of those who survived and came home, often wounded, frostbitten or stricken by illness. Letters from the front told the same grim tale.

The reaction at the top of the Nazi hierarchy was muted. It so happened that 30 January 1943, one of the last days for the survivors surrounded at Stalingrad, was also the tenth anniversary of Hitler's taking power as Chancellor in 1933. Hitler himself chose not to speak – a marked omission in itself; and Goebbels read the text of his speech on the radio. There was only one reference to Stalingrad, and then not by name. 'The heroic struggle of our soldiers on the Volga should be a warning for everybody to do the utmost for the struggle for Germany's freedom and the future of our people, and thus in a wider sense for the maintenance of our entire continent.' This obscure sentence at least hinted that the times of conquest were over, and that Germany must now undertake a war of defence.

effects on German morale

Throughout the whole country, the news from Stalingrad produced a reaction of dismay and depression. The Gestapo reported that the nation was 'deeply shaken'. In Nuremberg crowds around the newspaper stands shouted openly that Hitler had lied to them for months – a sign that the Führer's immunity from criticism was beginning to fail. When Hitler eventually broadcast to the nation on 21 March, Heroes' Memorial Day, he again did not mention Stalingrad by name, and his speech met with an unprecedented degree of adverse criticism among his listeners. Ian Kershaw sums up the public mood: 'sullenly depressed, anxious about the present, fearful of the future, above all else weary of the war – though not rebellious.' Stalingrad had dealt a blow to German morale from which it never recovered.

When all was over, Hitler tried to pretend that Stalingrad had never happened, and it is said that he never mentioned it again. But of course Stalingrad *had* happened, and it was the Führer's own strategy that had come to grief. It was Hitler who had decided to try for both the conquest of the Caucasian oilfields and the capture of Stalingrad, and had achieved neither. It was Hitler who had staked his own prestige on victory at Stalingrad, and had claimed that it was within his grasp, only to fail at the last. It was Hitler who had ordered Paulus to hold Stalingrad rather than break out, and then to fight to the last rather than surrender, only to see his newly promoted Field Marshal capitulate. Hitler had repeatedly insisted on the power of the will, but had found that in an equal conflict of wills

Hitler's strategy failed

the weight of numbers and war material prevailed in the long run. Before Stalingrad, Hitler had often overruled his generals, and been proved right. But this time he had been proved disastrously wrong. Hitler had staked everything, not least his own prestige, on Stalingrad and had lost.

On the Soviet side, the picture was reversed. The German sense of defeat was matched by a realisation of victory. As early as the opening of the Soviet offensive on 19 November 1942, many participants felt that a turning point had come. When the battle was over, the whole country felt a surge in confidence. A saying at the time, much repeated, was: 'You cannot stop an army which has done Stalingrad.' Hitler's loss of prestige was more than matched by Stalin's gain. Stalin assumed the rank of Marshal of the Soviet Union, ostensibly at the behest of the Presidium of the Supreme Soviet – which was rather like promoting himself, though with an apparent modesty. Victory at Stalingrad, the city which bore his name, removed any doubts that had clung to his reputation from the defeats of 1941 and the summer of 1942. He now emerged beyond all doubt as the great war leader, stern yet benevolent, whose face appeared everywhere in cinema newsreels and photographs.

Spread of Soviet power / support

The fame of Stalingrad and the prestige of Stalin himself spread far outside the Soviet Union. In Britain, Red Army Day was celebrated on 23 February 1943 with official ceremonies and enthusiastic public support, and with a strong focus on Stalin as the hero of the hour. As a mark of public tribute to the city and battle of Stalingrad, the Stalingrad Sword was commissioned by the government and specially forged, bearing the inscription: 'To the steel-hearted citizens of Stalingrad, the gift of King George VI, in token of the homage of the British people.' Almost half a million people filed past this symbolic weapon during the 33 days during which it was on display up and down Britain. In Nazi-occupied Europe there could of course be no such public shows of admiration, but Stalin's name flourished in the clandestine press and among the resistance movements. The prestige of Stalin and of communism thus achieved a new and lasting impetus. It was now certain that the Red Army would emerge as the strongest military force in Europe, and that the Soviet Union would exercise a profound influence over much of the continent.

It may well be argued, as Richard Overy has done, that Stalingrad alone was not in a military sense a decisive turning point in the Second World War, but rather that it laid the foundations for later victories in 1943. In such a perspective, the Battle of Kursk (July–August 1943) appears as 'the most important single victory of the war', because it was the first German defeat in high summer (as against winter, when the climatic conditions favoured the Russians), and because it was a decisive victory for Soviet armoured forces over the German Panzers in the biggest tank battle of the war. This is true enough, but even so Stalingrad deserves a place as a major turning point in the whole war.

First, Stalingrad was a decisive military victory. A whole German army was not just defeated but ceased to exist, with its battle-hardened troops and all its high-ranking officers, headed by a Field Marshal. This was a moral as well as a material blow. The German reputation for invincibility, which was an arm of war in itself, was destroyed. In a wider strategic sense, the whole German campaign in Russia was left directionless. Hitler's two aims for 1942 – to capture the oil of the Caucasus and the city of Stalingrad – had both been frustrated; and there was no clear objective to take their place. In plain words, 'Germany no longer had a grand strategy'.

why Stalingrad is a turning point

That was not all, even on the military side. The strategic affects of Stalingrad spread far beyond Russia and the Eastern Front. On 1 January 1943 General Brooke, the Chief of the Imperial General Staff, reflected in his diary on the contrast with the position a year ago:

> I felt Russia could never hold, Caucasus was bound to be penetrated, and Abadan (our Achilles heel) would be captured with the consequent collapse of Middle East, India, etc. After Russia's defeat how were we to handle the German land and air forces liberated? England would be again bombarded, threat of invasion revived. . . . And now! We start 1943 under conditions I would never have dared to hope. Russia has held, Egypt for the present is safe. There is a hope of clearing North Africa of Germans in the near future. . . . Russia is scoring wonderful successes in Southern Russia.

The transformation that Brooke described here was very largely the result of the battle of Stalingrad. The British, of course, won their own battle at El Alamein in Egypt in November 1942, which rightly figures prominently in British and Commonwealth accounts of the Second World War. But there were only about 50,000 German troops at El Alamein, whereas the Germans actually *lost* 200,000, killed and captured, at Stalingrad. 'The Hinge of Fate', as Churchill entitled the fourth volume of his war memoirs, swung primarily at Stalingrad.

The Soviets were skilled at turning military victory into propaganda triumph, especially through the use of film. Camera crews followed the street fighting in Stalingrad, accepting all the risks and casualties of their dangerous trade – in the whole war, no fewer than 40 Soviet cameramen were killed on the Eastern Front. It was for good reason that large numbers of Soviet troops were used to re-enact the closing of the ring around the Germans trapped in Stalingrad in November 1942; and when the final victory came the newsreels made the most of it. Using striking graphics, the swastika was shown being swallowed up by the hammer and sickle, against a background of the gaunt ruins of Stalingrad's buildings. The scale of the Soviet victory was driven home by film of long lines of prisoners winding interminably across the snow. Stalingrad marked a psychological as well as a military turning point, and Soviet propaganda hammered home the message with stunning effect.

Politics followed strategy and propaganda. Stalin's prestige was now enormous, putting the Soviet leader in a strong position when he dealt with Churchill and Roosevelt, and particularly when the three statesmen met face to face for the first time in Teheran at the end of November 1943. Admiration for Stalin naturally rubbed off on to the country he ruled and the communist system by which it was organised. British public opinion was deeply impressed by the achievements of the Soviet Union in winning the war on the Eastern Front, especially at a time when Britain's own contribution to the land campaigns was comparatively limited. Across much of occupied Europe, the prestige and role of Communist parties in resistance movements were further enhanced. Victory brought its own endorsement and justification for the Soviet regime. For strategic, propaganda and political reasons, Stalingrad takes its place as one of the decisive turning points of the Second World War – and perhaps the greatest of them all.

CHAPTER SEVEN

CONVOYS AND WOLF PACKS
DECISION IN THE ATLANTIC, MARCH–MAY 1943

The Battle of Stalingrad typified the war on the Eastern Front – an immense struggle, involving hundreds of thousands of men and vast amounts of equipment and munitions. By comparison, the Battle of the Atlantic was a small-scale affair. The Germans built just over 1,150 U-boats during the whole war, manned by 40,900 men; and not all of these ships and men served in the Atlantic area. On the Allied side, even during the most intense stages of the conflict, there were no more than a dozen convoys at sea at any one time – perhaps about 500 merchant ships. But the importance of the battle was far greater than the numbers of ships and men involved. On the Allied side, Britain faced economic strangulation and physical starvation if its Atlantic lifeline for supplies from North America was cut. For the United States, the Atlantic was geographically the only way they could bring their forces to bear in Europe – quite simply, the American Army could not invade western Europe without crossing the Atlantic first. The Atlantic sea lanes also carried supplies for the Soviet Union, to be sent on by the Arctic route to northern Russia – support that was of the highest military and political importance for the anti-German alliance. For the Germans, their only chance of defeating the British when invasion and bombing failed was to cut off their seaborne supplies. For both sides, therefore, the fate of the war rested on those comparatively few men who fought the arduous Battle of the Atlantic.

It was Churchill who gave this great struggle its name. Early in March 1941, he told Admiral Pound, the First Sea Lord: 'I am going to proclaim "the Battle of the Atlantic"', using this striking phrase as a signal to concentrate attention on the U-boat war. One of his first steps was to set up a committee, the Battle of the Atlantic Committee, bringing together all the relevant armed services and civilian departments (for example, the Ministries of Food and Transport), meeting at first every week, often with Churchill himself as chairman. This apparently humdrum measure was in fact of key importance. On the German side, it would never have occurred to Hitler to set up a committee as the best way to conduct a great battle. Instead, he kept all the different commanders and administrators apart, dealing with them separately, and often causing muddle and contradictions in consequence. The British method of putting everyone concerned around a table did not always work, but it was a good start.

Churchill's choice of name stuck. 'The Battle of the Atlantic' has entered the language, becoming almost as famous as the Battle of Trafalgar. But these were completely different events. Trafalgar was a battle in the conventional sense, fought at a particular place and on a specific date. The Battle of the Atlantic lasted as long as the war in the west, from September 1939 to May 1945. It was waged over three continents and a vast expanse of ocean. It drew in all sorts of men and women: hardy merchant seamen and intellectual code-breakers; high-ranking naval officers and Wrens, who kept charts of the Atlantic up to date; the crews of solitary aircraft and the crowded vessels of a convoy. It was the only campaign in which the most important events were non-events. Most convoys crossed the Atlantic without being attacked at all, and each marked a significant victory – 'Happy is the convoy that has no history'.

In all these ways the Battle of the Atlantic was a complex and extraordinary set of events – not so much a battle as a campaign, or even a war in its own right, with its own form and character. For almost three years, from July 1940 (when the Germans began to use the French Atlantic ports) to May 1943, the struggle was indecisive, swaying this way and that as one side or the other gained an advantage. Then suddenly the turning point came in three weeks, from 4 to 24 May 1943, when the German U-boats lost the battle and the Allies won it. We can only understand this transformation if we look first at the whole nature of the conflict and how it was fought. We can only see the drama of the denouement when we have set the scene and followed the early acts.

For almost the whole of the Atlantic battle, the Germans were the attackers, and the British, Canadians and Americans were the defenders. The Germans had a range of weapons at their disposal. Surface ships, whether warships or armed merchantmen, proved less effective than they had hoped. Aircraft were very successful in the early years, sinking 580,000 tons of British shipping in 1940 and over a million tons in 1941, with the long-range Focke-Wulf Condors flying far over the Atlantic. But the main killer of merchant ships was the submarine. The main ocean-going U-boats were the Type VII and Type IX, vessels of 700 to 1,100 tons, with ranges varying between 6,500 and 13,450 miles, and a top speed on the surface of 17 to 19 knots, which was fast enough to catch most merchant ships and outrun many escort vessels. These types of U-boat, with modifications, formed the bulk of German forces engaged in the Atlantic throughout the war.

The commander of the German U-boat force was Admiral Karl Dönitz, who had himself been a U-boat captain towards the end of the Great War, and had commanded the first flotilla of U-boats formed in 1935 as Germany rearmed. He was a keen thinker about submarine warfare, and early in 1939 published a book on U-boat tactics advocating night attacks on the surface, using boats in groups (or packs) – a significant volume, which British Naval Intelligence seems to have missed. In manner he was formal, even stiff; and he bore the loss of his two sons in action with

18 The attackers. German U-boat on the surface.

19 U-boat Admiral Karl Dönitz. His principal tactic was night attack by 'wolfpacks', operating on the surface.

fortitude. But he knew about U-boat warfare at first hand, and was deeply concerned about the welfare and morale of his men. In 1940 he set up his headquarters near Lorient, in Brittany, and made a point of meeting returning U-boats and talking to their crews, which had a powerful effect on morale. A British historian has described him as 'one of the great commanders' of the war.

For all his qualities, Dönitz laboured under serious disadvantages. At crucial times he did not have enough U-boats to do the job he had undertaken; and he worked with too small a staff – the entire U-boat command could be transported in a few cars and a single lorry carrying a radio transmitter. This showed an admirable determination to reduce bureaucracy, but proved inadequate to deal with the complex nature of the U-boat war. (The British, with a larger staff and a wide-ranging scientific approach to anti-submarine warfare, achieved better results.) On 30 January 1943 Dönitz replaced Grand Admiral Raeder as Commander-in-Chief of the whole German Navy, while retaining the command of the U-boat fleet for himself, leaving the day-to-day conduct of operations to his chief of staff. In practice, Dönitz had to shift his headquarters to Berlin, and lost his regular contact with the U-boat crews. This was a crucial time, bcause the U-boat fleet had suffered such casualties that captains were mostly in their twenties, and their crews were even younger. On average, U-boats survived no more than three or four patrols before being sunk, leaving their crews with little chance of survival. The demands on the courage of these crews grew steadily greater, and Dönitz's influence on morale diminished at the very time when it was needed most.

On the British side, the Admiralty began the war with a sense of confidence that they could deal with submarine attack. In the Great War, the U-boat campaign of 1917 had eventually been defeated by the convoy system, in which merchant ships had sailed in groups under the escort of warships. Between the wars, the organisation for establishing convoys had been maintained and improved, and there was a belief amounting to certainty that the U-boats themselves could be dealt with by the device called Asdic, which could detect a submarine under the surface by emitting a sound pulse and picking up the rebound; although it had the limitation of revealing the direction and distance but not the depth of a submarine. Moreover, the Royal Navy did not have enough escort vessels to protect the convoys when they were organised.

Despite these difficulties, the convoy system that was introduced at the start of the war was the mainstay of the defence of shipping. A convoy might comprise somewhere between 30 and 80 merchant ships. It was axiomatic that a convoy moved at the speed of the slowest ship, so that many faster ships sailed independently; but over the whole war the proportion of losses was 80 per cent among the 'independents' to only 20 per cent of ships in convoy – an eloquent statistic. The prime duty of the commander of an escort was 'the safe and timely arrival of the convoy'; sinking a U-boat was a bonus, but took second place. Operational research, based on scientific principles, was increasingly used to work out the optimum size for convoys and the best way to use their escorts. (Dönitz, by contrast, had no operational research unit in his staff.)

As the war progressed, new types of escort vessels came into service, notably the fast and powerful sloops, and the workhorse corvettes, which were easy to build in large numbers but too slow to compete with a U-boat on the surface. The Canadians brought into being a whole new escort fleet – the Royal Canadian Navy consisted of a mere 6 warships in 1939, but grew to over 400 by 1945. Air cover proved to be of crucial importance for convoy protection, because the mere presence of a hostile aircraft forced U-boats to dive, and so deprived them of the advantages of operating on the surface.

20 Convoy at sea in the North Atlantic – the best method of protecting merchant ships, although they were still vulnerable to night attack by U-boats.

In the utmost secrecy, a key role in the Battle of the Atlantic was played by the Code and Cipher School at Bletchley Park, a Victorian mansion halfway between Oxford and Cambridge, where a staff of about 150 in 1939 and over 10,000 by 1945 worked with intense concentration and ingenuity to break enemy ciphers. The varying success and failure of Bletchley Park in breaking the German naval cipher did much to shift the balance of the conflict to and fro. For example, the British were reading German signals for most of 1941, so that the Admiralty could direct convoys away from known concentrations of U-boats; but that advantage was lost for most of 1942. On the other side, the Germans too worked hard at signals intelligence, and could read the British cipher for convoy traffic for much of the war. By a striking coincidence, each side had an unshakeable confidence in its own ciphers, and both were wrong!

All this immense and varied British effort in anti-submarine warfare was directed by the Western Approaches Command, which set up its headquarters at Liverpool in 1941. The Western Approaches staff was established and run with unobtrusive efficiency by Admiral Sir Percy Noble, who was succeeded in November 1942 by the more dynamic figure of Admiral Sir Max Horton. Horton had been a submarine commander in the Great War, when he torpedoed a German cruiser as early as 13 September 1914, and later operated in the German-dominated Baltic Sea. In 1939 he was in command of the Navy's submarine branch, and was thus familiar with submarine warfare in both action and administration. He was a man of formidable character, described by one of his staff as 'absolutely ruthless but so astute that he could see through a brick wall'. He made his own routine at Western Approaches HQ – golf at Hoylake most afternoons,

21 Admiral Sir Max Horton, the dynamic commander, Western Approaches. He understood the vital importance of air power in the Atlantic battle.

dinner and bridge in the evening, and then to the operations room, where he was prepared to stay all night if need be, driving his staff hard and keeping morale high. He understood the role of air power in anti-submarine warfare, and at one stage (April–May 1943) he pushed through the installation of anti-submarine rockets on to aircraft in a mere eight weeks, including fitting, training and the first sinking of a U-boat – a remarkable demonstration of the impulse he brought to his command. It would be misleading to see the Atlantic campaign in terms of the two admirals, Dönitz versus Horton, because in fact the two only confronted one another directly for a short time, before Dönitz moved to Berlin as Commander-in-Chief of the whole fleet; but in retrospect Horton thought that there had been a duel, and said that, even if offered the post of First Sea Lord, he would have declined it – 'I had got Dönitz where I wanted him and I intended to keep him there until the war was won.'

For both sides, the Battle of the Atlantic was dominated by the moods of the sea and the weather, which were often hostile in the extreme. One U-boat sailor wrote that in the trough of the waves 'We do not look down on to the sea, but up out of it, enveloped in water like swimmers. Whenever we are pulled down into its valleys, we have to stretch our heads up and back; we see with the eyes of the sea . . .'. And a U-boat captain wrote: 'North Atlantic weather! In such weather waging war stops of its own accord because everyone has enough on his hands without it . . .'. The crews of escort vessels led much the same wretched life. 'Gumboots fall upon their sides and fill with water. Trousers get soaked and press dankly upon one's legs. Shirts are sodden. Duffel coats are soggy sacks.' Merchant-ship captains were hard pressed to keep station in the convoys, and orders to 'Keep closed up' were often impossible to obey. One officer recalled: '. . . the attitude to convoy work? . . . we HATED it! The soul-destroying frus-tration; the physical strain of watch-keeping and station-keeping in convoy was one of the worst aspects of wartime seafaring.' Amid all these hardships there was an additional penalty when a vessel was sunk: a seaman's pay ceased from the day of sinking, often with disastrous conse-quences for his dependants. The merchant seamen (who were after all civilians) bore the burden of the battle with an endurance that too often went unrecognised and unrewarded. All in all, it was one of the marvels of the war that all the combatant groups – German U-boat men, Allied escort and air crews, and merchant seamen – stuck to their arduous and perilous tasks with such tenacity and courage.

The U-boat campaign against British shipping began on 3 September 1939, when the U-30 sank the passenger liner *Athenia*. But it was in 1940 that the Atlantic battle assumed the form it was to take for the next four years. The German occupation of Norway in April–May 1940 gave U-boats a short and secure northern route to the Atlantic. More important, the defeat of France provided the Germans with direct access to the ocean from the French ports in Brittany and the Bay of Biscay – Brest, Lorient, St Nazaire and La Pallice. Lorient was brought into operation as a U-boat base on 5 July, and was working as a dockyard for refitting submarines by the beginning of August. The use of these ports added two weeks to the duration of a normal U-boat operational cruise, increasing the number of U-boats on station at any one time. Meanwhile, with the conclusion of the Franco-German armistice, the French fleet, with its strong force of escort ships, dropped out of the fight. Moreover, for a time the British faced the threat of invasion, and had to concentrate their destroyers to cover the Channel crossings, thus weakening the defence of the convoys.

In these advantageous conditions, in the autumn of 1940 Dönitz was able to put into action his plans to use night attacks on the surface as the main tactic against convoys. This meant locating a convoy, usually by signals intelligence, which told the Germans where convoys were being routed; concentrating a group of U-boats against it; and sending the whole group into the attack on a single night. The Germans called this *die Rudeltaktik*, 'the wolf tactic', and the British soon called the groups 'wolf packs', a striking name with menacing undertones. The British speedily found that they had no defence against the wolf packs, because U-boats on the surface were faster than any escort ships except modern destroyers, which were rarely available for convoy duty. The attacking submarines could pass through the escort screen, and then pick their targets, almost at leisure, from *within* the convoy itself. These advantages gave the U-boats their first 'happy time', from June to October 1940, in which they sank no fewer than 274 merchant ships, totalling nearly 1.4 million tons. In October, one slow convoy (SC 7, eastbound) lost 21 ships out of 30, while another (HX 79, westbound) lost 12 out of 49.

The period between autumn 1940 and spring 1941 offered the Germans a valuable chance to achieve a decisive strategic result in the Battle of the Atlantic, but they were unable to take it because they had too few U-boats. The number of ocean-going U-boats actually declined from 27 in August 1940 to 21 in February 1941; and only about one-third of these were on station at any particular time, the others being on passage or in port.

Dönitz had long argued that he needed a total of 300 ocean-going U-boats to cut off British seaborne trade – indeed, 300 became for him of talismanic number. In fact a large-scale building programme only got under way in 1941, mainly because Hitler thought in 1940 that the British were sure to give up the fight. U-boat building actually declined in the summer and autumn of that year. As a result, Dönitz did not get his 300 U-boats until January 1943. The best U-boat tactics in the world were not enough when the Germans did not have the numbers to clinch their success.

The British, of course, were not aware of these German difficulties, and were only too conscious of their own troubles, which was why Churchill proclaimed the Battle of the Atlantic in March 1941. As it happened, the British scored some marked successes that same month. On 8 March, U-47, commanded by Gunter Prien (who in 1939 had made his name by sinking the battleship *Royal Oak* right inside the naval base at Scapa Flow), was sunk, and Prien killed. On 15 March two more U-boats were sunk, one rammed by a destroyer and the other caught by depth charges; both boats being commanded by much-decorated 'aces'. That meant the loss of three U-boat 'aces' within a week, and brought Dönitz's plans for a spring offensive to a temporary halt. Moreover, in May 1941 the 'escort gap' in mid-Atlantic (the zone where no escorts were provided, even for ships in convoy) was closed when an escort force was based in Newfoundland, and for the first time a convoy was continuously escorted across the Atlantic, with a handover at a meeting point south-west of Iceland. However, the 'air gap' (the zone that could not be covered by aircraft flying from either side of the Atlantic) was *not* closed at the same time, and the few very long-range Liberator bombers that could have done this crucial job were used by Bomber Command, arguably for less useful purposes.

There was another key event in May 1941, on the intelligence front. A German Enigma machine, along with signal logs and other papers, was captured intact aboard a U-boat which surrendered to a British warship. This boat, the U-110, later sank while being towed towards Iceland, so that no news of its capture reached the Germans. At the same time, the code-breakers at Bletchley Park introduced a new electro-mechanical device, referred to as a 'bombe', which simulated the Enigma by trying out scrambler settings at a rapid rate. By June 1941 these developments allowed Bletchley Park code-breakers to read German U-boat traffic rapidly, and sometimes as soon as its German recipients. The capture of a German weather ship in July provided more information. There were still some problems, but the British were able to read most U-boat signals for the rest of the year, so that the Admiralty was able to route convoys around areas where wolf packs and their scouting screens were known to be stationed.

At the same time, the British Western Approaches Command, set up in February 1941, was introducing new escort tactics for screening convoys against the wolf-pack attacks, and forming escort groups that trained together to pursue new methods of dealing with attacking U-boats. The United States, though still a neutral power, began to escort convoys as far as Iceland in September 1941, releasing British and Canadian warships for other duties.

All these developments, coming within a few months of each other, tilted the balance of the struggle in Britain's favour. Sinkings of merchant ships, which were running at about 300,000 tons per month in early 1941, were down to 120,000 tons per month by the end of the year. On the German side, Dönitz was encouraged by an increase in U-boat numbers, from about 80 at the start of 1941 to 250 at the end of the year, but he was unable to translate this growth in numbers into more sinkings of merchant ships. This was partly because the Allies brought more escort vessels into the conflict, and partly because in mid-1941 Dönitz had to transfer many

22 Rear plugging of a 'bombe' decoding device at Bletchley Park.

of his submarines to the Mediterranean, to support the Italians and Erwin Rommel's *Afrika Korps*, and to Norway, to support the invasion of the Soviet Union. The demands of these other theatres of war were so great that in November 1941 U-boat operations in the Atlantic virtually ceased. Dönitz protested, but Hitler ignored him.

The year 1942 began with a bang in the western Atlantic. Germany declared war on the USA in December 1941, and in January 1942 Dönitz despatched five long-range U-boats to operate off the east coast of America. This was a tiny force – one German historian has a chapter heading 'Five Boats versus the United States'; and over the next six months the Germans could maintain an average of only eight U-boats on the American coast. But they achieved results out of all proportion to their numbers. Not until April 1942 did the American government impose a black-out on the east-coast cities; and until then the U-boats could sight merchant ships silhouetted against the glow of the city lights, and pick them off like targets at a funfair. The Americans did not begin to set up a convoy system until May, concentrating instead on so-called offensive sweeps to hunt the U-boats, with paltry results – they sank none at all for three months, and only two in April and May. Meanwhile, in the same five months, U-boats sank 362 merchant ships, most of them on the American east coast; and Allied tonnage losses averaged about 500,000 tons per month. Even when convoys began on the east coast, the U-boats moved into the Caribbean and the Gulf of Mexico, and carried on sinking defenceless ships. This was the second 'happy time' for the U-boats, handed to them on a plate by astonishing American blunders, which were not fully put right until August 1942, when an interlocking convoy system for the whole of the Caribbean and east coast was established. At the same time, the Germans gained an intelligence advantage by the introduction, in February 1942, of a fourth rotor to their Enigma machines, producing a cipher impenetrable to the code-breakers at Bletchley Park, and rendering U-boat signals traffic unreadable for the rest of the year.

On 15 May 1942 Dönitz visited Hitler at his eastern headquarters at Rastenberg, and reported on the remarkable U-boat successes off the east coast of America. He was optimistic about the Battle of the Atlantic in general, with U-boats being built at the rate of about 20 per month, and sinkings of all kinds (by Germans, Italians and Japanese, and by aircraft and surface ships as well as submarines) reaching a peak of 700,000 tons in one month. But the Germans too had suffered losses. By the end of August 1942, 105 out of the 304 U-boats commissioned since the beginning of the war had been lost, and some 3,700 officers and men had been killed or taken prisoner. These losses, especially among experienced officers, were hard to make good. Moreover, so many new U-boats were coming into service that it was difficult to find crews, and some had to be manned by drafts from the Luftwaffe, with a decline in the high standards of the submarine service.

In the summer of 1942 the balance of power in the Atlantic was less favourable to the Germans than Dönitz indicated to Hitler. German U-boat numbers were increasing, but so were the numbers of Allied escorts. In August 1942 the British and Canadians together had 150 destroyers and nearly 200 corvettes available for escort duties, together with 30 sloops and a few of the new frigates. They were still stretched too thinly over all the convoys to provide complete protection, but their strength was increasing steadily, and the Americans were preparing to bring new escorts into action. Above all, the Allies brought four light aircraft carriers into operation toward the end of 1942, so that some escort groups could provide their own air cover. These escort carriers did not come into action on the convoy routes until spring 1943, but their very existence was ominous for the Germans.

In the background to these developments lay a crucial new element. American ship building was increasing at a formidable rate. When Dönitz went to see Hitler on 28 September 1942, to make another report on the U-boat war, the Führer took over the discussion at one point to insist that the enemy would not be able to replace shipping losses by new construction, because the Americans simply could not build as many ships as they claimed in public – it was, he said, mere propaganda. Not for the first time, Hitler was wrong, perhaps judging American propaganda by the standards of Dr Goebbels. The programme of 'Liberty Ships', devised by the industrialist Henry Kaiser, had seen its first vessel launched on 27 September 1941. After that, these 10,500-ton ships were 'built by the mile and chopped off by the yard', using a simple design which allowed them to be prefabricated by unskilled labour. By the end of December 1941, 35 Liberty Ships had been completed. In 1942 they were being built at the rate of over 60 a month; and there were more to come, at an even higher rate, in 1943. The Americans had other shipyards at work as well, so that their total production in 1943 reached six million tons. British and Commonwealth production reached a million tons for the same year. With Allied shipbuilding attaining these figures, the Germans ultimately had no hope of sinking more ships than the Allies could build. In the hidden competition between building and sinking, 1942 formed an important stage; though

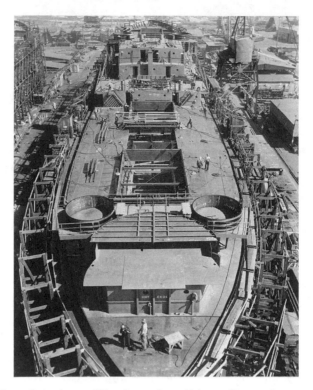

23 Built by the mile and cut off by the yard – a Liberty Ship under construction. The Americans mass-produced merchant ships using a simple design and unskilled labour.

the point at which construction overtook sinkings did not come until July 1943.

During 1942 the Allies introduced a range of new devices and methods to use against U-boats. Many escort vessels were fitted with High-Frequency Direction Finders (HF/DF from the initials, and Huff-Duff for short), which could pick up even the briefest U-boat radio transmission and fix its direction, though not its distance. (One German intelligence branch deduced the existence of Huff-Duff, or something like it, but put the information into a routine report where its significance was lost.) Centimetric radar, small enough to be fitted to escort ships without the cumbersome equipment previously required, could detect surfaced U-boats at night, diminishing one of the main advantages of the wolf packs. Depth charges were made more effective by operational research on the optimum depths at which they should explode. In the air, a simple but effective measure was to paint the underside of Coastal Command aircraft white, so that they were less visible to a U-boat look-out man against a cloudy sky. Powerful searchlights (Leigh Lights, after the name of their inventor) were fitted to bombers operating against U-boats by night.

On the other side, the Germans held the advantage in signals intelligence for most of 1942, being able to read the Allied cipher for the North Atlantic convoys, while Bletchley Park code-breakers were still grappling with the problems raised by the fourth rotor attached to the German Enigma machines in February 1942. But at the end of October the British had a stroke of fortune when the German submarine U-559 was sunk off Port Said in the Mediterranean, and her attackers managed to salvage a copy of the U-boat weather code and some valuable equipment. Along with improvements in code-breaking machinery, this enabled Bletchley Park code-breakers to resume reading U-boat signals from the middle of December 1942, restoring the balance in the intelligence war.

The importance of these developments, mostly telling against the U-boats and in favour of the Allies, has become plain in retrospect. But at the time the picture was darker for the Allies. In the six months from July to December 1942, U-boats sank, in all areas, no fewer than 575 merchant ships, totalling three million tons. In the whole year, U-boat sinkings amounted to 1,160 ships of over six million tons. November 1942 was a particularly bad month, with 128 ships lost, mostly sailing independently, but 35 in convoys. This was at a time when the Allies were carrying out Operation TORCH, the invasion of French North Africa, for which many of the forces sailed from North America, crossing the Atlantic before landing in Morocco and Algeria on 8 November. This placed an extra demand on escorts, and the Allies had to suspend the whole convoy system in the southern Atlantic, re-routing all shipping by way of North America as well as providing fewer escorts on those routes.

What we can now see with hindsight is the tilting of the balance against Germany in the course of 1942; but what the Allied high command saw at the end of that year was a tightening German grip on the passage of men and supplies across the Atlantic. At the Anglo-American conference at Casablanca in January 1943 General Brooke, Chief of the Imperial General Staff, reported that the scarcity of shipping was putting 'a strangle-hold on all offensive operations'. Churchill and Roosevelt, seeking the best strategy to defeat the Axis, concluded that nothing could be done until the Atlantic battle was won. The build-up of American forces in Britain in preparation for an invasion of France was already behind schedule, and the Allies needed more ships to get troops and equipment across the Atlantic. For a successful invasion of France to be launched, the Battle of the Atlantic had 'to be won and stay won'. To almost everyone's surprise, that was what happened in the following five months.

At the beginning of 1943 the German U-boat arm attained its greatest numerical strength so far. On 1 January there were 300 U-boats in commission – the number that Dönitz had set as his target in 1940. In February there were 178 U-boats in the Atlantic area, of which 70 were on station. In March the Germans had four groups of U-boats stationed across the northern convoy routes, on the edges of the air gap, and desperate convoy battles were fought. The slow convoy SC 121, westbound, lost 13 ships to U-boats, without sinking any of the attackers. In a five-day battle (16–20 March) around the convoys SC 122 and HX 229, 40 U-boats sank 21 ships for the loss of only one U-boat. In the whole of March 1943 the Germans located all the North Atlantic convoys, attacked half of them, and sank 22 per cent of the ships sailing in them. In the first 20 days of that month the U-boats sank 71 ships, amounting to nearly 510,000 tons, with cargoes of vital importance to Britain. One of the ships sunk in HX 229 was the Liberty ship *William Eustis*, with 7,000 tons of sugar aboard – one of her officers was horrified to think that they had lost about three weeks' sugar ration for the British people! Another vessel, the *Nariva*, sank with a cargo of meat, and an eyewitness recalled that: 'The surface of the sea all around the ship was littered with still-frozen carcasses of lamb and mutton . . .'.

The German successes were so great that a sense of crisis became intense in the Admiralty in London. One day in late March, a senior official visited Admiral Horton at his Liverpool headquarters to tell him that they were considering abandoning convoys and instructing all merchant ships to sail independently. As the Naval Staff summed up later: 'It appeared possible that we should not be able to continue [to regard] convoy as an effective system of defence.' This would mean disaster, because convoy was the essential basis for the defence of trade, and there was nothing to put in its place. The British official historian commented later that 'they must have felt, though no-one admitted it, that defeat then stared them in the face'. It was a moment fraught with danger.

And yet almost at the same time the balance of the battle was beginning to tilt against the Germans. April was a less successful month for the U-boats than March, with 270,000 tons of shipping sunk. Moreover, British intelligence detected a decline in the morale of the U-boat crews, with some captains failing to press home their attacks. Intercepts revealed that Dönitz was reprimanding some of his commanders for not sinking enough ships. By May the British had recovered their confidence. They were ready to abandon their defensive strategy of avoiding the U-boats by evasive routing, and take on the wolf packs head to head, and defeat them outright. And that is what happened. In a fierce battle around convoy ONS 5 (4–6 May 1943), the Germans sank no fewer than 12 merchant ships, but they themselves lost 9 U-boats sunk and 5 badly damaged out of 41 engaged – a formidable rate of loss. Admiral Godt, Dönitz's chief of staff, was compelled to break off the action. The escort crews who fought this battle sensed that it was a turning point, because no force could sustain casualties on such a scale. A Canadian historian later judged that: 'In one action the mystique of the Wolf Pack had been broken.'

So it proved. In the next few days, one convoy battle after another followed a similar pattern. On 11–13 May a group of seven U-boats attacked convoy HX 237, and met not only the convoy's escort but also a support group including the light aircraft carrier HMS *Biter*. One U-boat captain found to his surprise that he was being attacked from the air by a *small* aeroplane, and rightly deduced the presence of a carrier – an ominous development. The U-boats sank three merchantmen (all stragglers), but lost three of their own number – an unacceptable rate of exchange. After two days, the German U-boat commander called off the attack. Meanwhile, on 12 May no fewer than 25 U-boats were ordered to intercept a slow convoy, SC 129. Twelve made contact with the convoy, but all were found and attacked by the escort, again reinforced by *Biter*'s support group. Only two merchant ships were lost (both stragglers); two U-boats were sunk and others damaged. Admiral Godt again broke off the action. On 18–20 May a total of 30 U-boats attacked slow convoy SC 130, which was protected by continuous air cover. Five U-boats were lost, without a single merchantman being sunk. (One of the U-boats destroyed carried Dönitz's younger son among its officers – the Admiral's second son to be killed in action.) The U-boat commander again broke off the attack. On 22–23 May U-boats attacked convoy HX 239, and lost two of their number, both to aircraft from escort carriers, one American and one British. No merchantmen were sunk. The outcome was by then familiar. Godt called off the attack. The losses were too high.

In the two weeks from 10 to 24 May 1943, ten convoys comprising 370 merchant ships passed through the German wolf packs, losing only six ships. Thirteen U-boats were sunk; while seven more were lost to aircraft attack as they crossed the Bay of Biscay. It was a decisive Allied victory. Dönitz was reluctant to accept defeat, and on 21 May he signalled to all his U-boat commanders that anyone who thought it was impossible to defeat the convoys was 'a weakling and no real U-boat commander'. But on 24 May he bowed to the inevitable and ordered the U-boats to withdraw west of the Azores, out of range of shore-based aircraft, and not to attack convoys except under especially favourable circumstances. He intended this to be only a temporary measure, while the U-boats recovered their strength; but in the event there proved to be no way back. On the Allied side, Admiral Horton understood very well what had happened, and signalled to his forces on 1 June that: 'The last two months of the Battle of the Atlantic [have] undergone a decisive change in our favour . . . . The climax of the battle has been surmounted.'

The Battle of the Atlantic had been a war of attrition, lasting in its most intense form for three years, and yet the final victory came in an astonishing three months. March 1943 was one of the worst months in the war for the Allies, and the best for the U-boats, but by the end of May Dönitz had withdrawn his U-boats from the battle. What had happened?

There was no single cause for the change. In some ways the shift had been coming for some time, but had been hidden beneath the surface of events. The Allies had been building large numbers of escort ships and developing new devices, weapons and tactics. Centimetric radar, High-Frequency Direction Finders, better depth charges – all these were introduced slowly and were available by spring 1943 in sufficient quantities to tip the balance of the Atlantic battle decisively in favour of the Allies.

These gradual changes were accompanied in late March 1943 by a decisive intervention by Admiral Horton, who persuaded Churchill to stop the Arctic convoys to the Soviet Union for a time, and use the destroyers and frigates so saved to form five support groups for the Atlantic convoys. These groups were available to support any convoy under attack, and could shift quickly from one convoy battle to another. By May 1943 two or three of these groups included a light aircraft carrier, providing instant air cover and driving the U-boats under the surface.

In fact, air power was the most important single element in the victory. The 'air gap' in mid-Atlantic offered the U-boats the freedom to operate on the surface, and the wolf packs often gathered around the edges of the air gap. In 1942 the RAF had occasionally used Very Long Range (VLR) Liberator bombers to cover this gap, but only in May 1943 did RAF Coastal Command begin to operate nine VLR Liberators regularly from Iceland, and another nine 'ordinary' Liberators from Northern Ireland. These few aircraft had an effect out of all proportion to their numbers. For the Germans, the sight of a single aircraft was enough to make a U-boat crash-dive, while the Allied escort crews were revitalised. An American destroyer officer remembered his feelings: 'I recall the joy when we first saw an aircraft with us. At about the time they came out to cover us we had decided that

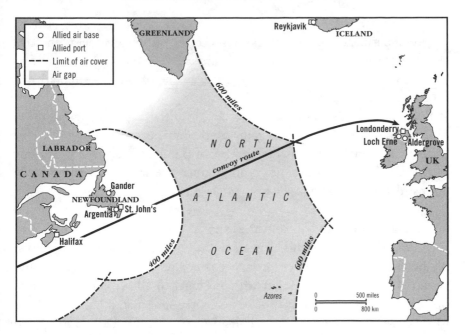

Map 9 North Atlantic 'Air Gap', 1942.

this convoy experience would last forever and that the Atlantic really had no "other side". We gave a real cheer when that first aircraft was spotted.' The proof of the pudding was in the sinking, as well as in the cheering – some 60 per cent of the U-boats sunk in May 1943 fell to aircraft, or a combination of aircraft and ships. Aircraft attacks also accounted for a substantial proportion of the U-boats that were forced to abandon their patrols and return to port without getting into action – the RAF made crossing the Bay of Biscay a dangerous as well as a rough passage.

Support groups and air power were directed by intelligence provided by the code-breakers at Bletchley Park, who had resumed their reading of U-boat signals from December 1942 onwards. There was a short break in this ULTRA intelligence material in the first three weeks in March 1943, which corresponded with the most successful German attacks on convoys; but after that the flow of information was resumed. For neither side was intelligence alone enough to secure victory. At the time of their Atlantic defeat in May 1943, the Germans were still reading the Admiralty cipher; but it was of little advantage for them to know where the Allied convoys were if they could not sink the ships. For the Allies, it was the combination of good intelligence with air power and improvements in weapons and tactics that achieved decisive results.

All these elements – new weapons and tactics, escort aircraft carriers, long-range Liberators, code-breaking successes – came together with decisive effect in May 1943. The long and arduous battle of attrition came to a sudden climax in an Allied victory. It was one of the most remarkable turning points in the whole war.

Far away from the battles at sea, the battle of the shipyards was also won in 1943. In July 1943 the Allied gains from new construction overtook their losses at sea, and after that the margin of building over sinking steadily increased. The tonnage war was won at much the same time as the battle against the wolf packs at sea.

The remainder of the U-boat war in the Atlantic was a low-key affair. In June 1943 Dönitz moved his U-boats to the South Atlantic, south and west of the Azores, out of range of land-based aircraft. But the British and Americans made an agreement with Portugal to allow Allied aircraft to operate from the Azores themselves, and the first planes began to fly in October 1943, extending the area of land-based air cover. Dönitz attempted a fresh offensive in autumn 1943, using new acoustic torpedoes, which homed in on propeller noises to improve the chances of a hit. U-boats scored a modest success with these weapons in September, sinking six merchantmen and three escorts for the loss of only two U-boats. But in October the Germans lost 26 U-boats, while sinking only 12 merchantmen.

In early 1944 the Germans still had nearly 200 operational U-boats, of which an average of 66 were at sea at any one time; but they found it very difficult to get into action. Their voyages were slow, taking a month to cross the Atlantic instead of a week in earlier times, because they had to remain submerged for long periods; and they were usually forced to operate alone instead of in packs. New types of submarine were being developed, capable of high underwater speeds and fitted with snorkels (combined air intake and exhaust gas outlets) to permit the U-boats to remain submerged for long periods. But construction was slow, and the production of snorkels was so disrupted by bombing attacks that by June 1944 there were only five snorkel boats in Norway and eight in France. The Allies expected that the Germans would attempt a strong, and if necessary suicidal, attack on the Normandy invasion fleet in June 1944, and made their defensive preparations accordingly, with intensive air patrols and no fewer than ten groups of surface ships to protect the invasion armada. In fact, Dönitz ordered 49 U-boats into action, but with little success. Two British frigates were sunk on one day, and three Liberty ships on another – a tiny proportion of the vessels involved in the invasion and its follow-up. In August 1944 the Allied break-out from the Normandy bridgehead forced the Germans to abandon their French U-boat bases and fall back on Norway or home ports.

Even so, the U-boats never gave up. In the last year of the war, from May 1944 to May 1945, their sinkings of merchant ships averaged some 50,000 tons a month – nothing like the total being built, but a considerable success under the circumstances. In April 1945 Dönitz even attempted a last wolf-pack operation, despatching 7 U-boats into the North Atlantic convoy routes. They were met by a massive force of 4 escort aircraft carriers and 40 destroyers, and lost 5 boats sunk, leaving 2 to surrender at the end of hostilities. As late as 5 May 1945, with the war almost over, there were still 25 U-boats in British waters or on passage, and the Allies were still deploying about 400 anti-submarine vessels and 800 aircraft against them.

The losses on both sides in the Battle of the Atlantic were severe, and in some cases horrific. In all, 2,828 Allied merchant ships and 148 warships were sunk by submarines. Casualties among merchant seamen are difficult to ascertain, but the total dead certainly numbered over 50,000, with about two-thirds killed by U-boat attack – a formidable figure for a supposedly 'civilian' body of men. On the German side, 1,131 U-boats were commissioned, 862 sailed on operations, and 754 were sunk. A U-boat memorial bears the names of 27,491 dead out of a total of nearly 41,000 who served in submarines – almost two-thirds in all, an enormous casualty rate.

The battle lasted six years from start to finish, though its intensity varied greatly from one period to another. What was at stake in this long and costly struggle was nothing less than the fate of the war in the west. Churchill put the issue plainly in his war memoirs. 'The only thing that ever really frightened me during the war was the U-boat peril. . . . Either the food, supplies and arms from the New World and from the British Empire arrived across the oceans, or they failed.' If they had failed, the British people would have faced starvation, and Britain could not have continued the war. After that, it is hard to see how the United States could have carried out an invasion of France without a British base. The Soviet Union would have lost the supplies that came across the Atlantic, and would have suffered heavily if there had been no Normandy landings. The Battle of the Atlantic was probably the least conspicuous conflict of the whole war, but surely the most vital in its outcome.

CHAPTER EIGHT

'THE PROPER APPLICATION OF OVERWHELMING FORCE'

THE BATTLE OF THE FACTORIES

Writing in his war memoirs, Churchill recalled his sense of relief when the United States was thrown into the war by the Japanese attack on Pearl Harbor on 7 December 1941. 'So we had won after all! . . . All the rest was merely the proper application of overwhelming force.' Stalin had said something similar on 6 November 1941: 'Modern war is a war of motors. The war will be won by whichever side produces the most motors.' He went on to claim that the combined American, British and Soviet production of motors was at least three times that of Germany – which, if true, seemed to leave the issue in no doubt. But in fact there was a good deal of doubt. The entry of the United States into the war was followed by one disaster after another for the Americans and British; and with the Germans advancing on Moscow, Stalin was by no means confident of victory, whatever the figures for the production of motors. Even so, the combined opinions of Churchill and Stalin carry great weight, and were justified by later events, when the economic resources of the United States, Britain and the Soviet Union were eventually translated into overwhelming power; and the side with the greater resources and heavier armaments won the war.

Yet this progression was by no means inevitable. History demonstrates that even overwhelming force does not always guarantee victory in war. In the Vietnam War of 1965–73, the Americans possessed immense material superiority over their opponents, but they eventually lost the war because they lost the will to win it. In Afghanistan between 1979 and 1988, the Soviet Union deployed superior force against their opponents but failed to crush them; and eventually the Soviets gave up the struggle and pulled out. In both these cases, morale and determination counted for more than numbers and weight of material. Moreover, quality of armaments can often be more important than quantity – for example, in Normandy in 1944 the German Tiger tanks were so powerful that a single well-placed Tiger could halt a strong Allied attack.

So numbers of men and weight of weaponry do not by themselves bring victory. But if other conditions are roughly equal, they can go a long way towards it; and they certainly did much to decide the outcome of the Second World War. It is true that there was no single dramatic turning point in the battle of the factories, like the German victory over France in six weeks in 1940; but the broad outline of events reveals a distinct period in which the balance of war production tilted decisively in favour of the Allies. The Second World War, despite its many complications, fell into two clearly defined phases: the initial triumph of the Axis, from 1939 to late 1942; and the victory of the Grand Alliance, from late 1942 to 1945. In the first phase, Germany and Japan scored striking victories over powers that on any reckoning of resources were economically superior; and surprise, speed and fighting power carried them through to the verge of final victory. But they failed to clinch their success, and in the second phase of the war the Allies first held their own, and then brought their immense resources to bear with overwhelming effect. The turning point in the battle of production and resources is to be found at the hinge between these two great phases of the war, at the end of 1942 and the beginning of 1943. The story starts with the war economies of the individual belligerent powers, and then moves on to bring out the comparative performance of the combatants which ultimately decided the issue.

2 distinct phases of 2ND WW

War Production: Germany and Japan

Germany was preparing for war well before the outbreak of hostilities in 1939. From the beginning of 1933 (when Hitler came to power) to the end of 1938 (the last full year of peace), the share of German industrial output devoted to arms production rose from a mere 1 per cent to 20 per cent. The aircraft industry grew at dizzying speed. Under the Treaty of Versailles of 1919, the Germans were forbidden to possess any military aircraft at all – a prohibition which they evaded, but only on a small scale, so that in 1932 the German aircraft industry produced no more than about 100 planes for military purposes. Expansion was then so rapid that by 1939 the production of military aircraft reached 8,295, and by 1940 it had reached 10,247. In a similar way, tank production started from almost nil in 1933, and reached 1,300 in 1939 and 2,200 in 1940.

German rearmament

To carry out the first strong push of its armaments programme, Germany possessed a strong industrial base and a skilled factory workforce. It had ample supplies of coal, and acquired more in 1940 by conquering the coalfields of Belgium and north-east France. On the minus side, the Germans lacked good-quality iron ore, and even after capturing the iron mines of Lorraine they remained heavily dependent on imports of iron ore from Sweden. Even more serious for a country preparing for war was lack of access to oil, the life-blood of modern warfare. In the 1930s Germany imported most of its oil from the Americas, sources that were at once cut off by the Allied naval blockade when war began. Germany's only secure source of oil was Rumania, which by 1940 was entirely under German control; and Germany imported between 2 and 3 million tons of oil per year from Rumania between 1940 and 1943. The Germans also seized large stocks of oil in western Europe by their conquests in 1940. In the long run, however, they relied increasingly on the production of synthetic oil by the chemical firm I.G. Farben; and in 1940 Germany produced 4 million tons of synthetic oil, rising to 6.5 million in 1943. The Germans also lacked supplies of rubber, which was mainly produced in Malaya and the Dutch East Indies; and again the Germans had to rely largely on synthetic production by I.G. Farben.

Germany's war economy thus showed a rough balance of strengths and weaknesses. Germany was basically a medium economic power, heavily reliant on its chemical industry and on imports of oil from Rumania and iron ore from Sweden. If the Germans became involved in war against the Soviet Union and the United States – which is what happened by the end of 1941 – then the balance of economic power would be heavily against them.

After the dramatic victories in 1940, Germany slowed down in some aspects of war production. Aircraft production rose only slowly from 10,247 in 1940 to 11,776 in 1941; and U-boat production actually declined in mid-1940. Tank production, on the other hand, more than doubled from 2,200 in 1940 to 5,200 in 1941, in preparation for the invasion of the Soviet Union. This slackening of pace in armaments production was mainly due to the euphoria created by the astonishing victory over France in 1940, and a natural though mistaken belief that the war was effectively over. Even the attack on the Soviet Union in 1941 was expected to bring another easy victory. For a time, even Hitler let industry take its foot off the accelerator. Moreover the Nazi regime, despite all its machinery of dictatorship and repression, sought to conciliate German

public opinion by protecting workers' hours of work and standard of living. *put resources into keeping civilians happy*
A German historian writes of 'an almost paranoid sensitivity to popular
sentiment', which may be going too far; but it was certainly true that the
Nazi government remained cautious in its treatment of German industrial
workers until well into 1942. It is striking that in 1941 nearly all German
war factories were working only one shift per day.

· This slackening of German industrial effort came to an end in 1942,
when war production put on a new spurt. On 22 January 1942, facing
setbacks on the Eastern Front, Hitler issued a directive mobilising all
possible resources for the armed forces and the arms industries. In
February he appointed Albert Speer (his chief architectural adviser and a
close political confidant) as Armaments Minister, with orders to increase
arms production. Speer quickly improved economic organisation by setting
up a Central Planning Committee to coordinate the work of the different
bodies concerned with war production. But it was the disastrous defeat at
Stalingrad in the winter of 1942–43 that led to more drastic measures. On
22 January 1943 Speer announced the Adolf Hitler Panzer Programme,
launched with a great propaganda fanfare, which aimed to boost the
production of tanks and self-propelled guns. On 18 February 1943
Goebbels made a striking effort to stimulate sentiment on the home front
by a dramatic speech at the *Sportspalast* in Berlin, calling for total war and
universal sacrifices.

There was a difficulty in this call for total war. The German workforce
was already at full stretch. It has sometimes been argued that there was
slack to be taken up, in that the Germans made less effective use of women
in the war economy than the British and Americans, because Nazi
ideology stressed the role of women in the home and family. But in fact as
early as 1939 the level of participation of women in the German workforce *Germans didn't involve their women as much in the war effort*
was already higher than it was to be in Britain and the United States *even
at the end of the war*. It was true that the majority of women workers were
in agriculture rather than industry, but farm work and food production
made a vital contribution to the war effort. In 1943 the German Ministry
of Labour undertook a registration of women aged between 16 and 45 for
total war, but found a potential of only an extra 1.5 million women
workers, of whom 700,000 could only work part-time. The Ministry
compared German figures for women workers with those in Britain and
the USA, and found that the share of women in war work was 34 per cent
in Germany, 33.1 per cent in Britain, and only 25.4 per cent in the United
States. So there was some slack to be taken up by recruiting more women,

but not much. Meanwhile, the numbers of German men in the war economy was declining, as more had to be called up into the Army to make up for casualties on the Russian Front. The only remaining resources were the use of foreign labour from the countries of occupied Europe, and employing Jews as forced labour before extermination.

labor shortages in Germany

Despite these difficulties, the Germans made a great spurt in war production in 1943–44. Aircraft production rose at a remarkable rate, from about 15,000 in 1942 to nearly 25,000 in 1943, and nearly 40,000 in 1944 – though some of this increase was achieved at the cost of quality, by building types that had slipped behind their enemies in performance. (The Me109, for example, was still a good aircraft, but by 1944 was inferior to the long-range Mustang fighters which were escorting American daylight bombing raids.) Tank production also increased: from 9,200 in 1942 to 17,300 in 1943, and 22,100 in 1944 – and many of these were powerful Tigers and Panthers. The production of guns more than trebled, from 12,000 in 1943 to 41,000 in 1944. There is some dispute as to how much of this achievement was due to the efforts of Speer himself. Certainly much of the 1943 production was the result of changes that were under way before Speer took charge; and Speer was undoubtedly adept at securing propaganda coverage for his efforts. In any case, whatever the role of Speer in person, the achievement itself was real. The trouble was that it was nothing like enough to meet Germany's needs. The Germans pushed their aircraft production up to nearly 40,000 in 1944; but the USA alone built 96,000 in the same year, to which the USSR added 40,000 and Britain 26,000, making 162,000 in all, or *four times* the German production. Moreover, the annual figures disguised the fact that the German effort peaked in the course of 1944. The production of aircraft began to decline in the summer; ammunition production fell away in September; and tank production dropped later in the year. Allied bombing, transport difficulties, and pressure on manpower all took their toll. The Germans also suffered from a growing shortage of oil, and there was little point in building aircraft if they were to be grounded for lack of fuel. The revived German war effort was not enough.

Moreover, it was too late, because Germany had passed the point of decision in 1942. At the beginning of that year, Hitler still hoped he could conquer the Caucasus in the next few months, and so secure enough oil to wage a long war. But if not, the economic resources ranged against Germany by the Russians, the Americans and the British would be overwhelming. Speer himself told the Central Planning Committee on 30 October 1942 that unless the war in the east was won that winter, by 1944

Germany would face what he euphemistically called 'a different situation'. In fact, Germany had lost the war of production by the end of 1942.

For much of the war, Germany was in the awkward position of having to carry a passenger, in the shape of Italy, which became an extra drain on German resources. Italy produced no oil, though ironically there were vast undiscovered deposits in Tripoli, then an Italian colony. By the end of 1942 Italian oil stocks were exhausted, and warships were unable to put to sea because they were out of fuel. The Italian aircraft industry was modest in output – 10,500 planes between January 1940 and April 1943 – and most of these aircraft were no match for their opponents. Tank production was low, and the tanks themselves were poorly armed and armoured. Italy thus proved to be a liability rather than an asset to the Axis war effort.

Italy was useless [handwritten margin note]

At first sight, the position of Japan was very different. The Japanese economy was partially on a war footing as early as 1937, to sustain the campaign in China. Then at the end of 1941 and early in 1942 the Japanese conquered the whole of South-East Asia, capturing ample resources of oil, rubber, tin and foodstuffs, and achieving something close to self-sufficiency. But in the event the Japanese were unable to make the most of these early triumphs. In the home base of Japan, Korea and Manchuria together, production of steel and coal remained steady between 1941 and 1944. Steel production (the basis for most armaments) reached a high point of 6.3 million tons in 1943, but fell to only 4.6 million in 1944. Coal production remained stuck at about 54 to 55 million tons in 1941–43, and fell to 49.3 million in 1944.

In land armaments, tank production was low. Its high point was 1,191 in 1942, falling away to a mere 401 in 1944. The tanks themselves were mostly light and poorly armed. Aircraft production did better, rising from 5,088 in 1941 to a peak of 28,180 in 1944. But these figures were much lower than American production, which reached 96,000 planes in 1944 – *over three times* the Japanese production, though of course many of the American aircraft were used against Germany. In naval production, Japan built only 438 major warships between 1942 and 1944, against 6,755 American. The cumulative effect of this disparity was overwhelming.

As the war went on, the whole Japanese effort was crippled at sea. There was little point in the Japanese controlling the oil and rubber resources of the Dutch East Indies and Malaya if they could not transport these materials by sea to Japan. The Americans began a submarine campaign against Japanese sea communications as early as 1942, at first with only modest success. But in 1943 the American submarines became more numerous, and in that year sank a total of 1.3 million tons of Japanese shipping. In 1944 sinkings rose to 2.7 million tons, which was far more than the Japanese could replace. The Americans increasingly concentrated their attacks on Japanese oil tankers, so that by the end of 1944 the total available tonnage of tankers was only 200,000 tons. The result was a near-strangulation of Japanese oil supplies, with disastrous effects on the whole war effort. The Japanese attempt at self-sufficiency, which was the object of all their early conquests, failed under an assault by American submarines which has been rather overshadowed by the more dramatic aspects of the defeat of Japan. What the German U-boats tried to do in the North Atlantic, the Americans actually achieved in Far Eastern waters.

War Production: The Allied Powers

Of the three principal powers making up the Grand Alliance, Britain was the smallest in size and material power but had the distinction of fighting the war from start to finish, from 1939 to 1945. As the war went on, the British achieved a remarkable degree of mobilisation of manpower. From December 1941 onwards, all men between the ages of 18 and 50, and women aged between 20 and 40, were called up for national service. By 1944, out of a total active population of 32,250,000, no fewer than 23,500,000 men and women were taking part in the war effort, either in the war economy or in the armed forces – 4.5 million of them in the Army. In this mobilisation, women played a vital role. The figures tell an important part of the story. Late in 1943, about 2 million women were employed in war industries – engineering, metal industries, explosives, chemicals and shipbuilding. In addition, 470,000 were in the ranks of the women's services or in the nursing corps, and 80,000 in the Land Army. Behind these statistics lay an immense change in the role of women in society, the effects of which were felt long after the war was over.

This degree of mobilisation was achieved by a remarkable feat of government organisation, drawing on the experience of the 1914–18 war, and enjoying the active support of the vast majority of the population. In 1941 Churchill streamlined the system of committees that ran the domestic war effort, reducing the number to only three: the Lord President's Committee on the home economy; the Production Executive, under Ernest Bevin, the Minister of Labour; and the Import Executive, which dealt with imports and shipping. In all this administrative work, the role of Bevin, a resolute patriot and the most formidable trade-union leader of his day, was pre-eminent; and he was largely responsible for the impressive fact that, whereas in 1915–18 an average of 4.2 million working days per year were lost in strikes, in 1940–45 the figure was only 1.8 million per year. The government also maintained a system of food rationing which grew more severe as the war went on, but was widely accepted as being necessary and fair, and which kept the British people well fed and in good health.

British war production kept up at very steady rates throughout the war, despite German air attacks. Steel production totalled between 12.3 and 13 million tons per year, from 1940 to 1944 inclusive. This was only about half German steel production, but the British also had access to American production, whereas the Germans were on their own. Aircraft production rose from 15,049 in 1940 to 20,094 in 1941, and then to 23,672 in 1942 and 26,263 in 1943, levelling off at 26,461 in 1944. From 1940 to 1943, the British out-built the Germans in aircraft, falling behind only in 1944, when the Germans turned out nearly 40,000 – too late. In many cases the British also produced better aircraft than their opponents – the Spitfire fighter, the rocket-firing Typhoon, the Mosquito light bomber and the Lancaster heavy bomber all outmatched anything the Germans produced. (Indeed, the Germans did not develop a heavy bomber at all.) Tanks were another matter. British tank production increased in the early years of the war: from 1,399 in 1940 to 4,841 in 1941, and 8,661 in 1942; but then fell away to 7,476 in 1943 and only 5,000 in 1944. Moreover, the British never produced a first-rate tank of their own, so that the Army became reliant on American tanks, especially the Sherman – though the Shermans themselves were no match for the German Tigers and Panthers.

The story of British war production was one of steady and unremitting effort, with no apparent turning points. But in reality the turning points were there, though they were not obvious at the time. The first was the introduction of the American Lend-Lease programme in 1941, which allowed the British to import vast quantities of materials of all kinds from the United States, even when they were unable to pay for them. The second was the victory over the U-boats in May 1943, which ensured that these imports from America could in fact get across the Atlantic. It was indeed the support of the United States, in the form of foodstuffs, raw materials, shipping, aircraft and military hardware of all kinds, that enabled the British to hold their own against Germany in the contest between the war economies of the two countries.

The Soviet Union was thrown into the war in June 1941, when the country was invaded by the Germans. In some ways, the Soviet economy

British war production was steady

was already on a war footing. In 1938–39 the military budget made up about 26 per cent of the total budget, a proportion that increased to nearly 33 per cent in 1940. The Soviet Union had the advantages of a vast territory, important natural resources (notably oil and minerals), and a high degree of self-sufficiency. But in comparison with Germany, Soviet industry was relatively backward in sophisticated technology and production methods. Moreover, under economic agreements signed in February and April 1941, the Soviet Union actually provided the Germans with large quantities of cereals, oil and raw materials, which only strengthened the German war economy. The Soviets faithfully carried out these agreements up to the very eve of the German invasion, and Soviet goods trains were still rolling westwards during the night of 21–22 June 1941, passing through German forces massed for Operation BARBAROSSA. It was an extraordinary scene, which still beggars belief even after so many years.

When the German blow fell, it crippled the Soviet war economy. Between June 1941 and August 1942, the Germans captured the most productive areas of the USSR, including about 55 per cent of Soviet agricultural production, 65 per cent of its coal, and 60 per cent of steel and aluminium production. The Soviet government made prodigious efforts to save something from the wreck. As early as 24 June, only two days after the German invasion began, an Evacuation Council was set up to organise the transfer of men, machinery and materials to the east. According to Russian estimates in the 1990s, something like 2,500 factories, with perhaps 25 million workers and their families, were moved to destinations in the Ural Mountains, Siberia, the Volga district and Kazakhstan. Sometimes these human cargoes were discharged into open countryside in the middle of winter, and had to improvise dugouts and huts to live in while they rebuilt the dismantled factories. The suffering was appalling, and in August and September 1941 there was very little war production at all, because many factories were being transported across the country. But the final result was a striking recovery in arms production in 1942.

Everyone and everything were mobilised for the war effort. By the end of 1941 about 11 million men had been drafted into the army from employment in industry and agriculture, which in turn suffered grievous shortages of manpower. Women were drafted into factories and farms, and by the end of the war they made up 55 per cent of the total workforce. On the collective farms, four out of every five workers were women,

24 Russian women workers making shells. They were vital in taking the place of men drafted into the army.

often working by hand because tractors and horses were requisitioned for the Army or for industry. Agricultural production fell drastically, and by 1945 Soviet farms were producing only some 60 per cent of their output in 1940. There were severe shortages of food, and even the Spartan provisions allocated under the rationing system were not always delivered.

The result of this mobilisation, despite all the hardships and difficulties, was a success. By the end of 1942 there was a remarkable spurt in armaments manufacture. Figures for six-month periods in 1941–42 tell their own story.

huge increase in war production

	July–December 1941	January–June 1942	July–December 1942
Aircraft	8,200	8,300	13,400
Tanks	4,800	11,200	13,300
Mortars	19,100	55,400	70,100

But what these figures do not reveal by themselves was more extraordinary still. In 1942 the Soviets were far outbuilding the Germans. That year, the USSR built nearly 25,000 tanks, but Germany only 9,200; the Soviets produced 21,700 aircraft, but the Germans only 15,400. It was a remarkable achievement.

In this way, Soviet war production passed a crucial turning point by the end of 1942. This success was then consolidated in 1943, when the Soviets continued to outbuild the Germans in all the main forms of weaponry: 35,000 aircraft as against 25,000; 24,000 tanks against 17,000; 130,000 guns against 27,000. Moreover, the Soviets went ahead or at least stayed level in quality. Their new light bomber, the Sturmovic, was a better plane than the Ju-87 Stuka, which had been in service since before the war. In tanks, the Soviets and Germans were evenly matched. The Russians produced improved models of the T-34 medium tank in 1943, and introduced a new heavy tank, the Josef Stalin, in 1944. The Germans introduced the powerful Tiger I in 1942, and the manoeuvrable Panther in 1943. Even in 1944, which was a year of almost constant Soviet victories, the Germans destroyed about 17,000 Soviet tanks; so the Red Army needed all the tanks its factories could build.

Soviet war production was supplemented by aid from Britain, Canada and above all the United States, at first in only small quantities but making a substantial contribution by 1943. American lorries were particularly important – Stalin said that he needed trucks more than tanks. Aircraft too arrived in large numbers from the Western powers, equivalent to about one-fifth of Soviet production in 1943–44.

This turning point in Soviet war production and increasing Allied help came at the turn of the years 1942 and 1943, coinciding with the long drawn-

Soviets established material superiority in Battle of Stalingrad

25 Soviet T-34 tanks being assembled in a railway marshalling-yard for shipment to the army. The T-34, sturdy and reliable, was the main battle tank used by the Red Army.

out battle of Stalingrad. Soviet industry provided the material for victory on the battlefield, and established a material superiority which was never lost.

Of all the belligerent powers, the United States proved to be the greatest industrial giant, and American war production exceeded that of any other country. This was achieved despite the Americans starting virtually from nothing. In 1940 the United States possessed immense resources of raw materials and oil, and advanced factories and industrial methods; but these vast resources were hardly used at all for military purposes. The entire American armed forces comprised only 700,000 men in 1940. Tank production for the year was a mere 400. The air forces, military and naval, were made up of only 1,700 aircraft, many of them obsolescent, though the aircraft industry was beginning to expand under the impulse of orders from France and Britain – production was 5,856 in 1939, rising to 12,804 in 1940. The navy was strong, but in need of modernisation. Perhaps even more important, the Americans were not a militarised people, and saw no reason to fear for their own safety.

US was the greatest industrial giant

This situation began to change in 1940, when the fall of France and the apparently imminent defeat of Britain put the security of the United States in jeopardy. In March 1941 Roosevelt steered the Lend-Lease legislation through Congress, and began providing supplies to Britain, and later to Russia. When the United States was suddenly plunged into war with the Japanese attack on Pearl Harbor of 7 December 1941, the Americans responded with extraordinary speed. In January 1942 Roosevelt set out an ambitious programme for arms production, aiming for 60,000 aircraft and 45,000 tanks per year. Astonishingly, the aircraft industry far outstripped its target within two years, reaching nearly 86,000 planes in 1943. Tank production fell short of Roosevelt's aim, reaching just over 29,000 in 1943, but this was still a great achievement for an industry that was virtually starting from scratch. Meanwhile the Americans also produced over 72,000 guns in 1942, and over 67,000 in 1943.

These remarkable feats of production were achieved by a mixture of government direction, private enterprise and sheer improvisation. In January 1942 the head of the Office of Production Management, a government agency, called a meeting of businessmen, read out a list of military products, and 'simply asked for volunteers to produce them'. This was free-wheeling American-style planning, and it worked. Henry Ford set an example on the largest possible scale by establishing a completely new aircraft factory south of Detroit, to build heavy bombers (B-24 Liberators) on mass-production

how the US achieved feats of production

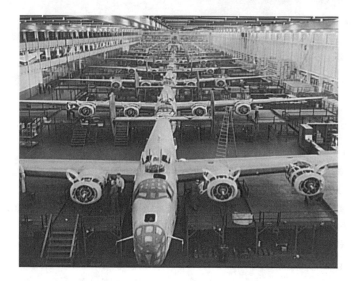

26 B-24 Liberators under construction. Henry Ford, the car manufacturer, set out to build a bomber every hour in his new factory near Detroit. Using mass-production methods, he achieved his aim by 1944.

lines. He undertook to build a bomber every hour, and at one point in 1944 this extraordinary aim was achieved, with the plant producing planes at an average of one every 63 minutes! This success was sometimes achieved *despite*, as well as by means of, Ford's highly individual approach – at one point he insisted on shifting part of the factory to avoid including a county that voted Democrat. Chrysler made a similar effort, starting with a cornfield near Detroit and building a factory that produced 100 medium tanks per week.

The government also stepped in directly when necessary. In 1942 German U-boats were sinking American oil tankers in dangerous numbers, and Harold Ickes (appointed Oil Commissioner by Roosevelt) set out to move oil overland, building an oil pipeline all the way from Texas to Phoenixville, Pennsylvania – 1,380 miles in all. The pipeline, called 'Big Inch', was in fact 24 inches in diameter, and could carry 15 million tons of oil per year across country. Inevitably, some plans went wrong. For example, the government converted locomotive factories to build tanks, only to find later that it needed more locomotives, including some to send to Russia. Naval shipbuilders naturally concentrated on building warships, only for the strategic planners to find in 1943 that they were desperately short of landing craft for amphibious operations.

But American war production was beyond doubt a success story, creating a vast war economy from a very low base within the space of a year

American war production emerged fast and out of nothing

or two. The Americans called up 14 million men into the armed forces by 1944, and filled the factories with black workers and women. By 1944 there were over 19 million women in the American workforce, as against 14 million in 1940, and 'Rosie the Riveter' (whose slogan was 'We Can Do It') was a reality as well as a propaganda figure. As early as 1942 the United States was out-producing Germany and Japan together in the main categories of war production – aircraft, tanks and guns. The Americans also built, in vast quantities, the workaday vehicles that kept the armies moving – trucks, jeeps and half-track lorries. The jeep, perhaps even more than the tank, was the key vehicle of the war, and the USA built more than 650,000 of them. The Americans were more than the armourers of the Grand Alliance – they kept the armies moving as well.

In all this effort, the Americans enjoyed the immense advantage of almost total freedom from enemy attack. With the exception of a few months of U-boat successes on the east coast in the first part of 1942, the American mainland was safe from attack, and American factories suffered no aerial bombardment. With this secure base, the Americans could simply get on with producing the materials and weaponry of war, which they did in vast quantities.

US advantages

War Production: The Key Contests

The separate stories of war production by each of the main belligerent powers must be set in the context of the war as a whole. The Soviet Union was unique, in that the Russians essentially had only one enemy, Germany; so that the whole weight of its massive war production could be concentrated on one front and one struggle. All the other countries had to fight more than one enemy, and on more than one front. From 1941 onwards Germany was committed to a two-front war, against the Soviets in the east and the British, and later the Americans, in the west; and German war production had to be divided accordingly. The British fought on a number of fronts – the North Atlantic, the Middle East and Mediterranean, and the Far East – and they had to make their limited resources go a long way. The Americans had to divide their efforts between two massive areas – the Atlantic and western Europe on the one hand, and the Pacific and South-East Asia on the other – and their immense productive capacity allowed them to do this.

Soviets = only grap fighting on one front

Within this broad framework, there were three key economic and industrial contests: first, between Germany and the Soviet Union; second, between Germany and the Western Allies (Britain and the USA); and third, between Japan and the United States.

In the contest between Germany and the Soviet Union, the production of the main categories of weaponry (aircraft, tanks and artillery) by the two powers, between 1941 and 1944, were as follows.

AIRCRAFT	1941	1942	1943	1944
Germany	11,766	15,409	24,807	39,807
Soviet Union	15,735	25,436	34,900	40,300

TANKS	1941	1942	1943	1944
Germany	5,200	9,200	17,300	22,100
Soviet Union	6,590	24,446	24,089	28,963

ARTILLERY	1941	1942	1943	1944
Germany	7,000	12,000	27,000	41,000
Soviet Union	42,300	127,000	130,000	122,400

The key point arising from these figures is that the Soviets consistently out-built the Germans in numbers of weapons. Only at one stage and in one category – aircraft production in 1944 – did the Germans approach parity; and by then most of their planes were used for home defence or could not get off the ground through lack of fuel. In the early stages of the conflict, Soviet superiority in production was more than offset by German advantages in speed, flexibility and fighting power; but as the Red Army came to match the Germans in all these respects, weight of material and numbers of weapons turned the scale decisively against Germany. This change came about over a long period, but the decisive stage was in the latter part of 1942 and early 1943, when war production provided the material means to win the battle of Stalingrad – a victory that was won on the ground, but was prepared in the factories.

In the contest of production between Germany and the Western Allies, the figures show that the British and Americans out-built the Germans, sometimes by a wide margin – in aircraft, the Germans were often out-produced by four or five to one. The exception to this was in tank production in 1944, when the Germans attained near-equal numbers as well as having outstanding tanks in the Tiger and the Panther; but, of course, the

Germans still had to face the Soviet production of tanks, which left them well behind overall.

AIRCRAFT	1941	1942	1943	1944
Britain	20,094	23,672	26,263	26,461
USA	27,277	47,828	85,998	96,318
Germany	11,776	15,409	24,807	39,807

TANKS	1941	1942	1943	1944
Britain	4,841	8,611	4,746	5,000
USA	4,052	24,997	29,497	17,565
Germany	5,200	9,200	17,300	22,100

near equal tank production

ARTILLERY	1941	1942	1943	1944
Britain	5,300	6,600	12,200	12,400
USA	29,615	72,658	67,554	33,558
Germany	7,000	12,000	27,000	41,000

When American war production really got under way in 1942 and 1943, the Germans had no chance of competing in sheer numbers, while the Allied victory over the U-boats in May 1943 ensured that the results of American output would get safely across the Atlantic. So, as with the German-Soviet contest, the turning point, or at any rate the critical stage, can be placed at the end of 1942 and the first part of 1943.

In the Pacific and East Asia, Japan fought single handedly against the USA and its British and Australian allies. In war production, this was a contest between at best a medium-weight (Japan) and a heavyweight (the USA). In the war at sea and in the air, the American superiority in ship-building and aircraft production was overwhelming. The production figures tell their own tale.

Even though the Americans had to divide their forces between Pacific and Atlantic theatres of war, their output was big enough to secure superiority in both zones. It is true that the Japanese fought with such tenacity and fanaticism that they were hard to beat, and the American Army and Marines suffered heavy casualties in individual battles, such as Iwo Jima in

MAJOR WARSHIPS	1941	1942	1943	1944
USA	544	1,854	2,247	1,513
Japan	49	68	122	248
AIRCRAFT	1941	1942	1943	1944
USA	26,227	47,826	85,998	96,318
Japan	5,008	8,861	16,693	28,180

February–March 1945; but in material terms the Pacific War was a one-sided contest, as long as the Americans did not waver. In that respect, the initial Japanese attack at Pearl Harbor in December 1941 proved to be a short-term success but a long-term disaster. The Americans never forgot Pearl Harbor, and their determination to wipe out the humiliation of 'the day that will live in infamy' sustained them to the end of the road. In this conflict there was no wearying or turning back.

In these various contests of war production, there was a decisive shift in the balance of power over a period between late 1942 and mid-1943. Before that time, the Germans and Japanese had used surprise, boldness and speed of movement to score dramatic victories over opponents who were even at that stage economically superior. But these victories came to an end, and the Axis advances were brought to a halt. There followed a war of attrition, in which Allied material superiority was increasingly brought to bear, on the Eastern Front, in North Africa and across the Atlantic and Pacific Oceans. The growth of Allied power behind the scenes in the hidden battle of the factories and shipyards was translated into victory on the battlefields. By 1943 the output of the three Allied powers exceeded that of Germany and Japan by an extent varying between three to one and four to one in different categories of war material. When this degree of material superiority was properly applied, victory for the Allies became as certain as anything can be among the hazards of war.

In sum, therefore, by 1943 the three powers of the Grand Alliance had established massive superiority in the output of war materials and weaponry. This meant that they were almost sure to win the war, *unless* the alliance broke down through some internal dispute; or the Anglo-American invasion of France, which was planned for 1944, failed; or in some way war weariness set in and their determination faltered. These were very real possibilities, and the story of the Second World War was therefore far from over.

CHAPTER NINE

THE TEHERAN CONFERENCE, 28 NOVEMBER–1 DECEMBER 1943
TURNING POINT FOR THE GRAND ALLIANCE

At the end of November 1943 Stalin, Roosevelt and Churchill met for a conference in the somewhat unlikely location of Teheran, the capital of Iran. It was the first time that they had all gathered together. Churchill and Roosevelt had met frequently, and established what appeared to be close personal relations. Churchill had once ventured to Moscow, to meet Stalin on his home ground. Roosevelt and Stalin had yet to meet, though this was not for any want of trying on Roosevelt's part.

This first meeting of the Big Three was a momentous occasion, because coalition warfare is an extremely difficult form of diplomacy and strategy. The partners in an alliance are held together by the need to defeat their enemy; but at the same time each individual country pursues its own interests, waging the war and preparing for the peace settlement to its own advantage. For example, the European 'Grand Alliance' against Louis XIV of France, to which Churchill often liked to refer because it had been orchestrated by his ancestor the Duke of Marlborough, had been riven with disputes and eventually broke down before achieving a final victory. The new Grand Alliance that waged the Second World War on Germany was subject to the inevitable stresses and strains of coalition warfare, and was also troubled by ideological differences. The Soviet Union was the world's first socialist state, and Stalin was a standard-bearer for Marxism-Leninism as well as being a hard-headed and realistic statesman. Britain and the United States were both liberal democracies, with much in common in their ideals and traditions; but the Americans (not least President Roosevelt himself) were ardently anti-imperialist, whereas Britain still ruled a vast empire, which Churchill was determined to maintain.

27 Stalin, Roosevelt and Churchill at the Teheran Conference, surrounded by photographers. The meeting was held in secret, but all three leaders knew the importance of publicity and propaganda.

In these circumstances, the first meeting of the three leaders of the United States, Great Britain and the Soviet Union was at one and the same time an urgent necessity in order to consolidate their alliance and determine their strategy, and also fraught with danger given that the tensions generated by such a meeting might bring concealed divisions and disputes into the open. The gathering of the Big Three was thus both a great opportunity and an alarming risk. It was a step into the unknown.

For the three great men to get to Teheran was an adventure in itself. On 27 November Churchill flew into Teheran aerodrome from Cairo, and then drove by car to the British Legation in the city, along roads crowded with people and guarded only by Iranian cavalrymen, stationed every 50 yards or so. As Churchill observed: 'The men on horseback advertised the route, but could provide no protection at all.' Fortunately, Churchill was not easily dismayed: '. . . nothing happened. I grinned at the crowd, and on the whole they grinned at me.' He eventually arrived at the Legation, and the safety of a guard provided by a Sikh battalion of the Indian Army.

On the same day, President Roosevelt also flew into Teheran, and made his way by a less conspicuous route to the American Embassy. It was for him the last stage of a journey of 9,000 miles from Washington, which had seen its own moment of danger when the battleship *Iowa*, with Roosevelt on board, had been missed by a torpedo fired accidentally by one of her escorting destroyers. The miss was by a clear thousand yards, but it was too close for comfort. General Arnold, of the US Army Air Force, scored his own hit by asking Admiral King, the Commander-in-Chief, US Fleet: 'Tell me, Ernest, does this happen often in your navy?' It must have been an unwelcome joke.

Stalin took his own form of risk to reach Teheran. He was afraid of flying, and went to Baku by train. But there was no railway line from Baku to Teheran, so he had no choice. He took to the air for the first time in his life, in a plane piloted by a Soviet air-force colonel. After he had safely managed the return trip, on 2 December, he never flew again.

The three leaders who met at Teheran were similar in age, but very different in background and experience. Churchill, the oldest of the three, was to celebrate his 69th birthday during the conference, on 30 November. Stalin was 67, and Roosevelt 61. Churchill had been a professional soldier, and had seen action in the Sudan and South Africa, and on the Western Front; his political career had lasted nearly 40 years, during which he had held most of the great British offices of state. Roosevelt came from a distinguished American political family, and with steely determination he had restored his political career after being struck by poliomyelitis at the age of 39. He never walked again, but by a convention carefully observed by the American press and films, he was never shown being carried in public. He developed an immense physical and mental stamina, but it was inevitable that he found long air journeys difficult. Stalin stood in marked contrast to both these Western establishment figures. For part of his life he had been a hard-bitten clandestine revolutionary. In the late 1920s he had emerged as the dictator of the Soviet Union; and in the 1930s he had become the ruthless mass murderer of his own people. When the Teheran Conference met, he was at the height of his power, having survived the disasters of 1941 and having led his country to recovery in 1943.

(margin note: Churchill/ Roos - pair / Stalin = odd man out)

These three statesmen did not form a coherent triumvirate, but something more like a pair and an odd man out. Churchill and Roosevelt made up the pair. Since 1940, Churchill had cultivated close relations with Roosevelt by constant correspondence and lengthy conferences; he believed that Britain and the United States were in many ways natural associates, sharing political traditions as well as interests. His relations with the Soviet Union were quite another thing. In 1919 Churchill had been an ardent advocate of intervention against the Bolsheviks in Russia, and he had never wavered in his hostility to communism. But this ideological enmity was accompanied by a strong dose of political realism. In March 1938 Churchill had gone out of his way to explain to Ivan Maisky, the Soviet Ambassador in London, that he had previously opposed communism with all his strength, because it was the greatest danger to the British Empire; but that now Nazi Germany presented the greatest danger, and therefore Churchill opposed Hitler with all his strength. This might change again in the future, but not yet – 'For this period of time we and you share the same path.' It was as clear a statement of political realism as one could wish to see. Since 1941 Churchill had sought to make personal contact with Stalin, and during a visit to Moscow in August 1942 he believed that he had somehow got through to the Soviet leader during a late-night session of talking and drinking. He tried to introduce a personal note in their correspondence, and he offered gestures of friendship – for example, by persuading Dunhill, the tobacco firm, to send Stalin some of their distinctive pipes.

So Churchill added a dash of personal contact to his basic policy of political realism when dealing with Stalin. Roosevelt on the other hand reversed these proportions, pinning high hopes on his charm of manner and the 'Roosevelt touch'. As early as 18 March 1942 he had written to Churchill: 'I know you will not mind my being brutally frank when I tell you I think I can personally handle Stalin better than your Foreign Office or my State Department. Stalin hates the guts of all your top people. I think he likes me better, and I hope he will continue to do so.' Twice during 1942, and again in May 1943, he had suggested to Stalin that they should meet somewhere near the Bering Strait to get to know one another, *without* Churchill being present. Stalin first put the matter off, and then declined the proposal; so what would have been an intriguing summit meeting never came about. But Roosevelt's proposals formed a vital aspect of the background to the Teheran Conference, where the President finally achieved his man-to-man meetings with Stalin.

Stalin himself was a stern and enigmatic figure. Anthony Eden, the British Foreign Secretary, who was a shrewd and experienced judge of character, rated him highly as a negotiator:

> . . . if I had to pick a team for going into a conference room, Stalin would be my first choice. Of course the man was ruthless and of course he knew his purpose. He never wasted a word. He never stormed, he was seldom even irritated. Hooded, calm, never raising his voice, he avoided the repeated negatives of Molotov which were so exasperating to listen to. By more subtle methods he got what he wanted without having seemed so obdurate.

Similarly, General Brooke, the Chief of the Imperial General Staff, rated Stalin highly as a strategist:

> I rapidly grew to appreciate the fact that he had a military brain of the very highest calibre. Never once in any of his statements did he made any strategic error, nor did he ever fail to appreciate all the implications of a situation with a quick and a unerring eye.

Stalin was a formidable man to deal with in conference. He also had the advantage of secret intelligence sources of a high order, with Soviet agents in high places in both London and Washington. Stalin's views on foreign policy were in some ways strikingly simple. His main purpose was to ensure the security of the Soviet Union by holding the territories gained in 1939 and 1940 (eastern Poland, the Baltic states and parts of Rumania), and adding a zone of Soviet predominance beyond them. When Eden met him in Moscow in December 1941, with the Germans still no great distance from the city, Stalin calmly presented a list of territorial demands which would take the Soviet Union back to the frontiers of autumn 1939, plus some additions. That was when the Soviet military position was at its weakest. By the end of 1943, when the Teheran Conference met, the military position had become so strong that Stalin could be sure that the territories he wanted would soon be within the grasp of the Red Army. There was no need to negotiate about them. This hard-headed concern with territorial advantage stood in sharp contrast to Roosevelt's vague talk of making personal contact; but in fact Stalin was well able to play the game of vagueness to his own advantage, knowing that the longer a definitive settlement of eastern European affairs could be put off, the stronger his position would become. There was no likelihood that Stalin would trade any of his territorial claims for any nebulous goodwill. He was not that sort of negotiator.

So the Big Three gathered in Teheran, which for a few days, 28 November–1 December, became the nerve centre of the alliance against Nazi Germany. They met in favourable strategic circumstances. On the Eastern Front, the Red Army had completed its victory at Stalingrad in February 1943; and in July the Soviets had scored a major success in the Battle of Kursk – the biggest tank battle of the war, which stopped the German summer offensive almost as soon as it began. The Soviet Army had thus established a superiority over the *Wehrmacht* which it was to maintain to the end of the war. In May 1943, German and Italian forces totalling some 300,000 men had surrendered to the British and Americans in Tunisia. In the Atlantic, the Allies had won the battle against the U-boats by the end of the same month. The struggle for Europe was far from over, but the war map had assumed a distinctly favourable look.

But in the background to these strategic successes, the three-power alliance faced serious problems. There was still no 'second front', in the sense in which Stalin used those words – an Allied cross-Channel invasion of France. Even victorious campaigns in North Africa and Italy were no substitute for the real thing. Stalin had used the phrase 'second front' in a message to Churchill as early as 3 September 1941, and it rapidly assumed a symbolic as well as a military significance. In Britain, 'Second Front Now' was scrawled on many a wall and hoarding. In May 1942 President Roosevelt virtually promised Vyacheslav Molotov, the Soviet Foreign Minister, that there would be a landing in France that year; but there was not. At that time only the British could carry out such an operation, and they were certain that it would end in disaster, so they refused to attempt it. Churchill courageously went to Moscow in person to break the news to Stalin that there would be no cross-Channel invasion in 1942. It was, he wrote, 'like carrying a large lump of ice to the North Pole'. Stalin could only accept the fact, but he resented it none the less. Towards the end of 1943, the question of the second front was still festering within the Grand Alliance.

The second front was a public problem, constantly debated in the press; but there was another issue, largely hidden and best kept out of the newspapers. The USA and Britain were at war with Japan, but the Soviet Union was not. This state of affairs suited the USSR and Japan well enough. Japanese neutrality allowed Stalin to move troops safely from Siberia to execute the Soviet counter-offensive at Stalingrad in November 1942. In addition, nearly half the supplies sent by the Western Allies to the Soviet Union in 1943 went by way of Vladivostok and other Siberian ports, sailing past northern Japan without let or hindrance. The Japanese for their part had enough on their plate in the Pacific, South-East Asia and China, without looking for a further war with the Russians; and they were glad to receive assurances that the Soviet Union would not allow the Americans to use its airbases to bomb Japan. Both countries therefore found this rather odd arrangement mutually advantageous; but their respective allies found it exasperating. The Germans were dismayed that Japan refused to cut the Allied supply line to Vladivostok. The Americans were acutely aware that at some point in the future they would need Soviet support in the war against Japan, by invading Manchuria or even Japan itself. They therefore wished to draw Stalin into a commitment to go to war with Japan at some point in the future; and this became a constant though inconspicuous element in American-Soviet relations.

Within the Grand Alliance itself, the year 1943 saw a shift in the balance of power between the allied countries. The Soviet Union had established its military predominance on the Eastern Front, while the United States was outstripping Britain not only in economic power but also in military capacity. These changes demonstrated to Roosevelt that in future the Soviet Union would be a more important partner for the USA than Britain, in peace as well as in war, and this assumption underlay much of his policy at the Teheran Conference.

These developments accentuated problems that had long troubled Anglo-American relations, notably the question of empire and imperialism. Roosevelt was in principle opposed to imperialism – or at any rate he was opposed to other countries' empires, while ensuring that he maintained American predominance in the Caribbean and Latin America, and prepared to control the Pacific after the war. He had insisted that the right of peoples to choose their own government should be included in the Atlantic Charter of August 1941; and he intended to dismantle parts of the French Empire, planning to put Dakar (in West Africa) and French Indo-China under international trusteeship – in effect, under American influence. In 1942 he had pressed the cause of Indian independence, and urged the British to move more rapidly in that direction. In all these matters he crossed swords with Churchill, who was a lifelong imperialist with no intention of applying the Atlantic Charter to British colonies, and who had declared openly that he had not become the King's First Minister to preside over the dissolution of the British Empire. This difference of view produced an undercurrent of dissension between the two men, which Roosevelt was to exploit for his own purposes during the Teheran Conference. It was, incidentally, a curious fact that Roosevelt seemed to have no qualms about the existence of a Soviet Empire, in which peoples were not merely denied the right of self-determination but were deported or killed in vast numbers.

For most of 1943, these problems in Anglo-American relations were by no means obvious. In the first nine months of the year, Churchill and Roosevelt had held three long meetings – at Casablanca in January, at Washington in May, and at Quebec and Washington in August–September – a total of 50 days in all. As time went by, Stalin's absence from these meetings came to seem like exclusion, and presented a danger to the cohesion of the alliance. The British press was highly critical of the lack of any Soviet representation at the Quebec Conference, and Churchill felt bound to point out that the discussions had been mainly concerned with the war against Japan, in which the Soviet Union was not involved – an explanation which only drew attention to a difficulty that was usually left unmentioned. In mid-July 1943 the Soviet government recalled its ambassadors in London (Ivan Maisky) and Washington (Maxim Litvinov) to Moscow, which was another ominous sign of dissension within the alliance.

All this demonstrated that a three-power meeting was becoming urgent. In fact, Roosevelt and Churchill had invited Stalin to join them at Casablanca in January 1943, but he declined, explaining that he had to remain in close contact with the fighting on the Russian front. (In the event, the Casablanca Conference coincided with the final phases of the Battle of Stalingrad.) Then in June Churchill had suggested a meeting at Scapa Flow, in the Orkneys – a bleak venue, but one where he would be the host – but Stalin again declined. In August 1943 Stalin had himself taken the initiative, telling Churchill and Roosevelt that a three-power meeting was desirable 'at the first opportunity', and proposing a conference of 'responsible representatives' (in the event, Foreign Ministers) to prepare the way for a meeting of the Big Three. There followed some discussion about dates and possible meeting places. On 8 September Stalin had proposed the end of November as the date, and Teheran as the place, and eventually he got his way on both counts. The Foreign Ministers of the three countries (Cordell Hull for the USA, Eden for Britain, and Molotov for the Soviet Union) were to meet in Moscow from 19 to 30 October, and the Big Three in Teheran from 28 November to 1 December.

In principle, the Moscow Conference of Foreign Ministers was no more than a preliminary meeting, to prepare the ground for later decisions by the three great men. But in practice it was of crucial importance. It was the first formal Allied conference to be held in Moscow, with the Soviet government as host and with Molotov as chairman. These arrangements conferred a diplomatic prestige on the Soviet Union to match the military reputation achieved at Stalingrad and Kursk. They also allowed Molotov to impose his own order of priorities at the conference. When the British and Americans presented lists of subjects for discussion, Molotov proposed only one – 'Measures to shorten the war against Germany and its Allies in Europe', or in other words the second front. And in fact, on only the second day of the conference, the British and Americans assured their hosts that the invasion of France was being planned for the spring of 1944.

The conference itself lasted for 12 days. The United States gained important objectives, notably acceptance of an American proposal for a Declaration on the Post-War World, outlining a new international organisation to succeed the League of Nations. Moreover, at a banquet on the final evening of the conference, Stalin delighted Cordell Hull, the American Secretary of State, by assuring him (without being asked) that the Soviet Union would enter the war against Japan after Germany was defeated. This was only a verbal undertaking, and expressed in general terms, but it was well worth having. Eden, the British Foreign Secretary, was less successful. Notably, his carefully prepared proposals for an eastern European settlement based on confederations between Poland and Czechoslovakia and between Yugoslavia and Greece were rejected by Molotov. On the positive side, Eden gained an agreement to set up a three-power European Advisory Commission, based in London, to discuss ideas for a post-war settlement – a body that later devised the occupation zones in a defeated Germany. Molotov, by rejecting Eden's proposals for confederations in eastern Europe, secured by implication a free hand for the USSR in the area. But his great achievement lay in the success of the conference itself, and the glowing tributes he received as chairman, especially from Eden, a polished diplomat and an old hand at conferences. The Soviet Union had established a new, stronger, position in the working of the three-power alliance.

When all was over, the published communiqué emphasised the close cooperation between the participants, and the confidence that prevailed among them. Stalin, in a speech on 6 November (the anniversary of the Bolshevik Revolution), went out of his way to stress the success of the conference in consolidating the anti-Hitler coalition. In the USA, Hull was given a hero's welcome, and received the unusual distinction for a Secretary of State of addressing a joint session of Congress, where he spoke enthusiastically of the understanding and confidence that prevailed at the conference. Eden, who on balance scored no more than half points at the conference, put on a good front when he presented the results to the House of Commons. These public displays were of the highest importance. The Foreign Ministers' Conference, once it had been convened and announced, simply *had* to be a success. There could be no half measures, and no compromises in the public view. The same was true, only more so, for the meeting of the Big Three that followed.

In the last few days before the Teheran Conference, Churchill and Roosevelt met in Cairo for a meeting (23–26 November 1943) which was mainly concerned with the war against Japan. Churchill tried to use this opportunity to prepare the ground for Teheran by holding talks with Roosevelt before they met Stalin; but Roosevelt would have none of it, and was determined to avoid even an appearance of 'ganging up' against Stalin before the main conference. Instead he held long talks with the Chinese leader, Chiang Kai-shek, leaving almost no time for talks with Churchill before setting off for Teheran. Churchill was left fretting on the sidelines in fruitless agitation, and eventually had to set off for Teheran without holding serious conversations with the Americans. He even lost his voice by too much talking – though not with talking to Roosevelt. It was an ominous sign of things to come when the three-power conference began.

Before the Teheran Conference convened, it had already been settled that the Big Three should not work to a fixed agenda. The Americans had proposed this at the Moscow Conference of Foreign Ministers, and Molotov had agreed without demur – which implies that Stalin thought he could secure advantage from the arrangement. At Teheran therefore the main participants could raise or reject topics for discussion as they wished, and each could conduct the discussion in whatever style he preferred. This dismayed the British professionals, who preferred more orderly procedures. Sir Alexander Cadogan, the Permanent Under-Secretary at the Foreign Office, complained in his diary that '. . . this meeting looks like being all over the place, but that is ever the way with the Great Men'. General Brooke took the same view: '. . . we are heading towards chaos'.

But the Great Men themselves thought differently. Churchill welcomed the freedom to press his own case as hard and as often as he could; though

[margin note: Roosevelt determined not to gang up against Stalin]

[margin note: no fixed agenda]

unhappily he sometimes spoke at such length that he wearied his listeners rather than persuading them. Roosevelt was in his element, conscious of his ability in informal conversation, and also knowing when it was best to keep silent. Stalin proved an expert in both the formal sessions and in informal conversation. For example, in one after-dinner conversation he asked Churchill outright whether the English thought that Russia was going to swallow Poland – a blunt approach that no one else had cared to take. Churchill made no reply, which was in itself unusual. Eden wondered aloud how much of Poland the Russians would leave undigested, and left it at that. In fact, Stalin had delivered, apparently casually, a plain warning as to what he *could* do in Poland, with his troops already present on the ground. All further discussion of Poland between the British and the Soviets was conducted under the shadow of this warning.

While there was no formal agenda for the conference, there were certainly subjects that had to be discussed. The most prominent proved to be the date of the cross-Channel invasion, Operation OVERLORD, which in fact took up most of the formal sessions. Other topics included: the problem of Polish frontiers; the future treatment of a defeated Germany; the question of an international organisation to regulate the post-war world; and the issue of the Soviet Union entering the war against Japan. If there had been an agenda, it would have been crowded. As it was, the conference was, as Cadogan feared, 'all over the place', with much of its business being done in private talks and at social occasions.

This suited Roosevelt well, and he moved quickly to get on friendly terms with Stalin. In point of fact he made his opening move before the conference began, sending a telegram on 24 November actually asking Stalin where he should stay. After Roosevelt arrived in Teheran he spent one night at the American Embassy, and then on the following morning he accepted Stalin's invitation to move into the Soviet diplomatic compound, where the formal sessions were to be held, and where he stayed for the rest of the conference. This saved the President from awkward, and possibly dangerous, journeys between the American and Soviet Embassies; it also led him and his entourage into a building that was bound to be full of Soviet bugging devices. But Roosevelt had no doubt that he had gained an advantage. His presence in the Soviet Embassy gave him immediate access to private meetings with Stalin; and he believed that bugged conversations could be used to demonstrate American confidence in their Soviet hosts. At first, Churchill was apparently unperturbed by these arrangements – he thought at one point of inviting Roosevelt to stay at the

British Legation, but concluded that there would scarcely be room for everyone.

So Roosevelt moved in with the Russians on 28 November. He had a meeting alone with Stalin (each accompanied only by an interpreter) that same afternoon. Stalin observed the courtesies by asking Roosevelt whether he was comfortable and offering him a cigarette. Roosevelt assured Stalin he felt quite at home, but that he preferred to smoke his own brand of cigarette. The meeting lasted 45 minutes, with translation reducing the actual conversation time to half that. Even in this brief period, Roosevelt seized the opportunity to point out his differences from Churchill. He explained that he did not share Churchill's view that France would soon return to the rank of a great power. He suggested that French Indo-China should be brought under international trusteeship after the war, adding that Churchill was afraid of such a device being applied to British colonies. He criticised Churchill's views on India, and Stalin agreed that India was Churchill's sore spot. The talk moved quickly from one topic to another, without reaching any conclusion, but leaving a general impression that Roosevelt wanted to open the door to a close cooperation with Stalin.

The next day, 29 November, Roosevelt declined an invitation to lunch privately with Churchill, and instead held a second meeting with Stalin at 2.45 in the afternoon. This time the conversation, on Roosevelt's initiative, concentrated on the establishment of a new international organisation (the United Nations) after the war. Roosevelt remarked that he hoped American ground forces would be withdrawn from Europe soon after the end of the war – a point which Stalin doubtless noted with interest. Stalin for his part raised the question of the future of Germany, and emphasised the need for a severe peace settlement.

The next day, 1 December, Roosevelt held a third meeting alone with Stalin. This time, on his own initiative, he took up the question of the Polish frontiers, saying that he would like to see the Polish-Soviet frontier moved westwards, conceding former Polish territory to the USSR, while Poland should gain territory from Germany, moving its westward frontier to the River Oder. He explained to Stalin that he could not commit himself to these changes in public, because 1944 would be an election year and he could not afford to offend Polish-American voters. (Stalin's ideas on elections were rather different, and it would be interesting to know what he made of this.) Roosevelt also briefly raised the question of the former Baltic states (Estonia, Latvia and Lithuania), indicating that the USA would not make an issue of their incorporation into the

Soviet Union, though he hoped that the USSR would make some gesture towards the principle of self-determination. In short, Roosevelt had conceded, without being asked, Soviet territorial claims against Poland, and had tacitly accepted the Soviet annexation of the Baltic states.

Roosevelt's concessions

Roosevelt had thus held three private meetings with Stalin in the course of four days. He deliberately revealed to Stalin his differences from Churchill on France; on colonies in general; and on India in particular. He had also gone far towards accepting Soviet territorial gains in eastern Europe, despite his reputation as an idealist and an advocate of the self-determination of peoples. Whether he achieved the breakthrough in personal contact that he so earnestly desired was very doubtful; but it was not for want of trying.

Roosevelt also took another opportunity to distance himself from Churchill, this time during a large gathering at a dinner for the three delegations on the evening of 29 November. On this occasion, Stalin needled Churchill repeatedly, claiming that the Prime Minister really wanted to let the Germans off with a soft peace. Stalin declared that there must be harsh peace terms, including the liquidation of the whole of the German General Staff – 50,000 or even 100,000 officers. Churchill grew angry, and said he could not accept such a barbarous proposal. Roosevelt, who had sided with Stalin throughout, offered the weak joke that they could perhaps settle on killing 49,000. At that point Churchill left the table and went into an adjoining room, where Stalin and Molotov sought him out and persuaded him to return. It was a bad evening for Churchill, and for his relations with Roosevelt.

Churchill grew dismayed at his isolation during the conference, and the breach that was opening between himself and Roosevelt. He had his own moment of glory and attention on 29 November, at a ceremony in which he presented Stalin with the Stalingrad Sword as a symbol of British admiration for the heroic defence of the city. Stalin raised the sword to his lips in a theatrical gesture, before handing it to Marshal Voroshilov – who dropped it! This scene, played out for the newsreels and press photographers, was meant to emphasise the closeness of British-Soviet relations and displayed the ardent British admiration for the achievements of the Red Army. Nearly half a million people had filed past the Stalingrad Sword while it was on show in Britain, and many had been disappointed not to see it. This display of public admiration for the Red Army and the Soviet Union embodied in these vast crowds had two opposite effects on the British position at Teheran. On the one hand it helped Churchill by demonstrating the warmth of Anglo-Soviet relations; but on the other it weakened his

28 The Stalingrad Sword was a symbol of British admiration for the Red Army and the defence of Stalingrad. Churchill presented it to Stalin during the Teheran Conference, and Stalin raised it dramatically to his lips.

bargaining position by showing that he could not possibly allow the conference to fail, and then go home to face the public anger which would surely follow if it did so.

To counterbalance Roosevelt's private meetings with Stalin, Churchill arranged one of his own on 30 November, at which he tried to persuade Stalin of the need to postpone OVERLORD in order to mount an offensive in Italy. Stalin replied firmly that if the cross-Channel invasion were not launched in May 1944, the Red Army would be disappointed, and it would be very difficult for the Russian people to carry on – a menacing remark, perhaps hinting at the possibility of a separate peace with Hitler. In the event, Churchill got little out of his meeting with Stalin, and his influence at the conference, never great, was slipping away.

Meanwhile the formal work of the conference went ahead at the plenary sessions, held in the late afternoon each day, with Roosevelt as chairman.

[handwritten margin note: Stalin getting frustrated by delay of Second front]

At the first session, on 28 November, Roosevelt outlined the two-front war which the USA and Britain were waging in Europe and the Pacific. In Europe, their main operation was to be OVERLORD, which would be the most effective way of helping Russia by drawing German forces from the Eastern Front. He emphasised that he wanted this to go ahead with the least possible delay, and specifically asked Stalin for his views on what options the Western Allies should pursue in the meantime, before the landings in France took place. Roosevelt's remarks effectively invited Stalin to decide on the next stages of Allied strategy in Europe – an extraordinary move, which demonstrated Roosevelt's new views on the balance of influence within the Grand Alliance.

Roosevelt agreed to Overlord

Stalin began his reply by answering a question he had not been asked, except by implication: he repeated the undertaking he had given at the banquet to close the Moscow conference of Foreign Ministers – that the USSR would enter the war against Japan when Germany had been defeated. On the question of European operations, Stalin recognised that the Italian campaign had its advantages; but as a means of defeating Germany it had the fatal defect of leading to the unassailable barrier of the Alps. To beat the Germans, the best of all options was the cross-Channel attack, perhaps supported by a landing in southern France. Roosevelt had in effect asked Stalin to decide Allied strategy in western Europe, and in return Stalin had given the answer the Americans wanted. He backed OVERLORD, plus a landing in Provence. General Brooke commented: 'This conference is over when it has only just begun. Stalin has got the President in his pocket.' But for once he was mistaken. Roosevelt and Stalin *both* knew what they were doing, and each got what he wanted; and the British were left behind. When Churchill, later in the same session, urged his allies to postpone OVERLORD for a time, in order to undertake an offensive in Italy and new operations in the Aegean Sea, he made no headway. By that time, he was one against two, and Britain was visibly the weakest of the three powers.

Churchill got outnumbered. Stalin + Roos didn't want to delay invasion any more

The second plenary session, on 29 November, returned to the issue of OVERLORD, and went over some of the same ground again, arousing a degree of impatience, even anger, on Stalin's part. At one point he asked point-blank who was to be the commander of OVERLORD, to which Roosevelt could only reply that the appointment had not yet been made. This was in fact a delicate matter. The commander was certain to be an American, and the most likely choice seemed to be General Marshall, the Chief of Staff, who was actually present at the conference. But Roosevelt was deferring a decision, because he valued Marshall's personality and abilities as Chief of Staff too highly to lose him. None of this could be disclosed at the conference, especially in Marshall's own hearing. Roosevelt had to evade the question, only for Stalin to declare that unless a commander was nominated then nothing would come of the operation, and he could not take it seriously. Churchill made matters worse by reverting to his ideas for further operations in the Mediterranean, until Stalin lost patience (or appeared to), and asked Churchill outright whether the British really believed in OVERLORD, or were just using the plan to propitiate the Russians. Churchill replied that the British would carry out OVERLORD if the conditions were right. This seemed to be another evasive answer, though there were in fact crucial conditions that had to be right – for example, there had to be enough landing craft available. But the upshot was that Churchill's commitment to OVERLORD again seemed in doubt. Roosevelt remained silent for most of this session, watching Stalin wear Churchill down by his persistent questioning.

On the following day, 30 November, the British and American Chiefs of Staff met in the morning and agreed on a set of proposals: (1) that the Italian campaign should be pressed up to the Pisa-Rimini line, keeping landing craft in the Mediterranean until mid-January 1944, when they should be transferred to England; (2) a landing in southern France, to coincide with OVERLORD; and (3) OVERLORD itself to start on 1 June 1944. Roosevelt changed this last date to 'during May', to be more acceptable to Stalin; and these proposals were then put to a further plenary session that afternoon. The Big Three accepted all three points within an hour, and Roosevelt also undertook to announce the appointment of a commander for OVERLORD within three or four days. (In fact, the appointment of Dwight D. Eisenhower – not Marshall – was announced on 6 December.)

It was an extraordinary finish. The British and Americans had been arguing about when to launch a cross-Channel invasion for a year and a half, since May 1942. Stalin had now, in three sessions of the conference, fixed a date for the operation and ensured that a commander was to be nominated in the next few days. The Teheran Conference thus brought about a decisive development in Allied strategy – a crucial turning point in the war.

So OVERLORD was dealt with, to the satisfaction of the Soviets and the Americans, though not the British. There remained two major political issues that might have derailed the conference: the frontiers of Poland, and the future of Germany.

The question of Polish frontiers was complicated, with roots going far into the past; and recently to the German-Soviet agreements of August and September 1939, by which the Soviet Union had annexed large parts of eastern Poland, which Stalin was determined to retain. The Polish government in exile in London, on the contrary, insisted on the restoration of Polish territory as it had been in early 1939, before the Nazi-Soviet Pact. This left the frontier between Poland and the Soviet Union in dispute between the two countries. Britain was involved in this dispute, as an ally of Poland, the host to the Polish government in exile, and as a guarantor of Polish independence, though not of specific borders. The United States had no direct commitments in the matter, but was certain to be involved in the final peace settlement. If either Britain or the USA had chosen to support Polish claims to the frontier of early 1939, this dispute might well have split the three-power alliance.

But they did not. Essentially, this potential turning point was passed in two private conversations. First, Churchill and Eden discussed Poland with Stalin after dinner on the evening of 28 November, when Roosevelt had retired early to bed. Churchill suggested the possibility of meeting Soviet claims by moving Poland bodily westward, yielding territory to the Soviet Union in the east while gaining ground from Germany in the west – a proposal that he illustrated by using three matches, moving one from right to left to show how Poland could move from east to west. Two days later, in one of his private talks with Stalin, Roosevelt made a very similar proposal: that the Soviet-Polish frontier should run along the Curzon Line (a border proposed in 1920, when Lord Curzon was British Foreign Secretary), which was near the Molotov-Ribbentrop line of 1939; while in the west the Polish-German border should move to the River Oder. There was some trouble in locating the exact course of the Curzon Line on a map, but the basic proposal was clear enough. These two conversations brought about a substantial change of policy. For over three years the British and American governments had declined to recognise the Soviet annexation of Polish territory secured by the Nazi-Soviet agreements of 1939. Now, in the space of three days, Churchill and Roosevelt separately had agreed to accept the Soviet gains, without any conditions attached. The question of the Polish-Soviet frontier was not to be allowed to disrupt the Grand Alliance. It is hard to see how the British and Americans could have decided otherwise, even if the arrangement was difficult to square with the Atlantic Charter and Roosevelt's professed ideals about self-determination.

Other questions relating to Polish frontiers were postponed, as were any definite proposals about the future of Germany. The beginnings of a territorial settlement for Germany were in fact emerging piecemeal. The Soviet Union intended to annex the northern part of East Prussia, which the British and Americans agreed to. The proposal that Poland should move westward to the River Oder implied a substantial transfer of German territory. On the wider issue of the future shape of Germany, Churchill argued that Prussia lay at the root of German aggression, that it should be separated from the rest of Germany and dealt with severely. Stalin was sceptical about this, saying that Bavarians and Saxons fought every bit as hard as Prussians; and he thought that all Germany should be demilitarised and democratised – whatever that might mean. Roosevelt suggested splitting Germany into five parts, which would prevent its re-emergence as a great power, but he did not go into details. Nothing was decided, and the subject was deferred.

When all was over, the balance sheet of the Teheran Conference was plain enough. Stalin had done well. He had ensured that the date for OVER-LORD was settled for May 1944, with a commander to be named shortly. In eastern Europe, the Soviet annexation of Polish territory in 1939 was accepted by the British and Americans. The annexation of the former Baltic states was settled virtually by default, after a brief mention in one of Roosevelt's meetings with Stalin. These all represented solid Soviet gains. The postponement of other Polish border questions, and of decisions about Germany, were likely to work out to Stalin's advantage, as the Red Army advanced into eastern Europe.

As for the United States, Roosevelt secured a further verbal confirmation that the Soviet Union would enter the war against Japan after Germany was defeated, though no details were settled. The Soviets also repeated their support, already given at the Moscow Conference, for a new international organisation to replace the League of Nations. But Roosevelt's main aim at the conference had been the intangible one of making a personal contact with Stalin which would open the way to close cooperation in future. Roosevelt believed he had done this. Broadcasting to the American people on Christmas Eve 1943, he was confident. 'I may say that I "got along fine" with Marshal Stalin. He is a man who combines a tremendous relentless determination with a stalwart good humour. I believe he is truly representative of the heart and soul of Russia; and I believe that we are going to get along very well with him and the Russian people – very well indeed.' Roosevelt's so-called 'fireside chats' on the radio were very carefully considered, and this represented his firm conviction. We now know that he erred on the side of optimism, as he often did.

For Britain, the balance sheet was depressing. Churchill was defeated in his attempt to postpone the date of OVERLORD, and his proposals for further operations in the eastern Mediterranean were brushed aside. Moreover, Roosevelt's new understanding with Stalin was established at the cost of his relations with Churchill, which emerged badly damaged from the Teheran meetings. For Churchill, and for British influence in the Grand Alliance, this was an ominous turning point.

The balance sheet had other entries, less tangible but every bit as important. The conference was a publicity and propaganda success. A Three-Power Declaration, agreed at the conference and published on 8 December, proclaimed: 'We have concerted our plans for the destruction of the German forces . . . . No power on earth can prevent our destroying the German armies by land, their U-boats by sea, and their war plants from the air.' And it ended: 'We came here with hope and determination. We leave here friends in fact, in spirit and in purpose.' In a speech on New Year's Day 1944, Stalin described the conference as: 'The greatest event of our days, an historic landmark in the struggle against the German aggressor.' And he again emphasised the theme of unity: 'The leaders of the three Great Powers reached full agreement on matters of war and peace.'

Joseph Goebbels, that master of propaganda, thought there was nothing much in the Allied Declaration – indeed, so little that the German people could be allowed to read it. He was mistaken. The language of the Declaration may have been flat, and its sentiments may have seemed commonplace. But in essence the Declaration was simple, powerful and truthful – that vital element in propaganda. The threat of overwhelming force ('No power on earth can prevent our destroying the German armies . . .') was steadily carried out as the strategic plans agreed at Teheran were put into action. The political unity of the three powers was tested at Teheran, as Roosevelt and Stalin redrew the lines of force within the alliance, but unity survived. It was the essential condition for Allied victory, and Teheran confirmed that unity. It was a conference where much could have gone wrong, and some things did. But more than enough went right to ensure that it was a turning point on the road to victory. The Grand Alliance had been put to the test of a difficult conference, and had come through intact.

CHAPTER TEN

D-DAY AND THE BATTLE OF NORMANDY, JUNE–JULY 1944

On 6 June 1944 (D-Day in the military parlance of the time), British, American and Canadian troops landed in Normandy. It was the greatest seaborne invasion in the history of warfare. In retrospect, the fact that the technical term 'D-Day' has entered the English language is a lasting sign of the significance of the event. At the time, there was no doubt in anyone's mind that it was to be a decisive event in the Second World War, and probably in the history of the world. In October 1941 Churchill had instructed Admiral Lord Louis Mountbatten, the Chief of Combined Operations: 'You are to prepare for the invasion of Europe, for unless we can go and land and fight Hitler and beat his forces on land, we shall never win this war.' On the other side, Hitler himself thought along the same lines, observing to members of his headquarters in December 1943 that: 'If they [the Allies] attack in the west, that attack will decide the war.' By that time, there was really no 'if' about the invasion, which was certainly on its way. In March 1944, Admiral Kirk, the commander of the American naval Task Force due to take part in the invasion, knew what was coming, and that the great event might go either way. 'If this is successful', he wrote in a private letter, 'the war is won, if this fails it may go on for years.' On the actual eve of action, on 5 June 1944, an American private soldier waiting in a landing craft unknowingly echoed Churchill's remark to Mountbatten: 'Well, sergeant, the only way this war is ever going to end – we're going to have to cross the Channel and we're going to have to end it.'

All these men, from the Prime Minister and the Nazi dictator to the GI Joe, got it right, and the passing years have confirmed their convictions. Looking back, one historian has rightly claimed that: 'The struggle for Normandy was the decisive western battle of the Second World War, the last moment at which the German army might conceivably have saved Hitler from catastrophe.'

The stakes were high for both sides. For the Germans, defeat in France would undermine their whole position in western Europe – for example, by losing their U-boat bases in France – and it would demand the transfer of forces from their hard-pressed armies on the Eastern Front. For the Allies, the consequences of defeat were incalculable. Could they try again in 1945? The Americans almost certainly could, because they still had reserves of manpower; but the task would have been more difficult the second time round, and their base in Britain might have been less secure. The British probably could not, because their reserves were used up. On the home front, the British people would have faced the prospect of months of bombardment by the German V-1 flying bombs and V-2 rockets – a threat more daunting than the earlier bombing to which they had become inured. At the same time, the Germans would have been free to move forces to the Eastern Front, giving them a chance of halting the Soviet advance. If despite this the Russians had still been victorious, the Red Army might well have pushed through to the Rhine or even the Atlantic, and the history of Europe and the world would have been changed utterly.

We now know that the landings succeeded, and with that knowledge there has grown an impression of the certainty of Allied victory in the cross-Channel attack. But at the time fears loomed large, not least in Churchill's mind and spirit. Lord Cherwell, Churchill's scientific adviser and confidant, once told General Marshall, the American Chief of Staff, 'You must remember you are fighting our losses on the Somme' – meaning the terrible battle in 1916, which had left a scar on the collective memory of the British people. General Ismay, the Secretary to the Chiefs of Staff Committee, recalled Churchill's 'ingrained dread' of repeating the disasters of the Great War at Gallipoli in the Dardanelles (where an amphibious operation had gone badly wrong in 1915) and Passchendaele (where the British army had been worn down in the mud in 1917). These experiences – not shared by the Americans – had bitten deep into the British memory. Churchill could not dispel visions of the landing beaches choked with bodies and the sea running red with blood – nightmares which haunted him right up to the eve of D-day, and which were fulfilled in scenes of casualty-strewn beaches and bloodstained tides when the landings took place.

General Brooke, the Chief of the Imperial General Staff and Churchill's principal military adviser, shared these fears, writing in his diary on 5 June 1944:

It is very hard to believe that in a few hours the cross Channel invasion starts! I am very uneasy about the whole operation. At the best it will fall so very far short of the expectation of the bulk of the people, namely all those who know nothing of its difficulties. At the worst it may be the most ghastly disaster of the whole war. I wish to God it were safely over.

Admiral Ramsay, who commanded the naval aspect of the whole operation, and who four years earlier had organised the evacuation from Dunkirk, was well aware of the dangers. He wrote in his diary on 5 June, when the decision to launch the attack had been made: 'I am under no delusions as to the risks involved in this most difficult of all operations . . .'.

Most telling of all, the Supreme Allied Commander, General Eisenhower, wrote in his own hand a note for a communiqué to the press and radio in the event of failure:

Our landings in the Cherbourg-Havre area have failed to gain a satisfactory foothold and I have withdrawn the troops. My decision to attack at this time and place was based on the best information available. The troops, the air and the navy did all that bravery and devotion to duty could do. If any blame or fault attaches to the attempt it is mine alone.

In the stress of the occasion he misdated this note 5 July instead of June. He then put it in his wallet, and never needed to use it.

The risks involved in the Normandy landings were only too real. Looking back, Brooke attached a note to his diary entry for 5 June: 'I knew too well all the weak points in the plan of operations.' First he put the weather, and the danger that 'a sudden storm might wreck it all'. Next there were the immense complexities of a great amphibious operation, which might go wrong at any point. Finally he recalled his close – almost too close – knowledge of the various commanders involved, and his anxiety that some of them might crack under the strain.

There was much else for the Allies to worry about. Reports from the code-breakers at Bletchley Park indicated that the German armed forces were still powerful, and likely to become more so in the near future. Several SS Panzer divisions were in the course of formation and training, equipped with the new Tiger and Panther tanks. A jet-propelled fighter, the Me262, superior in speed to any Allied aircraft, was being developed, and in fact began to come into service in July 1944. At sea, the first snorkel U-boat, capable of operating under the surface for long periods, had made its appearance in January 1944, and was threatening to challenge the domination over the U-boat created by Allied air power. In the background, the existence of the German V-weapons (flying bombs and rockets) was known to the Allies, though they had not yet come into action.

German V-weapons [handwritten margin note]

As for the strength of the German land forces that could be brought to bear against an invasion, Allied intelligence estimated there were 53 German divisions in France and the Low Countries in January 1944. Some of these were static coastal defence formations, of doubtful quality; but there were also five or six Panzer divisions. Whatever the actual German strength, it was magnified in British minds by the fear which had struck deep in 1940 and 1941, and still in part persisted, that the German Army was invincible. The British were painfully conscious that between 1940 and 1944 they had rarely defeated the Germans when the two sides were of roughly equal strength. The Americans were more confident, but they too knew that their inexperienced troops had been badly shaken by the Germans in Tunisia in early 1943. Indeed, at that time, the Allied commanders in the Mediterranean had developed an excessive respect for their opponents. In April 1943 Churchill had exploded in anger when he was warned that the presence of only *two* German divisions in Sicily might make the capture of the island impossible. 'What Stalin would think of this', he wrote, 'when he has 185 German divisions on his front, I cannot imagine.'

high estimates of German military strength [handwritten margin note]

These estimates of German military strength meant that the Allies were acutely conscious that they needed a wide margin of superiority in numbers at the actual points of landing. Then, once ashore, they would have to build up their strength by sea more quickly than the Germans could increase theirs by land. The Allies would have to despatch men, vehicles and supplies across the Channel, while using air attack and sabotage by French Resistance groups to impede the movement of German reinforcements. They also planned to exploit the weapon of deception, to persuade the Germans to believe that the Normandy landing was a feint, and that the main invasion was still to come, in the area of the Pas de Calais, or even as far away as Norway, and so keep substantial German forces in idleness elsewhere.

To accomplish all this was a tall order. Many of the troops involved in the invasion had to cross the Atlantic, from the USA and Canada. Between January 1943 and May 1944, 1.4 million American servicemen were shipped to Britain; and in the first half of 1944 nearly 9 million tons of supplies crossed the Atlantic. To carry out the landings, the Allies assembled some 7,000 warships, transport vessels and landing craft. To follow up with men and material, they planned to capture the port of Cherbourg as quickly as possible; but they also intended to do without a port by constructing their own artificial harbours (code-named 'Mulberries') to provide shelter and docking facilities to all kinds of vessels, from small landing craft to big transports. In all, the Mulberries required the building of 400 separate concrete caissons and breakwaters, which all had to be towed long distances to the Normandy coast. At any point in these preparations something could have gone badly wrong, starting a chain reaction of error and failure. All in all, what has come to seem with hindsight an inevitable victory looked very different at the time, when the prospect of defeat looked only too likely.

The plans involved were of great complexity. Admiral Ramsay's final plan for the naval aspect of the invasion ran to 700 pages, which were distributed to the captains of some 400 vessels as early as 10 April 1944, under security cover that was never broken – in itself one of the most extraordinary aspects of the whole operation. According to Ramsay's plans, all the invasion shipping had to pass through an area to the south-east of the Isle of Wight (Area Z, nicknamed Piccadilly Circus) before heading towards Normandy. Again, at any stage these elaborate movements at sea might have been thrown into disarray.

Much of this naval planning depended on the tides and the moon. The forces landing by sea needed the best state of the tide to allow them to deal with the defensive obstacles that protected the beaches, which in fact meant setting five different times (H-Hours) for the five different landing zones. The airborne landings, by parachute or gliders, required a full moon for good visibility. The best combination of tides and moon occurred in June 1944 on only two groups of three days each, the 5th to the 7th, and 18th to the 20th. Whichever date was chosen, some of the assault forces and the Mulberry components had to start moving no less than six days ahead, which complicated the timing still further.

Tides and moons were at any rate predictable. The weather in the Channel was not. Early in May, General Eisenhower set the date for the landings at 5 June, but early on the 4th the weather forecast for the next day was very poor, predicting low cloud and strong winds, bringing rough seas and high waves. This was too dangerous, and Eisenhower postponed

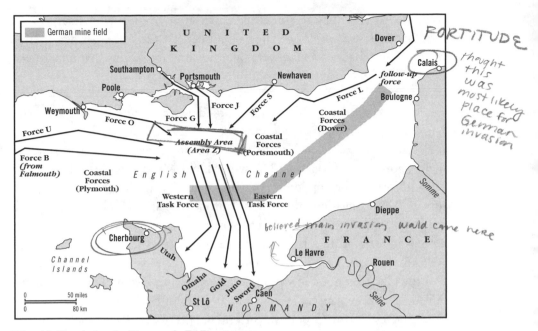

Map 10 Naval plan for Normandy D-Day invasion.

the operation for 24 hours, even though it meant recalling some ships already at sea. The new date for D-Day was set at 6 June; and if that had to be missed there was no other possible date before the 18th, with all the problems which that would entail for security and for men confined to their ships. Everything therefore depended on the weather for the 6th, which for practical purposes meant the predictions of the weather forecasters. Group Captain Stagg, the RAF meteorological officer on Eisenhower's staff, was confident enough to forecast feasible conditions for the landings, and Eisenhower had the moral courage to set the whole operation in motion. In the event, this proved absolutely right. On 5 June the weather would have been too severe for the landings to succeed; while the next suitable date, the 18th–19th, saw a gale in the Channel which would have led to either another postponement or disaster. At the point of embarkation, all the plans and preparations were at the mercy of the weather, and the notoriously uncertain predictions of the weathermen.

In short, in the run-up to the invasion the Allies faced a German Army that was still formidable, and of which they were still to some degree afraid. The task of building up their forces, first in Britain and then across the Channel, involved plans and preparations so vast and complicated that they might break down at any point, with fatal results. And in the last resort, everything depended on the uncertain weather in the English Channel. These were by no means conditions that guaranteed success.

On the other side, the Germans worked under some severe handicaps, but even so they had serious grounds for hope. The handicaps were in part self-imposed. The German high command made serious misjudgements, going as far back as 1942, when Field Marshal von Rundstedt and his staff formed the opinion that the Pas de Calais was the most likely place for an Allied invasion of western Europe. Their reasoning was logical: the area offered the shortest sea crossing and the closest distances for air cover; and if the landings succeeded the Allied forces would be well situated for an advance on Germany. All this was true. The trouble was that the Germans guessed wrong, and were encouraged in their error by the Allied deception plan, code-named FORTITUDE. Under this plan, a fictitious 2nd US Army Group was invented, and placed under the command of a real general, George Patton, for whom the Germans had a high regard. Dummy tanks, aircraft and landing craft were deployed, and intense signals traffic simulated the presence of no fewer than 11 divisions preparing for an invasion. All this succeeded beyond the Allies' expectations, partly through sheer effort and ingenuity, and partly because FORTITUDE was telling the Germans what they wanted to hear and believed to be true. In the event, the Germans were convinced until mid-July 1944 that the main invasion was still to come to the north of the Seine.

The Germans also suffered from divided opinions as to the best method of defeating an invasion when it came. Field Marshal Rommel, who was placed in command of the defence of France in January 1944, advocated defeating the Allied landings on the beaches, by means of strong defences and by stationing powerful armoured forces close to the coast for immediate action. General Guderian, who held the post of Inspector-General of Armoured Forces (in effect, the head of all Panzer formations), argued that it would be best to station the main Panzer forces inland, and to attack the Allied forces when it had become clear where the main landings were to be made. Rommel disagreed. He had fought in Africa under the handicaps imposed by British air superiority, and he was sure that it would be impossible to move armoured forces in daylight without their coming under attack. Guderian's ideas therefore simply would not work. But Guderian, von Rundstedt and (most important of all) Hitler did not accept Rommel's views about the effects of Allied air power, and refused to believe that it would be impossible to move large forces safely by day.

As between the two strategies, there was something to be said for each – *either* for defeating the landing forces on the beaches, so that they could not get a foothold, *or* for launching a heavy armoured counter-attack when the main landing had been identified. But there was almost nothing to be said in favour of the compromise which was in fact adopted, when Hitler arbitrated between Rommel and von Rundstedt at the end of March 1944. On Hitler's decision, three Panzer divisions were placed under Rommel's command; another three were held in southern France to guard the Mediterranean and Atlantic coasts; and four were stationed in northern France and Belgium, theoretically under von Rundstedt's command but in fact not to be committed to battle without Hitler's specific authority. This had the effect of scattering the German armoured forces across France, so that they neither defended the beaches nor formed a striking force for a concentrated counter-offensive.

In the event, Rommel was proved right about Allied air power and its effects. In the early months of 1944, the German air force had suffered a disastrous defeat, not over France but over Germany itself. American bombers operating in daylight were now escorted by long-range Mustang fighters, which proved overwhelmingly superior to their German opponents. In January 1944 the Germans lost 1,311 aircraft; in February, 2,121; and in March, 2,115. At the same time, trained pilots were killed more quickly than they could be replaced. The result was the virtual elimination of the Luftwaffe from the scene of the Normandy landings. On D-Day itself, the Germans flew only 319 sorties over the battle zone, without effect. They brought in reinforcements from Germany and Italy, and made some night attacks on Allied shipping; but their only serious success was to sink an American destroyer with a glider bomb. Meanwhile, Allied fighter-bombers flew unimpeded over France, attacking anything that moved.

So it happened that the Germans swallowed the Allied deception plan, largely because it corresponded with what they expected; they adopted a compromise strategy that dispersed rather than concentrated their armoured forces; and they had to fight under the severe disadvantage of complete Allied dominance of the air. In these circumstances, it may be surprising that they had any chance of success at all; but in fact they had some solid grounds for hope.

First, there were the beach defences. A common pattern comprised a line of so-called 'Belgian barn doors' – steel frames with mines attached to the uprights – followed by rows of concrete or wooden poles, again mined. Then there were 'hedgehogs', consisting of steel bars and ramps, also mined. Where the beach met the shore there were anti-tank ditches, concrete strong-points and gun emplacements. These defences were not always complete, but on most beaches they were quite strong enough to make the initial landings dangerous and difficult. Inland, open spaces that might be used for glider landings were defended by 'Rommel's asparagus' – posts designed to wreck gliders as they came in to land. Offshore, the best defensive weapon was the mine, including pressure mines which exploded under the water pressure set up by a vessel passing over them; though these were not used to the best effect, because the Germans did not wish to reveal them prematurely, and none were laid until the invasion was actually under way.

At sea, the Germans had a number of fast motor torpedo-boats (E-boats) based at Cherbourg and Le Havre. The capacity of these boats to create havoc among landing craft had been shown at Slapton Sands, in Devon, on the night of 27 April 1944, when a squadron of nine E-boats had attacked vessels taking part in a night-landing exercise, sunk three landing craft, and killed 750 American servicemen. Of course, this exercise was taking place without the intensive protection provided for the D-Day

2) Fast motor torpedo boats

29 German beach defences in Normandy, photographed by a reconnaissance mission on 6 May 1944, a month ahead of the Allied landings.

landing ships; but even so it was a disconcerting display of what German light craft could do. The Germans also assembled 36 U-boats in western France, of which 25 were despatched to attack the invasion fleet. Very few penetrated the strong Allied screen of aircraft and destroyers, but one sank three transport vessels off Selsey Bill on 29 June, which showed what the Germans might have achieved if more of their submarines had managed to get within striking range. The Germans thus had real, if slender, hopes of intervention at sea.

More important, the Germans could draw encouragement from events in the recent past. In August 1942 they had repulsed a large-scale raid on Dieppe, inflicting heavy casualties on the Canadian troops involved, and also on the supporting air forces. Then in January and February 1944 German forces had quickly checked an Anglo-American landing at Anzio, just south of Rome, again causing heavy casualties. The Germans could therefore look forward with some justification to achieving another Dieppe or Anzio when the cross-Channel invasion took place; and on the other side Churchill was afraid that the Normandy landings might repeat the failure at Anzio. Finally, the defence of northern France was directed by Field Marshal Rommel, one of the most dynamic and charismatic German commanders, who had instilled his own energy and determination into the men under his command. The Germans had some reasonable grounds for confidence as they waited for the invasion which everyone knew was coming, though no one knew exactly when or where.

3/encouragement from recent past

'When' proved to be 6 June 1944; 'where' was between the base of the Cotentin peninsula on the west and Ouistreham and the River Dives on the east. Towards this landing front of some 50 miles there sailed thousands of vessels, varying in size from massive British and American battleships to landing craft. The spectacle at first light was astonishing. Captain Duke of the US Navy, commanding a tank-landing ship, looked around him at the endless columns of ships and wondered 'How, in God's name, could it be a secret, could THIS be a secret from the enemy?' Yet it was so. The invasion came as a complete surprise to the Germans. In 1942 the German victory at Dieppe had come about in part because the landing force was spotted during the night by patrol boats. But in 1944 the German naval commander decided that the period from 4 to 6 June was unsuitable for an Allied landing, because the tides were unfavourable and the weather too rough. The German E-boats therefore stayed in port during the night of 5–6 June, and the Allied fleet crossed the Channel

30 Troops in landing-craft approaching the Normandy coast on D-Day. Many had been waiting in their ships for a whole day under stormy conditions.

undetected. Similarly, on land, von Rundstedt concluded on the evening of 5 June that there was nothing to indicate the invasion would come in the near future. Rommel was actually on leave in Germany, to mark his wife's birthday, confident in the belief that the weather around 5–6 June was too rough to allow a landing.

With the advantage of complete surprise, on 6 June the Allies secured the crucial success of getting ashore and establishing themselves on all five of the assault beaches – UTAH, OMAHA, GOLD, JUNO and SWORD. (The first two were American landings; JUNO Canadian; GOLD and SWORD British.) They also held total mastery of the air. The landing forces were supported by massive naval gunfire, from destroyers close inshore and battleships far out to sea. The heavy guns of the battleships could fire at very long range, so that concentrations of German tanks as far as 17 miles inland were bombarded by HMS *Rodney*'s 16-inch guns, with devastating effect. There were, however, limits to the Allied success. The British failed to capture Caen – one of the objectives for D-Day that proved too ambitious – and there were close-run battles which we will look at shortly. But in general the first day of the invasion proved a striking success for the Allied landing forces.

The early German response to the landings was slow and uncertain. Two Panzer divisions which might have intervened promptly against the British landing beaches were held under Hitler's direct control, and General Jodl refused to wake the Führer up early in the morning of 6 June. In fact, these divisions were not released until 4 p.m. that day, and did not get into action until the 7th. Moreover, requests from Rommel for reinforcements from forces stationed north of the Seine were refused, because both Hitler and von Rundstedt were convinced that Normandy was only a diversion before the real blow was struck in the north. So the Germans lost their best chance of a rapid armoured counter-attack, partly through their slow response to the landings, and partly through their insistence that the main assault was still to be launched around Calais. When the reserve Panzer divisions got into action, they were able to check the British advance around Caen but not to drive them back into the sea.

So the Allies achieved their first objective – to get ashore and establish a bridgehead. But in contrast to this broadly encouraging situation, there were two areas where the battle was a close-run thing, and the invading forces came close to defeat. One was at OMAHA beach, one of the two American assault landings. The beaches here had been carefully reconnoitred and were known to be difficult. The beach obstacles were particularly strong, and were overlooked by fortified positions on cliffs and hills close to the shore, subjecting the landing forces to dangerous crossfire. But the OMAHA zone was the only possible landing area between the westward beach at UTAH and the British at GOLD, so there was no choice, even though a hard fight and heavy casualties were foreseen. In the event, the difficulties of the landing were made greater by the unforeseen presence of two regiments of first-rate German troops from 352 Division, who strengthened the less efficient coastal defence forces. At OMAHA, the landings often went wrong, in contrast to the other beaches, where they mostly went right. The air bombardment, mostly by Liberator heavy bombers attacking through cloud, fell behind the German defences instead of upon them. Naval gunfire, though powerful and accurate, failed to knock out many of the concrete pill boxes and strongpoints, so that German machine guns and artillery were able to dominate the beaches with their fire. The amphibious Sherman tanks were launched about three and a half miles from the beach, and most of the first wave sank before reaching the shore, so that the infantry had to land without armoured support. Most of the infantry themselves were transferred from transport ships to landing craft 12 miles offshore, making a three-hour passage to the beach through some very rough seas. (The forces on the British and Canadian beaches transferred only seven miles out, and suffered less.) For reasons of their own, the Americans had declined to use the specialist armour devised by the British – for example, the flail tanks which exploded mines in their path by swinging chains – so that their infantry had to tackle German minefields unassisted.

The landings were going badly. An American soldier described the situation on his beach:

> At H-Hour the tide had been low; now it was coming in fast, narrowing the flat expanses of sand, and as it came swept the dead, the abandoned life-belts and the mess of wrecked equipment before it, tidying up the appalling scene like a huge broom. It also caught and drowned the wounded who were powerless to move. There was not much blood because the water was so cold and the sand acted as a blotter.

Offshore, General Bradley, the commander of the American Army Group engaged at D-Day, who had put to sea in an American warship to keep in close touch with the landings, thought that 'our forces had suffered an irreversible catastrophe'. The situation looked so grave that he briefly considered diverting the later waves of American assault craft to the other American beach at UTAH. This would have played havoc with the carefully planned movement of transports and landing craft at UTAH, and might well have meant the defeat of the OMAHA landings, which in turn would have left a wide gap in the Allied landing-front, putting the whole landing operation in danger. In the event, the Americans secured a foothold by heroic efforts and at a heavy cost. By the end of the day over 30,000 troops had got ashore, and the immediate danger of defeat had been overcome; but it had been a close-run thing.

Another close-run thing, less famous than the crisis at OMAHA but potentially just as dangerous, occurred just to the west of Ouistreham, between the seaside villages of Lion-sur-Mer and Luc-sur-Mer. Here, the German 21st Panzer Division got into action late on 6 June, and one of its tank battalions pushed into a gap between the 3rd British Division, on SWORD beach, and the 3rd Canadian Division, on JUNO. The Germans actually reached the shore at one point, and gazed with astonishment at

31 Americans getting ashore on OMAHA beach on D-Day. This was the most difficult landing of all, and showed what might have gone wrong with the whole operation.

the massive Allied fleet close offshore. If they could have held their ground and brought up reinforcements, they might have cut the British and Canadian landing forces off from one another. But in fact one of their armoured units, equipped with Mark IV tanks, less powerful than the Tigers and Panthers, was driven back by British Sherman tanks. Other German troops, actually at the shoreline, were dismayed by the sudden appearance overhead of a great force of aircraft and gliders. These were actually heading for another part of the front; but their appearance, along with the Shermans' counter-attack, caused the commander of the 21st Panzer Division, General Feuchtinger, to order a retreat. The Germans thus lost an opportunity to drive a wedge between the British and Canadians, which a more determined attack might have achieved. In fact, by the end of the day, the 21st Panzer Division was in retreat towards Caen, with the loss of about half its 127 tanks.

So the Allied forces made good their landings, and survived two danger-points which might have imperilled the whole operation. During the next few days the situation in Normandy settled down in the Allies' favour, and by 9 June even General Brooke's anxieties were beginning to diminish as the news got better. The key question was whether the Allies could build up their forces more quickly by sea than the Germans could by land. Estimates prepared in April 1944 had predicted that two weeks after D-Day (D plus 14, in the military language of the day), as many as 28 German divisions would be facing just over 19 Allied divisions, and that as late as D plus 30 the numbers might be 33 German divisions against 29 Allied ones. The bare figures, of course, said nothing about the strength, equipment and morale of divisions, but even so there was a dismaying possibility that the two sides would reach a balance and the campaign might settle into deadlock. In the event, the Allied build-up proved quicker than foreseen. By 16 June (D plus 10) the British had landed 7 divisions, including two armoured, and the Americans 11 divisions, including one armoured. In round numbers, these forces totalled 500,000 men and 77,000 vehicles. The Mulberry harbours had been put in place, one at OMAHA beach in the American sector, and one at Arromanches in the British, and were working well. Then the weather intervened, showing how the elements could play havoc with the most careful planning and preparation.

On 18 June the sea was calm and the scene of activity, with ships plying to and fro at the beaches, struck one participant as being 'like Margate on a Bank Holiday'. Then between the 19th and 21st the worst June storm in 40 years blew up in the Channel. The winds were not exceptionally severe, reaching gale force only in gusts. But the waves were short and steep, rising to 6 feet high even in sheltered anchorages, and beyond the capacity of landing craft to endure. Something like 800 craft of various kinds were driven ashore. In many cases vessels carried dangerous cargoes, and one captain received a signal: 'If the ship on your port bow is No. 269 she contains 3,000 tons of ammunition.' Even the return journey across the Channel was difficult – a tank-landing ship took four days to cover the 80 miles between Normandy and Southampton. The American Mulberry harbour began to break up on 19 June, and by the 21st was wrecked beyond repair; though some of its parts were towed to Arromanches to add to the British harbour, which fared better because it was protected by the configuration of the coast. The unloading of ships was not resumed until the evening of 22 June, which meant that the landing of men and supplies was halted for four days. At the same time, the Germans profited from the bad weather. High winds and low clouds drastically reduced Allied air strikes, and German forces could move more freely. The storm provided the clearest possible evidence of what might have gone wrong with the Normandy landings, simply through the effects of the weather. If the landings had been postponed for a fortnight, as seemed possible at one point when Eisenhower was weighing up the weather forecasts on 5 June, the vast invasion fleet might have headed straight into the storm, with potentially disastrous results.

The Allied forces needed a properly equipped port, and just after the storm ended, on 22 June, the Americans began to attack Cherbourg, which they captured within a week. The German garrison surrendered on 29 June, followed by outlying forces at Cap de la Hogue on 1 July. The port was of course sabotaged, but the Americans were able to clear it quite quickly, and the first cargoes were landed on 16 July. By the end of July as many as 12 or 14 cargo ships could use the docks at once, and the Allies were no longer reliant on the remaining Mulberry harbour and the beaches.

With large forces safely ashore, with a big port captured, and total command of the air and sea, the Allied position in Normandy was secure. General Montgomery, commanding all the Allied land forces, wrote to the Military Secretary at the War Office, one of his confidential correspondents: 'Now we are absolutely safe, under no conditions can we be pushed into the sea unless we make some frightful mistake which we shall not do.' Montgomery was sometimes prone to fits of over-optimism, but not on this occasion. The vast enterprise of landing on a hostile coast and establishing a firm bridgehead – one of the most dangerous and difficult of all military operations – had been successfully carried out. The crisis at OMAHA beach, the German push to the sea at Luc-sur-Mer, and the damage inflicted by the Channel storm had all been overcome. The first stage of the Normandy campaign had been won. But the Allies were still a long way from victory, and there remained a very real danger that the struggle might settle down into a stalemate – not as bad as a defeat, but falling well short of success.

The Allies faced serious problems. The British army in Normandy was weak in some vital respects. One was in numbers. The British were sustaining casualties, in some of the hardest fighting in the war, which could not be replaced with fresh troops. By the end of August 1944 the 59th Division had to be disbanded through lack of infantry replacements – a grave and telling step. The Canadian forces also suffered heavily, and in November the

Canadian government was compelled to introduce conscription, a measure that for domestic political reasons it had long sought to avoid. Moreover, some of the best British divisions were nearly exhausted. Montgomery had brought from the Mediterranean area three of the most experienced and successful divisions from the 8th Army – the 7th Armoured, the 50th Infantry and the 51st Highland. But the men of these formations were war-weary, and felt with much justification that they had done their bit. They had fought hard campaigns in Africa and Italy. It should now be someone else's turn to bear the burden. General Dempsey, commanding the British 2nd Army in Normandy, thought that the 7th Armoured Division was living on its reputation, and morale in the famous Highland Division was judged to be so low that Montgomery relieved its long-serving commander, General Erskine, from his post. Similar difficulties affected some of the American infantry divisions, so that the two airborne divisions had to fight in the front line all the way to Cherbourg, and the 82nd Airborne Division suffered particularly heavily in 33 days of constant action.

All the Allied troops laboured under one almost inescapable disadvantage – the superiority of the German Tiger and Panther tanks. The heavy Tiger tank, at 54 tons, with its almost impenetrable frontal armour and powerful 88-mm gun, outclassed anything the Allies could put against it. The Panther, rather lighter at 45 tons and armed with a 75-mm gun, was more mobile but still well protected against Allied fire. On the Allied side, the main battle tank was the American-built Sherman, which was under-gunned and inadequately armoured compared to the Tigers and Panthers. Shermans caught fire quickly, and often 'brewed up' (the terrifyingly casual phrase of the day) after only one hit. A graphic demonstration of what Tiger tanks could achieve came during a battle at the village of Villers-Bocage, near Caen, on 13 June. First, a single Tiger, commanded by Captain Michael Wittman, an SS officer, entered the main street of Villers-Bocage, and within five minutes knocked out three British tanks and disabled another. Later, Wittman led a group of five Tiger tanks and destroyed what remained of a British armoured brigade. 'Almost single-handedly, this one audacious and brilliant German tank commander had crushed the British advance around Villers-Bocage and forced the 7th Armoured Division onto the defensive.' Wittman's tactics were doubtless brilliant, but his tanks were also overwhelmingly superior. It is not surprising that British morale suffered accordingly.

By the second week in July, the Allies faced the prospect of a stalemate in Normandy. The British and Canadians had failed either to take Caen by direct assault or to envelop the city by flank attacks. (It was one such flanking movement that was halted by the Tigers at Villers-Bocage.) The Americans had attempted to break through the German line to the west, at the base of the Cotentin peninsula, but had failed. All the Allied forces found it almost impossible to make headway through the Normandy *bocage* – thick earth banks and hedgerows, virtually impenetrable by tanks and strong barriers against infantry. Not until mid-July did the Americans find a means of dealing with the problem by fitting strong saw-teeth to tanks, which could then cut through the hedgerows. The danger of stalemate was less serious than that of being defeated on the beaches, but it was real enough. The Allies had not mounted their immense invasion to become stuck in a bridgehead some 60 miles long and only a few miles deep in places. A stalemate on those lines would be a form of defeat.

This prospect loomed at the same time as a growing crisis of confidence within the Allied high command. Montgomery had always had his critics at Eisenhower's headquarters – indeed, some amounted to enemies, notably among the air commanders. Eisenhower himself once summed up his own view of Montgomery: 'Monty is a good man to serve under; a difficult man to serve with; and an impossible man to serve over.' By mid-July Eisenhower's patience was wearing thin, as one after another of Montgomery's offensives failed to achieve its stated objectives. Sometimes this failure came about in the full glare of publicity, as when (on 18 July) Montgomery publicly declared Operation GOODWOOD a complete success, only to leave his press officer to confess failure to the newspapermen the next day. The whole Normandy campaign was fought under the eyes of the press, radio and visiting politicians from three countries. Newspapers from England reached the troops in Normandy only a day or two after publication, with sometimes severe consequences for morale and confidence.

At the same time, British morale on the home front was suffering the new blow of attacks by German V-weapons. The first V-1 flying bombs were launched against London on 13 June, only a week after the D-Day landings, and by the end of the month 2,452 had been fired, of which about one-third landed in the London area. (Another third crashed or were shot down in flight, and the others fell outside the target zone.) On Sunday 18 June a V-1 hit the Guards Chapel at Wellington Barracks during Morning Service, killing 121 people and wounding another hundred. Eisenhower was so disturbed by this incident that he instructed the Allied air forces over northern France to give V-1 targets first priority over everything else except the urgent requirements of the land battle. The Minister for Home Security, Herbert Morrison, was so shaken that on 27 June he put to the War Cabinet a proposal for large-scale evacuations from London – though Churchill did not agree. In fact, large numbers of mothers and children left the capital in official parties, and more people simply got out. Some estimates put the number of people leaving the capital at different times as high as a million and a half. After five years of war, and when the rigours of 'normal' bombing seemed to be over, the new wave of attacks came at a bad time for Londoners. On the German side, Hitler refused to direct flying bombs against the south-coast ports used for supplying the armies in Normandy, or against the receiving ports and beaches – everything was to be aimed at London, and he was probably right. V-2 rockets were to follow, starting with one that fell at Chiswick in south London on 8 September. Captain Butcher, Eisenhower's naval staff officer, thought Londoners were dazed. A school teacher in Sevenoaks, Kent, noted that many children were being sent to safer areas, and that candidates for School and Higher Certificate were taking their examinations in dugouts. 'The whole of June', she wrote in her diary for 30 June, 'has been a month of deep, grey gloom and oppression.' On the home front, as well as in the fighting line, victory seemed a long way off.

Fortunately for the Allies, the Germans too had their troubles. As early as 10 June, Rommel concluded that his plan to defeat the landing forces immediately after they came ashore had failed, and that he would have to fall back on a holding action until he could build up reserves for a counter-offensive. But in fact the arrival of reinforcements was delayed and disrupted by air attack and sabotage by French Resistance groups on the railways, and continuous strikes by fighter-bombers on anything moving by road in daylight. The best Rommel could do was to use his reserves as they arrived, to plug gaps and make minor attacks, rather than build up a strong force, especially of armour. Rommel and von Rundstedt agreed on 11 June to report the gravity of the situation to Hitler. On 16–17 June Hitler actually journeyed to France, meeting the two field marshals on the 17th at Margival, near Soissons, where the Führer's train took shelter in a tunnel and bunker prepared when the invasion of England was being planned in the summer of 1940. In fact, this was Hitler's first visit to France since 1940; and it proved fruitless. For most of the time, he refused to discuss the military situation, talking at length about V-weapons and the jet aircraft that would soon come into service. At one stage he agreed to issue a new instruction that would allow von Rundstedt greater freedom of action, but this never actually materialised. While the meeting was in progress, there was an air-raid alarm, and Hitler and the field marshals had to take shelter; and at another point a V-1 flying bomb, whose direction-finding mechanism had failed, crashed within earshot of the conference. Hitler had just agreed to visit Rommel's headquarters to get a closer view of the situation in Normandy, but after the explosion of the rogue V-1 he refused to go. Instead he returned to Germany, leaving the military situation no better than when he arrived.

This did not mean that Hitler left the military men to do the best they could. Once the Allies were well established onshore, the best course for the Germans from a military point of view was probably to pull back to a line along the Seine and fight a defensive battle there. But Hitler's reaction to any crisis was to refuse to give up any inch of ground – all units must fight to the last round, and willpower would prevail. Indeed, he ordered his forces to take the offensive. On 27 June, in the midst of a British drive to surround Caen (Operation EPSOM), Hitler ordered von Rundstedt to shift his armoured forces to attack the Americans on the west of the Allied line. Von Rundstedt protested, explaining that he could not, in the midst of a battle, simply disengage his Panzer divisions from the defence of Caen and send them westward. Hitler then summoned both von Rundstedt and Rommel to meet him at his mountain retreat above Berchtesgaden on 29 June. After a long and dangerous drive, and then a long wait to see the Führer, they were sent back empty-handed. A few days later, on 2 July, Hitler dismissed von Rundstedt and replaced him by Field Marshal von Kluge, who arrived in France full of fire but quickly concluded that the battle in Normandy was lost. It was notable that Hitler's first directive to von Kluge predicted that the Allies would soon make a new landing to the north of the Seine – the Allied deception plans were still having their effect.

Even before D-Day, the intelligence staff at Montgomery's 21st Army Group headquarters had argued that the longer Hitler remained in power, the better it was for the Allies in a military sense. Long afterwards, looking back on the battle, General Quesada of the US Army Air Force commented that: 'One's imagination boggled at what the German army might have done to us without Hitler working so effectively for our side.' This was largely true, because under Hitler's control the German field commanders could never analyse the military situation objectively and act accordingly; though it is fair to add that Hitler's persistent belief that the main Allied landing would come in the Pas de Calais was shared by his generals.

[margin annotation: Hitler ordered OFFENSIVE rather than DEFENSIVE]

Meanwhile, the battle went on and German casualties mounted. By 13 July the forces under Rommel's command had suffered over 96,000 casualties (killed, wounded and missing) in the period since D-Day, and had received only 6,000 replacements. In the same period, Rommel had lost 225 tanks and received only 17, while knocked-out Allied tanks were quickly replaced. Such losses could not be sustained for long, and Rommel forecast to his naval colleague Admiral Ruge that the front would collapse within a month.

This proved just about right. On 25 July the American armies under General Bradley opened an offensive south of Carentan (Operation COBRA), which at last succeeded in breaking through the German defences. By the 30th the Americans reached Avranches, a communications centre at the south-east corner of the Cotentin peninsula, and were in a position to move westwards into Brittany and to drive eastwards in the rear of the German forces in Normandy. For the first time the German resistance was actually broken, and they were unable to restore the situation. Field Marshal von Kluge told his Chief of Staff on 31 July: 'Someone has to tell the Führer that if the Americans get through at Avranches they will be out of the woods and they'll be able to do what they want. . . . It's a crazy situation.' By that time the Americans were in fact through at Avranches, and finding very little to stop them.

Hitler's response was yet again to order an attack, this time at Mortain, to strike across the American line of advance, recapture Avranches and cut off the American forces that were moving into Brittany. On paper this seemed a feasible proposition. The distance involved was not great – about 20 miles from Mortain to the sea; the American supply lines along the coast road at Avranches looked vulnerable; and von Kluge was able to put together a group of four (admittedly weak) Panzer divisions to make the attack. But in fact the German offensive was doomed before it even started. Ultra intelligence informed Bradley's headquarters of German intentions 24 hours in advance, and air strikes were prepared well ahead of time. The Germans succeeded in recapturing Mortain, and pushed about seven miles further; but that was all. On the first day, the Germans lost 40 of their 70 tanks, mostly to air attack, and their offensive came to a halt. Hitler's last throw was doomed to failure, and it failed.

In the days that followed, large numbers of German troops were almost surrounded in the so-called 'Falaise pocket' – a euphemism for a situation that was more like a death-trap. In a battle lasting five days (16–20 August) the Germans lost about 10,000 dead and 50,000 taken prisoner, though between 20,000 and 30,000 men escaped and lived to fight another day. By the end of August the Normandy campaign was over. In three months the battle had been lost and won.

In those three months, from the beginning of June to the end of August 1944, the Allies had pulled off the greatest amphibious operation of all time, overcoming the hazards of the weather and the resistance of a dangerous opponent. This was a battle they had to win in order to win the war – and they had succeeded. On the other side, the Germans had a real if slender chance of winning a military victory that might have saved them from defeat in the war as a whole – but they failed to take it. A decisive turning point in the war had been reached and passed.

CHAPTER ELEVEN

'A FATEFUL CONFERENCE':

YALTA, 4–11 FEBRUARY 1945

On 8 January 1945, a month before the Big Three Allied leaders were due to meet at Yalta in the Crimea, Churchill telegraphed to Roosevelt: 'This may well be a fateful conference, coming at a moment when the great allies are so divided and the shadow of the war lengthens out before us.' Even allowing for Churchill's liking for dramatic language, this seemed at first sight a startlingly bleak assessment. After all, by the end of 1944 the issue of the war in Europe was surely decided. In the west, the Allies had won the battle of Normandy and liberated France. In the east, a Soviet offensive (code-named BAGRATION) had advanced hundreds of miles and inflicted disastrous casualties on the German armies. At the northern end of the Russian front, the Red Army had entered East Prussia, while in the south Soviet troops were fighting their way into Budapest. Looking at the war map at the turn of the year 1944–45, the main military issues seemed settled. Germany had lost the war.

This was true, but only up to a point. In fact, the war was not yet over. As long ago as 8 September 1944 Churchill had cast doubt on hopeful forecasts of an imminent German collapse, predicting that it was quite likely that the enemy would still be resisting when the New Year came – and indeed they were. Almost at once, in late September 1944, an Allied attempt to cross the lower Rhine at Arnhem by a daring airborne attack, in the hope of ending the war quickly, proved a costly failure. In mid-December the Germans struck a heavy and unexpected blow in the Ardennes, the scene of their victory in 1940, catching the Allied armies off balance and inflicting a sharp though temporary defeat upon them. Even when this attack came to a halt, the German armies fought doggedly on, holding substantial territories across central Europe. Meanwhile, in East Asia, the Japanese forces had

Map 11 Territories still held by Germany, January 1945.

inflicted heavy defeats on the Chinese Nationalists (May–December 1944), making it finally plain that Chiang Kai-shek's armies could not be relied upon for any major offensive contribution to the war against Japan. When the Americans looked for support in a future invasion of the Japanese home islands, they had to turn to Russia – a crucial strategic fact that lay behind all the deliberations at the Yalta Conference.

So the three Allied powers still faced military difficulties; and at the same time political problems crowded in upon them. Anglo-American relations were going through a rough passage. In the 14 months between the conferences at Teheran and Yalta, Roosevelt deliberately shifted the focus of his diplomatic attention away from Churchill and towards Stalin, whom he now regarded as his chief partner in the war and in the peace that was to come. After Teheran, Roosevelt and Churchill did not meet until the Quebec Conference in September 1944, and their correspondence lacked the warmth and comradeship that had marked its earlier stages.

The most difficult among several Anglo-American disputes concerned the plan (first code-named ANVIL, and later DRAGOON) for an invasion of southern France to support the landings in Normandy. This operation had been agreed upon at the Teheran Conference, and Roosevelt regarded it as a vital element in his efforts to establish trust between himself and Stalin, on which it was politically impossible to change his mind. On the military aspect of the operation, the American strategic planners wanted to bring all available forces to bear in France, rather than Italy, which increasingly seemed a dead end; and they also wanted to use the port of Marseilles to supply the Allied forces in France.

Churchill, on the contrary, opposed the operation tooth and nail. He was desperately anxious to maintain the campaign in Italy at high intensity, so that the British commander on the Italian front (General Alexander) could gain the prestige of winning a victory there. 'I am not going to give way about this for anybody', Churchill declared vigorously. 'Alexander is to have his campaign.' He even contemplated the astonishing step of threatening to resign on this issue, and actually drafted a telegram to Roosevelt including the broadest of hints: 'If my departure from the scene would ease matters, by tendering my resignation to the King . . .'. He thought better of it, and the telegram was never sent; but even the idea is revealing. General Brooke, the Chief of the Imperial General Staff, saw what was going on, and wrote in his diary on the same day the draft was prepared that Churchill 'looked like he wanted to fight the President'. In the event, all Churchill's protests were in vain. Roosevelt stood firm, and the invasion of southern France went ahead on 15 August 1944. Churchill finally made the best of it, and even turned up to watch the landing forces go in.

Another constant source of friction between the United States and Britain lay in their dealings with General de Gaulle, the leader of the Free French. Roosevelt had long displayed an intense hostility towards de Gaulle, and refused to extend any form of recognition to the French Committee of National Liberation (CNL), which aspired to become the Provisional Government of France. Churchill, who (to say the least) often had his own difficulties with de Gaulle, supported Roosevelt in refusing to recognise the CNL, though Anthony Eden and the Foreign Office argued strongly for recognition. Then suddenly, at a press conference on 11 July 1944, without even informing the British in advance, Roosevelt threw his policy into reverse and announced that he was ready to treat the Committee of National Liberation as the de facto administration for liberated France. Oliver Harvey, a senior Foreign Office official, observed in his diary: 'Both PM and AE [Anthony Eden] rather bitter at this sudden volte face without any warning.' Three months later, on 23–24 October 1944, Roosevelt pulled the same trick again, and the USA abruptly recognised de Gaulle's Committee as the Provisional Government of France. The British were given very little notice, and had to follow on as best they could. Churchill telegraphed to Roosevelt with remarkable restraint, 'I was naturally surprised at the very sharp turn taken by the State Department', which diverted blame from the President to officials; but this was no more than a polite fiction. In fact, Roosevelt had twice left Churchill in the lurch on a matter that concerned Britain closely. It was a clear sign of Churchill's diminished standing in his relations with Roosevelt.

Churchill was conscious of these growing difficulties with America, and tried to strengthen his position in the Grand Alliance by improving his relations with Stalin. He made a long visit to Moscow (9–19 October 1944), and took the opportunity to propose an agreement on spheres of influence in eastern and central Europe, which has become famous as the percentages agreement. Churchill suggested that in the immediate future the Soviet Union should exercise 90 per cent influence in Rumania and 75 per cent in Bulgaria; Britain should have 90 per cent influence in Greece; while in Hungary and Yugoslavia the two powers should go 50–50. It was not clear what these percentages might mean in practice; but the figures were thought important enough for Eden and Molotov to amend them by allotting the USSR 80 per cent influence in Hungary and Bulgaria.

When he made his first proposal, Churchill wrote the percentages down on a half-sheet of paper, and Stalin approved them by adding a big tick in blue

32 Carving up the Balkans and Hungary. The 'percentages agreement' between Churchill and Stalin allotting spheres of influence in the Balkans and Hungary. Stalin signified his assent with a large tick.

crayon. Churchill then wondered whether this document might be seen as rather cynical, and suggested burning the paper, but Stalin told him to keep it.

In his messages to Roosevelt, Churchill was careful not to mention the stark contents of these exchanges, referring vaguely to 'a common mind about the Balkans', and 'preliminary agreements . . . subject to further discussion and melting down with you'. He avoided using the words 'spheres of influence', knowing full well that Roosevelt opposed such a concept in principle – though, of course, the President had no intention of giving up the American spheres of influence in the Caribbean and Latin America.

In the event, the value of the 'percentages agreement' to Britain was demonstrated remarkably quickly. In November 1944 British troops landed in Greece after the Germans had withdrawn, and almost at once used force to prevent a *coup d'état* by the Communist forces in the Greek Resistance. There was at once an outcry in the House of Commons, and in *The Times* and the *Manchester Guardian*, denouncing the British intervention as a breach of the Atlantic Charter and an infringement of the right of the Greek people to choose their own government. Across the Atlantic, the American press was ardent in its denunciation of the British action, and the State Department issued a critical public statement. Roosevelt himself telegraphed to Churchill, explaining that he had to respect public opinion, and therefore the US government could not 'take a stand with you in the present course of events in Greece'. In striking contrast, Stalin and the Soviet press remained completely silent, at a time when they might have rendered the British position untenable. In Churchill's words: 'Stalin . . . adhered strictly to our agreement of October, and during all the long weeks of fighting the Communists in the streets of Athens not one word of reproach came from *Pravda* or *Isvestia*'.

The percentages agreement thus showed its value, and achieved the remarkable result of aligning Britain and the Soviet Union against the United States, to Churchill's immediate advantage in the Greek crisis. But it was an advantage that came at a price. When Stalin urged Churchill to keep the 'naughty document', he established a complicity between them, in which they both accepted a *Realpolitik*, power-politics method of conducting international diplomacy, as distinct from Roosevelt's idealistic approach. Later on, at the Yalta Conference, Stalin confronted Churchill with the same *Realpolitik* approach, this time over the Polish question; and the Prime Minister could scarcely complain. It was of course true that Roosevelt himself was a skilled, and, when necessary, a ruthless practitioner of power politics; but his idealism was real enough in itself, as well as being necesssary in his dealings with the American public.

During 1944 Roosevelt's foreign policy was largely directed towards his post-war ideals, and notably the organisation of the post-war world on lines far removed from power politics or spheres of influence. On economic affairs, a conference met at Bretton Woods (in New Hampshire) in July 1944, attended by 44 states, which agreed to set up two new economic organisations: the International Monetary Fund and the International Bank for Reconstruction and Development (later commonly called the World Bank). The conference also agreed to stabilise exchange rates between currencies, using either the gold-exchange standard or the US dollar as the common standard. In principle, the Soviet Union was hostile to all such capitalist devices, but in practice it attended the conference and signed its final agreement.

There followed a further conference at Dumbarton Oaks (a stately mansion in Washington), to prepare a framework for the United Nations

Organisation, the key element in Roosevelt's plans for a post-war political settlement. But this conference (August–October 1944) ended without agreement on two vital questions: which countries were to be accepted as members of the United Nations; and how votes were to be exercised in the Security Council, which was to be the principal executive body of the new organisation. As to membership, the United States proposed the signatories of the original Declaration on the United Nations in 1942 (the anti-Axis allies of that time), plus eight others, six of them in Latin America and so likely to be under American influence. The Soviet Union countered by proposing membership for all 15 of the Republics within the USSR (which in theory, though certainly not in practice, could conduct their own foreign policies), as well as for the Soviet Union itself, making a total of 16 Soviet members. As to voting in the Security Council, there was general agreement that the permanent members of the Council (at that stage, the USA, the USSR, Britain and China) should hold a power of veto, but not on the circumstances in which that veto might be used. The Dumbarton Oaks Conference thus ended in an impasse, with no obvious way out; and the United Nations Organisation was bound to be an important, and possibly dangerous topic at the Three-Power Conference.

These matters were in the public foreground of Allied relations. In the background, and more ominously, there lay the Polish question, and above all the problem of relations between the Soviet Union and Poland, which potentially threatened to disrupt the Grand Alliance. The British and American governments recognised the Polish government in exile in London as the legitimate government of Poland. Moreover, the Polish contribution to the war against Germany had been outstanding. Polish fighter pilots had fought with spectacular courage in the Battle of Britain. Polish warships had endured the rigours of the Battle of the Atlantic. A Polish Army Corps under General Anders had played a heroic part in the Italian campaign, notably in the struggle at Monte Cassino. A Polish Armoured Division had served in the Normandy campaign, and Polish paratroops had dropped at Arnhem. In the hidden war of secret intelligence, Polish sources had provided the British with vital information about the German Enigma cipher machine. It was a magnificent record, which amply deserved recognition and recompense on the part of the British, though in American minds it was less well-known and appreciated.

In 1943 a dangerous situation arose when the USSR broke off relations with the Polish government in London over the issue of the Katyn graves. In April 1943 the Germans announced the discovery of mass graves in the

Katyn forest, near Smolensk, where over 4,000 Polish officers had been shot and their corpses buried. The Germans claimed that the Soviets had killed these officers, but the Soviets denied this, and claimed that on the contrary the Germans were responsible. The Polish government in London (which had good reason to know that the Soviets were guilty) asked for an investigation by the International Red Cross. The Soviet government at once accused the Poles of siding with the Germans, and broke off diplomatic relations in retaliation. [didnt want investigation of who killed Polish officials)

At one level this breach could be dealt with as a diplomatic problem, open to a solution by diplomatic methods. But there were much wider implications. After breaking off relations with the London Poles, the Soviet government set up a Polish Committee of National Liberation, made up of communists in exile. This opened up the possibility of converting the Committee into a government, so that there would be two Polish governments, one in London and another in the Soviet Union. Moreover, behind these questions of diplomacy and politics there lay profound issues of morality and public opinion about the war. In 1943 and 1944 the reputation of the Soviet Union and the Red Army in the West was high, and Stalin himself was the focus of widespread public admiration. Yet if the Soviets had indeed massacred the Polish officers, that would be an atrocity like those committed by the Nazis, and the subsequent public reaction in Britain and the United States might well endanger the three-power alliance. In the event, the revelation of the Katyn graves passed without serious damage to the alliance. The key members of the British government who knew the facts about Katyn were 95 per cent certain that the Soviets were responsible for the massacre, but they preferred to keep silent and damp down public comment as far as possible. A few voices, notably in the Catholic press and in Scotland, where Polish troops had made a high reputation for themselves, took the Polish side on the Katyn affair; but they won little support in face of strong pro-Soviet opinion. In America, Roosevelt was informed of the evidence by the British government, but he too remained silent. The question of who was responsible for the Katyn massacre remained unresolved, but it did not endanger the alliance.

But that danger was ever-present in the background, and was revived in 1944 by two events: the Warsaw Rising by Polish Resistance forces; and the Soviet recognition of the Polish National Committee as the Provisional Government of Poland.

On 1 August 1944 the Polish Home Army, led by General Bor-Komorowski, began a rising to liberate Warsaw from the Germans in what they expected to be a brief interval between a German withdrawal and the

arrival of the Red Army. In the event, the Germans did not withdraw and
the Red Army did not arrive; and for two long months the Home Army
fought an unequal battle against the Germans, until General Bor-
Komorowski surrendered on 2 October. While this battle went on, the
Soviet forces stood within sight and sound of the fighting, on the eastern
bank of the Vistula River, without moving to help the Polish uprising.
Moreover, the Soviet government refused (except on one occasion) to allow
American aircraft to drop supplies to the Poles and then go on to land and
refuel at Russian airfields. The terrible struggle in Warsaw, and the Soviet
refusal to assist, provoked accusations that the Russians were deliberately
leaving the Polish Resistance to be destroyed, so as to ease the path for their
own occupation of Poland; but this was the reaction only of a minority. The
official line taken by the British and American governments was that the
Russians were in fact doing their best to help the Warsaw rising, and could
do no more. Neither Churchill nor Roosevelt was prepared to endanger the
three-power alliance by risking a public dispute with the Soviet Union over
the Warsaw rising. Public criticism of the USSR was more widespread than
in the case of the Katyn graves, but still not strong enough to affect government policy in London or Washington.

The Soviet recognition of the Polish National Committee was a less
dramatic affair, but still of far-reaching importance. On 27 December 1944
Stalin telegraphed to Roosevelt offering his good wishes for the New Year;
and at the same time he announced that the Soviet Union had decided to
recognise the Polish Committee as the Provisional Government of Poland.
Roosevelt protested, and appealed to Stalin to postpone recognition until the
three powers met in conference, only just over a month away. In reply Stalin
took the constitutional high ground, regretting that it was impossible for
him to meet Roosevelt's request, because the Praesidium of the Supreme
Soviet had undertaken that when the Poles had formed a government the
Soviet Union would recognise it. He could not go back on this commitment.
From time to time Roosevelt himself had explained to Stalin that the constitution of the United States would not allow him to do this or that; so Stalin
doubtless took some satisfaction in invoking this constitutional obstacle. In
the face of Stalin's negative, Roosevelt was effectively helpless. It was more
important to sustain the three-power alliance than to make a fuss about a
diplomatic move, even though it meant that there were now two Polish
governments, recognised by different partners in the Grand Alliance.

Looking back over the year 1944, there was much cause for anxiety
about the state of the Grand Alliance. Churchill and Roosevelt had been

involved in serious disputes that contrasted sharply with the friendship and cooperation of former years; and Churchill was having to cope with a new role as second fiddle, for which he was temperamentally ill-fitted. The Polish question had reached a dangerous stage, with two Polish governments in existence, one recognised by the British and Americans and the other by the Soviets. Public opinion had been disturbed by Soviet conduct at the time of the Warsaw Rising, and there might be worse to come – a serious outburst of anti-Soviet feeling in the press, or among Polish-Americans in the United States, would endanger the alliance. There was good reason for Churchill to think that the great allies were divided. Meanwhile the Germans, facing a worsening military situation, pinned their hopes on the break-up of what had always seemed an incongruous and difficult alliance. Yalta was indeed to be a fateful conference.

[margin handwritten note: threats/ background issues going into Yalta]

In February 1945 it was fourteen months since the Big Three had parted after their first conference at Teheran. During that time Roosevelt had become a changed man, bearing the marks of grave illness – photographs in the press showed him gaunt and hollow-cheeked. When Churchill met him at Malta en route for the Crimea, he felt that the President had only 'a slender contact with life'. Even so, in 1944 Roosevelt had fought and won a fourth presidential election, and his stamina and willpower still carried him through immense physical and mental exertions. He handled the new conference very differently from the previous one. At Teheran he had worked almost alone, but he went to Yalta with a strong team, including Edward Stettinius, the Secretary of State; James F. Byrnes, the Head of the Office of War Mobilisation and a former Senator; and Edward J. Flynn, a Democrat politician from New York and a prominent Catholic. Roosevelt was thus well prepared to present the results of the conference to the American public; and he was acutely conscious that there would have to be positive results to present.

Churchill too had suffered from ill health during the year, and he was feeling the strain of the long and unrelenting war, which he had been bearing for longer than either Stalin or Roosevelt. His response to fatigue was to drive himself (and those around him) harder than ever – he even spent Christmas 1944 at Athens, in the eye of the storm of Greek politics. At Yalta he was probably in better health than at Teheran, and his capacity for argument was certainly undiminished. When Molotov described Roosevelt and Churchill at Yalta as 'two tired old men', who had 'no choice but to give us what we wanted', he underestimated them. Roosevelt and Churchill both knew what they wanted, and did not give up easily.

33 Churchill, Roosevelt and Stalin at the Yalta Conference, 3 February 1945. Roosevelt, clearly a sick man, had not long to live.

There were some indications that Stalin too was feeling the strains of war, which in the particular circumstances of his dictatorship he had to bear almost alone. But he had an important advantage that was not available to Roosevelt and Churchill. For the two Western statesmen, and especially for Roosevelt, the triple alliance was absolutely essential in the war and in the peace to follow. For Stalin, the alliance was of decreasing value as the war went on, and the Red Army won one victory after another. If necessary, it would be difficult but not impossible for him to do without his allies; but they could not do without him. This was a very strong card to hold.

The Big Three met at Yalta only after much discussion of other venues. As early as September 1944 Churchill had suggested Invergordon, in the Orkney Islands, which would have been remote and secure, but somewhat bleak; Stalin declined. Roosevelt then proposed various meeting places in the Mediterranean, without success. Yalta, in the Crimea, had the crucial advantage for Stalin of being on Soviet territory. There were other points in its favour. It was a Black Sea resort of long standing, with plenty of accommodation; it was famous in literature as the setting for Chekhov's story, 'The Lady with the Little Dog'; and it had a good climate for a February meeting. So Yalta it was.

It was a meeting place that made formidable demands on Roosevelt: a long voyage by warship (the cruiser USS *Quincy*) from the USA to Malta; then a six-hour flight from Malta to Saki airfield in the Crimea, taking off at the wretched hour of 3.30 in the morning; and finally a trying 80-mile drive to Yalta on a rough road across snow-covered mountains. All this was endured by a man who was seriously ill, and it was a tribute to Roosevelt's courage and stamina that he arrived at all.

Churchill had a shorter but still a strenuous and hazardous journey. He flew from England to Malta, in a Skymaster aircraft, a gift from the American Air Force General Arnold. The rest of the Prime Minister's party flew in two other planes, one of which crashed into the Mediterranean, with only five survivors. Churchill met Roosevelt briefly at Malta on 2 February, and then followed a similar traverse, by air to Saki airfield, and finally a long drive to Yalta (broken by an elaborate lunch with Molotov). The last stage brought an encouraging change in the weather – 'As we crossed the mountains and descended towards the Black Sea we suddenly passed into warm and brilliant sunshine and a most genial climate.'

On arrival at Yalta, each of the Big Three had his own quarters. Stalin was established at the Koreis Villa, once a residence of Prince Yusupov, who had taken part in the assassination of Rasputin in 1916. From this villa Stalin kept up his demanding work of ruling the country and supervising the campaigns on the Eastern Front, as well as acting as host to the conference. Roosevelt and his principal colleagues were housed in the Livadia Palace, built for Tsar Nicholas II in 1910–11, and recently used (and knocked about) by the Germans. The President himself was comfortably settled, but the numerous members of his entourage found themselves short of bathrooms and irritated by bedbugs. Churchill and the main members of the British delegation were based in a palace built in the midnineteenth century for the Vorontsov family, whose members had included an ambassador to London and a Russian officer during the Crimean War. The British too had trouble with bedbugs, and Lord Moran (Churchill's physician) had to appeal for American help with DDT sprays. But there was plenty to eat and drink, and the Russians went out of their way to be good hosts, looking after the smallest details. A British naval signals officer noted in her diary that 'they had laid on the most terrific show for the British, which includes maids in caps, aprons and high-heeled shoes which they had never worn before . . .'. It was a strange, almost surreal, stage-set for the conference.

The plenary sessions of the conference were held at the Livadia Palace, so that Roosevelt was not put to the trouble of a daily journey. As at Teheran, Stalin proposed that Roosevelt should take the chair at the plenary sessions, ensuring that there should be no rotation of the presidency at the meetings, and also offering Roosevelt the role of impartial arbiter if there was opposition between Stalin and Churchill. The Big Three also followed the precedent of Teheran by agreeing to dispense with any formal agenda to settle what points were to be discussed and in what order. In the event, Stalin was able to direct the first plenary session towards the military situation, making sure that the Red Army was given full recognition for what he claimed was a selfless bringing forward of

34 The Yalta Conference in session at the Livadia Palace, formerly a residence of Tsar Nicholas II, recently vacated by the Germans.

its winter offensive – though in fact it had opened at a date long planned. There was a general recognition that the fighting was far from over, and General Antonov (the Soviet Deputy Chief of Staff) estimated that 1 July 1945 was the most likely date for the end of the war with Germany – which proved pessimistic in the event, but carried weight at the time.

Against this military background, the Big Three turned to the main political issues that lay before them. Stalin held the strongest bargaining position. A number of his immediate objectives had already been effectively secured by events on the ground and the advance of the Red Army, which had already established a Soviet sphere of influence in eastern Europe, from Finland to the Balkans. He also had other objectives, which depended on negotiations with the USA and Britain: an advantageous settlement of the fate of Germany; the need to ensure that the new world organisation (the United Nations) would recognise the Soviet Union's role as a great world power; and securing a high price for Soviet intervention in the war against Japan, which the United States had long been seeking. In all these matters Stalin held strong cards. The fate of Germany would at least in part be settled by the advance of the Red Army. The USSR had the power to block progress towards a world organisation simply by being difficult; and Stalin knew that Roosevelt needed Soviet help against Japan so desperately that he would certainly be prepared to pay for it. In the background, as at Teheran, Stalin still had the advantage of good intelligence on his allies, provided by Soviet agents in British and American governing circles.

Roosevelt was in a more difficult situation. The United States was economically and materially stronger than the Soviet Union, but that strength could not easily be brought to bear in the type of negotiations which were to take place at Yalta. Politically, Roosevelt was anxious to secure a firm foundation for the United Nations Organisation, which he regarded as the only means of establishing a permanent peace settlement. He therefore had to break the deadlock that had blocked progress at Dumbarton Oaks, and produce a framework for a world organisation acceptable to American public opinion.

Roosevelt's other great objective at Yalta was very different: to bring the Soviet Union into the war against Japan so as to secure victory and save American lives. This would mean paying a price that had nothing to do with ideals. After all, he could scarcely go to Stalin and say 'You have already suffered terrible losses in the war against Germany; will you now agree to suffer more, to save American casualties?' He must have something solid to offer in return for Soviet intervention. In such a bargain, Stalin would deal in territory, not ideals or goodwill; and the bargain would certainly have to be secret. So Roosevelt needed Soviet participation in the United Nations in a way acceptable to American public opinion; and he needed Soviet military action against Japan at a price that could not be made public at all. It was a tall order.

Of the Big Three, Churchill was in the weakest position – indeed, humourists were already referring to the Big Two-and-a-Half. The British and Imperial contribution to the fighting, on land, at sea and in the air, had been maintained at a remarkably high level, and so had British war production; but these efforts now came a clear third when compared with the immense resources deployed by the United States and the Soviet Union. At the personal level, Churchill's efforts to restore his relations with Roosevelt before the Yalta Conference came to nothing – they met at Malta, but only at social gatherings. It was already clear that if Roosevelt and Stalin got together, Churchill could do little against them. Perhaps fortunately, Churchill's objectives at Yalta were limited. As a matter of principle he was determined to ensure that Britain maintained its formal position in the Grand Alliance. On the German question, he was anxious to postpone any definite decisions as long as possible; meanwhile he wished to secure for France a role in the occupation of Germany, to take some of the weight of the occupation off British shoulders when the Americans left Europe, as they were expected to do before long. On Poland, Churchill recognised the strength of the Soviet position, but still hoped to save something for the Polish government in London.

It was against this background that Stalin, Roosevelt and Churchill approached the great issues of the Yalta Conference: to clear a path for the establishment of the United Nations Organisation; to work out a policy towards Germany, notably on the issues of partition and reparation payments; to settle the problems of Polish boundaries and the Polish government; and to decide when and on what terms the Soviet Union would enter the war against Japan.

Agreement on the United Nations Organisation came with surprising ease, and at an early stage of the conference. On 7 February, Molotov, the Foreign Minister, who so often acted as Stalin's 'No-man', unexpectedly announced that the Soviet request for 16 members of the UN would be reduced to three – the USSR itself, plus Ukraine and Belorussia, with a possible further claim for Lithuania which was later dropped. On the question of voting in the Security Council, the Soviet Union agreed that on matters of procedure (that is, how a particular matter should be dealt with) there would be no right of veto for permanent members; while on matters of substance, involving action by the Council, the permanent members would be able to exercise a veto, so preventing any action if they so wished. On both these matters, therefore, the Soviet Union agreed to arrangements that Roosevelt favoured. The President was delighted, greeting Molotov's statement as a great step forward. It was indeed a concession that allowed Roosevelt to gain just the sort of success that would please American public opinion. The establishment of the United Nations Organisation could go ahead, and its founding conference was scheduled to start in April at San Francisco.

The German question faced the three powers with a whole series of problems: where the German frontiers were to be drawn; whether Germany was to be partitioned, and if so into how many pieces; and how much Germany was to pay in reparations to her former enemies. Some of these matters had already been partially settled before the Yalta Conference met. At Teheran the three Allies had agreed that the Soviet Union was to annex the northern part of East Prussia, which was a step towards partition. During 1944 the European Advisory Commission (based in London, and made up of American, British and Soviet members), had agreed that Germany was to be divided into three occupation zones, each to be garrisoned by one of the great Allied powers, with an Allied Control Commission to administer Germany as a whole. This offered an outline of partition, but without settling anything.

At Yalta, Churchill proposed to alter these arrangements by allowing France to join the occupying powers, with an occupation zone and a representative on the Control Commission. Somewhat reluctantly, Stalin and Roosevelt agreed that a French occupation zone should be made up from the British and American zones.

This left the questions of partition and reparations. On the issue of partition (or dismemberment, which was the stronger term frequently used at the time), some decisions had already been made. Part of East Prussia was already to go to the Soviet Union; and it had been informally agreed at Teheran that Poland should gain former German territories up to the line of the River Oder and to one or other of the Rivers Neisse, either the eastern or the western. But this still left open the fate of the major part of Germany's pre-war territory. At Yalta, Roosevelt stuck to the view he had advocated at Teheran: that Germany should be divided into five separate states (though the shape of these states was left undefined). Churchill supported the principle of partition, but argued that it was too early to decide on details; so he proposed to postpone the question by referring it to a three-power committee, with Eden as chairman. Stalin was strongly in favour of dismemberment, but agreed to postpone a decision, which would strengthen his hand as the Red Army advanced into Germany.

As to reparations, there was at first an acute difference of opinion between the Soviet Union and the two western allies. The Soviet Union had suffered immense losses, in lives and material damage, and was determined to exact heavy reparations, in kind and in cash, to restore some of the damage and to punish the Germans for what they had done. Stalin therefore demanded that Germany should pay reparations to a total value of 20 billion US dollars, of which half should go to the Soviet Union. The Americans and British opposed this proposal, arguing that the attempt to extract large reparations from Germany at the end of the First World War, under the terms of the Treaty of Versailles, had been a failure, and in the long run had produced economic disaster for Europe. Naturally, this cut no ice with the Soviets, who were more interested in their present losses than in a historical debate about Versailles. Eventually, Roosevelt agreed that a three-power Reparations Commission should meet in Moscow, with Molotov as chairman, to consider the question, taking the figure of $20 billion as a basis for its discussions. Churchill continued to object, but he was overruled; and the Commission was duly established, which was a substantial success for Soviet policy.

With the framework for the United Nations Organisation agreed upon, and the German question largely postponed, the problems of Poland came to dominate the work of the conference, and might have led to its breakdown. The question of frontiers was already being settled piecemeal on the ground. The eastern frontier, between Poland and the USSR, had been largely fixed at the Teheran Conference, following the Curzon Line (the proposal for the Polish frontier made by Lord Curzon, then British Foreign Secretary, in 1920); and at Yalta all that remained was to accept the Soviet demand that this line should be so drawn as to incorporate Lwow in the USSR. The three allies also agreed without difficulty that Poland should annex the inland half of the former East Prussia. As to the western frontier, between Poland and Germany, the Big Three agreed that the border should at first run along the River Oder, and then follow the line of one of the two Rivers Neisse, eastern or western. Stalin favoured the Western Neisse, which would give Poland more territory;

while Roosevelt and Churchill preferred the Eastern Neisse for exactly the opposite reason – as Churchill put it, forcibly if inelegantly, 'It would be a great pity to stuff the Polish goose so full of German food that it died of indigestion.' No agreement was reached, and the question was postponed. (In the next few months it was settled in practice by the German population moving out of the area between the two rivers, and Soviet or Polish forces moving in.)

It is striking that none of these territorial questions, which involved the lives and fates of millions of people, was regarded by the great powers as being of sufficient importance to endanger their alliance. In this their conduct was doubtless cynical, but the fact was not in doubt.

The problems presented by the existence of two Polish governments were at once more difficult and more dangerous. The government in exile in London was the direct successor of the Polish government of 1939, and was recognised as legitimate by Britain, the USA and many other countries. The second government in Lublin had been constructed by the Soviet Union from Polish communists in exile, was recognised only by the USSR, and was firmly under Soviet control.

The British were under particular obligations to the London Poles. Britain had guaranteed the independence of Poland, which was hard to reconcile with the dependence of the Lublin government on Moscow, and the Polish contribution to the war had been outstanding. However, the Americans owed less obligation to the Polish efforts in the war, and Roosevelt felt little commitment to the Polish government in exile. Indeed at one stage he even remarked to Averell Harriman, the American Ambassador in Moscow, that 'he didn't care whether the countries bordering Russia were communized'.

At Yalta, therefore, the British and Americans faced a difficult choice. If they supported the Polish government in London, they risked an open breach with the Soviet Union on a matter of fundamental importance to the Soviets. On the other hand, if they abandoned the London Poles, then they would be open to accusations of betrayal, and of appeasing Stalin just as Neville Chamberlain had appeased Hitler at Munich in 1938. On their decision hung the fate of the Yalta Conference and the whole later course of the war.

The choice was painful, especially to Churchill, but in practice there was little doubt as to the outcome. Stalin held a formidably strong position. The Red Army already occupied almost the whole territory of the newly emerging Poland, with all the practical authority which that bestowed.

[margin handwritten note: Postponed final decisions on Polish territory]

Moreover, he held the tactical – almost moral – advantage in that Churchill had already concluded the 'percentages agreement' of October 1944, based solely on political expediency; so that the latter was in no position to take the high line of principle over Poland. Finally, the Polish contribution to the war, however splendid, weighed much less in the total balance of power than that of the Soviet Union.

There were long and anxious discussions at the conference, but in the end Churchill and Roosevelt accepted arrangements for the government of Poland that, under the cover of a superficial compromise, accepted the key Soviet demands. The wording finally agreed upon was:

Soviets won – provisional gov't in Poland

> The Provisional Government which is now functioning in Poland [that is, the Lublin Government] should ... be reorganised on a broader democratic basis with the inclusion of democratic leaders from Poland itself and from Poles abroad. This new Government should then be called the Polish Provisional Government of National Unity.

This new government was to hold 'free and unfettered elections as soon as possible', using a secret ballot and with all 'democratic and anti-Nazi parties having the right to take part'. This wording accepted the Lublin government as the basis of a new government, and did not even mention the London government by name, though it was understood that its members would be included in the reference to 'Poles abroad'. There was no definition of what the phrase 'democratic and anti-Nazi parties' would mean, though the British and Americans were well aware that the Soviet usage of the word 'democratic' differed radically from their own. In practice, the undertaking about 'free and unfettered elections' was worthless. So the apparent compromise gave Stalin all he wanted, and the Lublin government was set to become the basis of the future government of Poland. Faced with the choice between standing by their obligations to the London Poles and preserving their alliance with the Soviet Union, Churchill and Roosevelt chose to maintain the alliance It is hard to see how they could have done anything else.

In addition to these agreements on Poland, the Conference adopted, with the proposal of the United States, a Declaration on Liberated Europe, in which the three Allied governments undertook to assist the peoples of liberated countries, and also former German allies, to solve their problems by democratic means, to form interim authorities representative of all democratic elements, and to establish through free elections governments responsive to the will of the people. This was little more than a pious hope; but even so, Molotov grumbled to Stalin that the Americans were going too far in claiming to insist on free elections in eastern Europe. Stalin's reply was simple: 'We can deal with it in our own way later. The point is the correlation of forces.' Stalin knew he had only to wait for the presence of the Red Army across eastern Europe to produce the results that he required.

In the background to all these arrangements lay the issue of Soviet intervention in the war against Japan. For Roosevelt, this was as important in immediate strategic terms as was the United Nations Organisation for his long-term political aims. To defeat Japan by the invasion of the home islands was going to demand a massive military operation, with the certainty of heavy casualties; and the Americans needed the Red Army to take part in that operation and share the casualties. In principle, Soviet intervention had already been promised at the Moscow and Teheran Conferences in 1943; but these undertakings now had to be given specific shape and timing. To achieve this, Roosevelt had to pocket his ideals and pay in the hard coin of territorial advantage for the Soviet Union.

In this negotiation, Stalin took on the role of a Red Tsar, determined to regain the losses that Tsarist Russia had suffered in the war against Japan in 1904–5. His list of demands was lengthy: the return of South Sakhalin Island from Japan to Russia; the annexation of the Kuril Islands from Japan; the lease of Port Arthur in Manchuria as a Soviet naval base, and the establishment of Soviet rights in the neighbouring port of Dairen; and the recognition of Soviet rights in the South Manchurian and Chinese Eastern Railways in Manchuria. In addition, he required the maintenance of the status quo in Outer Mongolia – that is, the territory was to be accepted as a Soviet sphere of influence. In return, Stalin undertook to enter the war against Japan two or three months after the end of the war against Germany. Roosevelt accepted these terms, in a straightforward if cold-blooded act of power politics. Among the territories concerned, South Sakhalin and the Kuril Islands were Japanese, and therefore a reasonable price to be paid by a defeated enemy. Manchuria and Outer Mongolia, on the other hand, belonged to China, an ally (and supposedly a favoured ally) of the United States; but they had to be sacrificed, and by a curious provision Roosevelt actually undertook to secure Chiang Kai-shek's consent to the losses when Stalin requested it. The President presumably believed that Soviet intervention was worth the price – which was after all to be paid with other countries' territory. At the end of the conference, Churchill put his signature to this agreement, even though he had taken no part in negotiating it, on the ground that it would somehow maintain Britain's role as a power in the Far East.

In the early 1970s a musical play, *Yalta! Yalta!*, was staged at Zagreb, opening with these words: 'In February 1945 the leaders of the three great powers met at Yalta to divide the world.' They did not. They did not even divide Europe, though both claims are prominent among the myths that have clung to Yalta like barnacles to a wreck. The truth about Yalta is simpler and less dramatic. When the three statesmen left the Crimea, they could all claim to have achieved their main objectives. Roosevelt had cleared the way for the establishment of the United Nations Organisation, and received a firm undertaking by Stalin to enter the war against Japan. Stalin had secured a favourable arrangement on the make-up of a new Polish government; made a long step towards the acceptance of the Soviet claim to $10 billion in reparations from Germany; and obtained a good price in territory and other advantages for intervening against Japan. Even Churchill, in the weakest position of the three, had gained an occupation zone in Germany for the French, which he hoped would relieve Britain of some of the burden of the occupation. Each of them therefore came away from Yalta with something to show for his efforts. Moreover, difficulties and defects in the agreements could be reviewed at a later stage. Certainly Churchill and Roosevelt, and probably Stalin too, assumed that there would be a peace conference when the war was over.

Above all the Big Three achieved their crucial basic objective: they maintained the unity of the alliance. When Churchill reported to the House of Commons on 27 February 1945 he declared:

> The Crimea Conference leaves the Allies more closely united than before, both in the military and the diplomatic sphere. Let Germany ever recognise that it is futile to hope for division among the Allies and that nothing can avert her utter defeat.

This hit the nail on the head. The vital point at the Yalta Conference was that the three Allies should remain united. If they held together they would win the war. If they broke up, no one knew what would happen. That was why Roosevelt and Churchill had to accept Stalin's terms on Poland. That was why they largely gave way to Stalin's demands on reparations. In the end, the alliance held together and the war was won. There was a price to be paid for this unity, mainly by the Poles. But the price of the breakdown of the three-power alliance would have been far higher.

CHAPTER TWELVE

THE DEFEAT OF JAPAN AND THE ATOMIC BOMBS, 1945

The day of 6 August 1945 began quietly in Hiroshima. Michiko Hachiya, a physician at a hospital in the city, went home in the morning after spending the night there acting as an air-raid warden. He recalled the occasion clearly:

> The hour was early; the morning was still, warm and beautiful. . . . Suddenly, a strong flash of light startled me – and then another. So well does one recall little things that I remember vividly how a stone lantern in the garden became brilliantly lit and I debated whether this light was caused by a magnesium flare or sparks from a passing tram.

Hachiya was in fact witnessing the explosion of the first atomic bomb. What is striking about his account is its quiet, almost humdrum tone – 'sparks from a passing tram' seems an inadequate speculation on a world-shattering event.

Yet in some respects this was a true perspective. We now recognise the explosion of the two atomic bombs (the second, at Nagasaki, followed on 9 August) as a turning point in world history and the beginning of the nuclear age. But at the time, and in relation to the defeat of Japan and the end of the Second World War, the atomic bombs were simply weapons among many others. The defeat of Japan in 1945 was the result of an accumulation of events, rather than of two explosions, however powerful.

This accumulation began in August 1943, when the American Joint Chiefs of Staff presented an Anglo-American conference at Quebec (the QUADRANT Conference) with an outline plan for an offensive against Japan along two main lines: an advance across the South Pacific, by way of the Solomon Islands and New Guinea to the Philippines; and another thrust across the Central Pacific, by way of the Marshall Islands and the Carolines to the Marianas, which would provide airbases within bombing range of the Japanese home islands. The conference accepted these proposals, and agreed that the two lines of attack should be pursued simultaneously.

The southern offensive was already under way in the summer of 1943, when American forces commanded by General MacArthur and Admiral Halsey advanced into the Solomon Islands and New Guinea. By the end of the year the Americans had reached New Britain, and went on to attack New Guinea. They then prepared for a large-scale invasion of the Philippines, beginning with landings on the island of Leyte in October 1944 and moving on to Luzon in January 1945. These operations proved long and costly. The Americans landed over 200,000 men on Leyte, and took more than two months to conquer the island. Luzon proved an even harder nut to crack. General MacArthur publicly (and rashly) claimed victory as early as 6 January 1945, but in fact the Japanese held on in the north of the island until the end of the war in August.

These campaigns proved a slow and painful route to a victory in the Philippines which in strict military terms was of only limited value to the Americans. In fact their main purposes were not military but political – to liberate American territory, and to allow General MacArthur to score a victory and return to the Philippines, as he had promised to do when he left in 1942. These were important objectives in a war that was about prestige as much as about material aims. The Americans wanted to demonstrate that they could defeat the Japanese on land; and even MacArthur's theatrical performance when he waded ashore on Leyte Island in front of newsmen and cameramen had a serious purpose. Even bad theatre had its value in a war being waged by a democracy under the eyes of a demanding press and public.

In the event, the invasion of the Philippines paid a material dividend in a massive American naval victory at the Battle of Leyte Gulf (23–26 October 1944). The Japanese gathered a strong fleet, made up of six battleships (including the giant *Yamato* and *Musashi*, the biggest battleships ever built), four fleet aircraft carriers, 16 cruisers, and a number of smaller warships, to intercept the American invasion forces at sea. In a long and confused battle, the Japanese lost three of their battleships (including the *Musashi*), all four carriers, ten cruisers and nine destroyers. The Americans, for their part, lost only three small carriers and three destroyers. It was a crushing defeat for the Japanese, who had lost a large proportion of their remaining warships; and when all was over the American landing force got ashore safely.

The Battle of Leyte Gulf had another significance, introducing a new type of war at sea – the Japanese use of *kamikaze* tactics, suicide attacks, in which pilots crashed their aircraft and bomb-loads into American warships. In the long run, these tactics were suicidal in more ways than one, for trained pilots were hard to replace. But they scored some success in the battle (sinking a light aircraft carrier); and above all they brought home to the Americans the utter determination and fanaticism of their opponents – a factor that came to weigh heavily on their thinking.

All in all, the long campaigns in the South Pacific, from the Solomon Islands through to the Philippines, were much more than an ego-trip for MacArthur, as they sometimes appeared to be. They defeated strong Japanese land forces, destroying the aura of invincibility that had surrounded the Japanese since 1942; and at Leyte Gulf the Japanese lost a large part of their fleet. These were valuable gains, even if in themselves they were not going to win the war.

Meanwhile the Americans went ahead with the other prong of their offensive, across the Central Pacific towards the Mariana Islands. They began on a comparatively small scale with an attack on Tarawa, in the Gilbert Islands, in November 1943, which surprised the Americans by costing them about 3,000 killed and wounded to capture one small island – an ominous sign of the shape of things to come.

The next phase was an attack on the Marshall Islands in February 1944, which went more smoothly, and led to the capture of the Mariana Islands between February and August of the same year. The Marianas were about 1,200 miles from Tokyo, a long but feasible distance for the new B-29 bombers; and the Americans set themselves to build airfields at great speed, bringing them into active service in November.

This offensive across the Central Pacific culminated in two fiercely fought battles at Iwo Jima (February–March 1945) and Okinawa (April–June 1945). Iwo Jima was an island five miles long, heavily fortified and deeply tunnelled for defence. The Americans began their landings on 19 February, expecting to capture the island within 14 days. In fact they took 36 days. In all, 110,000 American marines landed on Iwo Jima, losing 5,931 killed and 17,372 wounded. The Japanese fought almost literally to the last man – out of a garrison of 22,000, all but a few hundred were killed. When all was over, the Americans had broken an important link in

Map 12 The Defeat of Japan, 1944–1945.

the defensive chain protecting the Japanese mainland and gained new airfields; but at terrible cost.

The next stage was an attack on Okinawa, in the Ryukyu Islands, about 350 miles south of Japan. This operation proved to be a re-run of the battle for Iwo Jima, on a larger scale. Okinawa was 60 miles long, and the fighting lasted 83 days, from 1 April to 22 June 1945. The Americans landed over 170,000 troops to attack about 77,000 Japanese. At the end of the battle, the American losses (land and naval forces together) totalled 12,513 dead and 36,631 wounded. The Japanese lost the enormous total of 70,000 killed and wounded. Only 7,000 surrendered. In the course of the fighting the Japanese threw in large numbers of *kamikaze* planes, sinking a number of warships and landing craft. All in all, it was an awe-inspiring demonstration of Japanese determination and fighting power.

Indeed, these two great battles of Iwo Jima and Okinawa made a profound impression on the Americans, of all arms and all ranks. To capture two islands of no great size they had lost about 18,000 dead and 54,000 wounded. The prospect of invading the Japanese home islands, where these losses might well be multiplied many times over, was daunting in the extreme, and weighed heavily on American minds and spirits.

In sum, these American offensives in the South and Central Pacific achieved great successes, regaining some of the territories lost in 1942, and breaching the Japanese defensive perimeter, designed to protect the home islands. The way was now open for the aerial bombardment of Japan and eventually for an invasion of the mainland.

These results had been achieved through almost complete command of the oceans and the air. By the end of 1944 the American Pacific Fleet outnumbered the Japanese Navy by about four to one in numbers of ships and more than that in striking power, a superiority which enabled the Americans to carry out their vast amphibious operations across the Pacific. In a less spectacular way American sea power was also able to cripple the Japanese economy, almost to the point of destruction, by means of submarine warfare.

In this submarine campaign against Japanese merchant shipping, the Americans got off to a slow start, partly because their submarine commanders were keen to attack Japanese warships rather than merchant ships. Not until 1943 did they seriously turn their efforts to merchantmen, and it was only in 1944 that they were actually ordered to concentrate on sinking oil tankers, a crucial element in the Japanese supply system. Fortunately for the Americans, the Japanese were even slower in organising their defences. The Japanese naval commanders were primarily concerned to engage their main enemy, the American fleet, rather than protecting merchant ships, which seemed a defensive and unheroic occupation for the Imperial Navy. Not until late 1943 did the Japanese begin to establish a convoy system, which they extended widely in March 1944; though at no time did they have enough escorts to protect convoys even when they were formed.

When the American submarines settled to their task, the results were devastating. In 1943 the Americans sank 1.8 million tons of Japanese merchant shipping; and in 1944 they sank a massive total of 3.9 million tons. In 1945, up to 15 August, their sinkings totalled another 1.8 million tons. Japanese losses of oil tankers during the whole war numbered 259 vessels, bringing oil traffic down to a trickle, so that by 1945 their warships were immobilised and aircraft grounded. Even this was not the whole story. In March 1945 the US Army Air Force was instructed to divert some of its heavy bombers from aerial bombardment to the less spectacular but useful task of laying mines in Japanese home waters. The Japanese had few minesweepers to counter this attack, and had to close one of their main sea routes for a fortnight, with disastrous results for their imports. The Americans code-named this mine-laying campaign Operation STARVATION, a warning of the hardships they could inflict on the Japanese population, almost at will.

The effects of the blockade affected the bulk of the Japanese people, especially the millions of city-dwellers. Factory workers spent time looking for food instead of being on the production lines, and weariness took its toll. The standard individual civilian ration in 1944 was a mere 1,900 calories per day, and in 1945 it was reduced to 1,680; for comparison, the British ration never fell below 2,800 calories. Gas and electricity supplies were often cut off except for a few hours each day. At the same time, military personnel in the home islands received higher rations, attracting a good deal of resentment.

The consequences of the Japanese losses in merchant ships and oil tankers were plain to more realistic members of the Japanese high command as early as 1944. Rear Admiral Tagaki, on the naval staff, argued in May 1944 that the current rate of shipping losses meant that Japan had no chance of winning the war and should therefore try for a compromise peace. Some members of the military general staff took a similar line in June, arguing that the war situation was getting steadily worse, and that Japan should try to end the war. No one explained exactly *how* Japan could end the war, or what sort of compromise might be considered – never mind whether the Allies would accept any sort of compromise at all. But doubts were growing in at least some Japanese military minds.

While submarines and mines were strangling the Japanese economy and threatening to starve the population, American bombers were subjecting Japanese cities to devastating air attacks. In 1944 the new B-29 Superfortress bomber came into service – a massive aircraft with a long range and a heavy bomb-load. At first these giant bombers could only reach Japan by flying from bases in India, refuelling in China en route. It was a long and hazardous flight which was wearing on the aircrews and proved almost useless in terms of bombs actually delivered. It was not until airfields were completed on the Mariana Islands that the Americans were able to begin serious bombing raids on Japan. The first B-29 attack took place on 29 November 1944, against an aircraft factory in Tokyo. The commander of the bombing force at that time, Brigadier-General Hansell, adopted a strategy of precision bombing by daylight against military targets; but General Arnold, commander of the US Army Air Force, had no faith in precision bombing, preferring instead night-time attacks against whole cities. The first operation of this kind was carried out against the city of Nagoya on 3 January 1945. On 20 January Arnold replaced Hansell by General Curtis LeMay, who had commanded American bombers operating against Germany from England, and now used that experience to introduce a strategy of large-scale night attacks on Japanese cities, using a high proportion of incendiary bombs, highly effective against towns that were largely made up of wooden buildings.

General LeMay launched the first big raid in this new strategy on the night of 9–10 March 1945, when over 300 B-29s dropped nearly half a million incendiary bombs on Tokyo in three hours, causing a fire-storm that destroyed about a quarter of the city (industrial and residential areas together), and killing somewhere between 85,000 and 100,000 people. An American airman described the scene from the bombers' point of view: 'The whole city of Tokyo was below us . . . ablaze in one enormous fire with yet more fountains of flame pouring down from the B-29s. The black smoke billowed up thousands of feet causing powerful thermal currents that buffeted our plane severely . . .'. The effects on the ground were devastating. An officer in attendance on Emperor Hirohito during a visit to the ruins of Tokyo found people 'digging through the rubble with empty expressions on their faces that became reproachful as the imperial motorcade went by'.

35 American B-29 bombers drop incendiary bombs on Yokohama, 29 May 1945. These 'conventional' raids caused more casualties and destruction than the atomic bombs dropped later.

General LeMay followed this raid up with a series of attacks in the next ten days, striking twice more at Tokyo, as well as at the cities of Nagoya, Kobe and Osaka. There was then a pause, while the B-29s switched their efforts to supporting the attack on Okinawa; but they resumed their offensive in mid-May, with nine raids on six major cities, including Tokyo yet again. In June LeMay varied his targeting by attacking no fewer than 60 smaller cities, spreading fire and ruin across the whole country.

By the end of July 1945 all but a very few cities in Japan had been bombed, with devastating results. War production had been drastically reduced, perhaps by a half. Many oil refineries had been put out of action. Civilian casualties were heavy – estimates varied between 300,000 and 800,000 dead, which meant that a true count was impossible. About eight million people had lost their homes. This destruction was on a scale greater than that which was wrought later by the atomic bombs, and it is not surprising that American strategists did not regard these new weapons as being exceptionally destructive, or their use as something very different from that of 'conventional' weapons.

Taken all together, these cumulative blows were almost fatal, leaving no doubt that Japan had lost the war on all fronts by the end of July 1945. Some of Japan's early conquests had been lost, and others cut off from the homeland. The fleet had been virtually destroyed. (Almost symbolically, the giant battleship *Yamato* had been sunk in the course of a suicidal attempt to help the defence of Okinawa, setting off with only enough fuel for the outward voyage, which she did not even complete.) Blockade had cut off most of Japan's imports, and threatened the population with starvation. Cities had been reduced to burned-out wrecks.

Japan had lost the war by a series of defeats, and yet the Japanese government had not *accepted* defeat, and was determined to continue the struggle, partly because surrender was unthinkable to the Japanese military mind, and partly in the slender hope that the Americans would refuse to accept the scale of casualties that would be involved in an invasion, and would prefer to reach some form of compromise peace. In effect, Japan was dead but would not lie down. What then could the Americans do to bring the Japanese to accept defeat? In theory they could continue with more of the same – more bombing raids and an intensified blockade – until the Japanese cracked. But in practice this was an unlikely course, partly because the Japanese might well hold on rather than crack, and partly because it would take too long. By mid-1945 the overwhelming sentiment in the United States (among political leaders, the high command, servicemen and citizens alike) was that the war must be brought to a speedy end. It had lasted too long already. A slow victory by 'more of the same' was not a serious option.

Another possibility – indeed, the logical outcome to the whole trans-Pacific offensive – was to invade the Japanese home islands. The Americans were in fact preparing plans, first for an attack on Kyushu, the southernmost island of Japan (Operation OLYMPIC); and next for the invasion of Honshu, the main island and the location of the capital, Tokyo (Operation CORONET). Under these plans, Kyushu was scheduled for November 1945, and Honshu for March 1946. The US First Army was actually being withdrawn from Europe and sent to the Far East, where its headquarters was reopened in Manila on 1 August. It was a grim prospect for men who had already fought from Normandy to Germany, and now faced the task of landing in Japan. The anticipated level of casualties in an invasion was terrifyingly high. The most recent evidence was that of the battles for Iwo Jima and Okinawa. Admiral Leahy, who provided the main liaison between the President and the Chiefs of Staff, put the American casualties at Okinawa at 35 per cent of the men involved. The force to invade Kyushu was to be 767,000, which at the same rate of losses would mean about 268,000 killed and wounded – a terrifying thought. Moreover, whatever the cost, results would be slow in coming, and a land battle on mainland Japan might stretch well into 1946.

The Americans therefore had good reason to look for some help in the invasion of Japan. They had long been seeking for Soviet intervention against Japan, and had secured general undertakings of Soviet participation in the war at the Moscow Conference of Foreign Ministers in October 1943, and again at the Teheran Conference in November. At Yalta in February 1945 Stalin had given a definite commitment that the Soviet Union would enter the war against Japan two or three months after the end of the war against Germany, and by the end of July 1945 the Soviet Union stood ready with an army of a million and a half men and an air force of 5,000 planes, ready to attack the Japanese in Inner Mongolia, Manchuria and Korea. Their assault, when it came, would be formidable.

There was more to come, in the shape of a completely new weapon: the atomic bomb. The idea of such a weapon had been in the air as early as 1939–40. In August 1939 a small group of American scientists persuaded Albert Einstein to write to President Roosevelt to warn him that Germany might be working on a bomb using nuclear fission; but even with the weight of Einstein's reputation behind it, this warning was not followed up with any urgency. In Britain, at the turn of the years 1939–40, two refugee scientists, Otto Frisch and Rudolf Peierls, made a strong case to the government that a bomb using nuclear fission was a feasible proposition, and that the Germans might well build one. The government was impressed, and in April 1940 set up a committee (code-named the MAUD Committee) to examine the whole matter.

The MAUD Committee reported in July 1941 that an atomic bomb could be built, and when built would probably decide the war. The British government (meaning in practice those very few people directly concerned) decided that they must build such a bomb before the Germans did; and they set up an organisation (code-named TUBE ALLOYS) to concentrate research and press on with the project as quickly and intensively as possible. American scientists who visited Britain in 1941 were so impressed by these British efforts that they strongly advised their own government to initiate a similar programme; and the German declaration of war in December 1941 concentrated American minds wonderfully. The United States government set about creating what became a vast organisation, code-named the MANHATTAN PROJECT, which at its full strength employed a workforce of over 600,000, and cost a total of over two thousand million dollars. The British recognised that they could not deploy anything like this weight of resources, and transferred their own atomic efforts to the United States, accepting their subordination to the vast American programme.

In the event, the Germans were much less successful in developing an atomic bomb than the Allies had feared. The Germans calculated (mistakenly, as it turned out) that it would not be feasible for them to assemble a uranium bomb. Instead, they concentrated their efforts on synthesising, in a nuclear reactor, a critical mass of plutonium 239. To control this process, they needed a 'moderator', and after early failed attempts with other materials, they settled on the use of heavy water – 'heavy' because the hydrogen in the water was replaced by a heavier isotope. For this purpose they used a plant for the manufacture of heavy water, a plant already in existence at Vemork, in Norway; but their project was seriously hampered and delayed by interventions from the Special Operations Executive, one against the plant itself, and another against a transport vessel carrying heavy water to Germany. As a result of these various setbacks, the German effort to build an atomic bomb fell far behind the progress being made by the Allies. In any case, it was doubtful whether the Germans could have found the resources, in terms of money, scientists or engineers to match the American effort; but it was not until the defeat of Germany in May 1945 that the fear of a German bomb was finally dispelled.

In all the work carried out by the Americans and British in the MANHATTAN PROJECT, there was no doubt that they were developing a weapon that was to be used, like other weapons and means of waging warfare that were constantly being introduced. It would have been used against Germany if it had been ready, and later it would be used against Japan. When Harry Truman suddenly became President of the United States on the death of Roosevelt in April 1945, he was informed by the Secretary for War, Henry Stimson, and the head of the MANHATTAN PROJECT, General Groves, of the tremendous secret of the atomic bomb, of which he had known nothing. In their discussions, there was no indication that they had to make any decision about the use of the bomb, but rather a tacit assumption that if the weapon was tested successfully it would be used against Japan, like the incendiary bombs and high explosives that were already destroying Japanese cities. The committee did debate whether to bring the Soviet Union into the atomic secret, and invite Soviet representatives to the testing of the new weapon; and whether to show the Japanese the immense power of the bomb by exploding it at some deserted site or island. Both suggestions were rejected. The Americans preferred to keep the secret of the atom bomb; and they ruled out a demonstration, mainly because it would not be effective; in the existing Japanese frame of mind, only the actual use of a bomb against a real target would work. On 1 June the Interim Committee recommended that the bomb should be used as soon as possible, the target being left to a military choice. This in effect let the existing assumption stand: the bomb was built to be used, and this would now be done.

At the end of July 1945 a tremendous array of forces were gathering against Japan. Naval blockade was exerting relentless pressure. Aerial bombardment had been almost incessant since March, with appalling results. The invasions of Kyushu and Honshu were being prepared. The Soviet Union was about to intervene with massive force. An atomic bomb had been successfully tested, and was ready for use. At that stage the Americans also made an effort to apply rough diplomatic pressure.

At the Three-Power Conference held in Potsdam in July 1945 a Declaration was drawn up to be presented to Japan. It began abruptly: 'Following are our terms. We will not deviate from them. There are no alternatives.' The most important points that followed were: the elimination of the authority of those who had misled the Japanese people into an attempt at world conquest; Japanese sovereignty to be limited to the home islands (that is, not Manchuria or Korea); the occupation of parts of Japan until a new political order was established; stern justice to be meted out to all war criminals; the establishment of a peacefully inclined and responsible government, 'in accordance with the freely expressed will of the Japanese people'. The Declaration concluded: 'We call upon the government of Japan to proclaim now the unconditional surrender of all Japanese armed forces. . . . The alternative for Japan is prompt and utter destruction.' This Declaration was issued on 26 July, signed by Truman and Churchill (and nominally by a Chinese representative), but not by Stalin – technically because the Soviet Union was not yet at war with Japan, in practice to keep the document in American hands. The Declaration was not communicated formally to the Japanese government through a neutral intermediary, but simply broadcast on the radio and published in the press.

Japanese ministers, military and naval leaders, and officials discussed this document on 27 July, to decide what (if any) reply to make. The Japanese noted that Stalin had not signed the Declaration, and thought that this kept open the chance of mediation by the Soviet Union. The prospect of unconditional surrender was unwelcome even to the so-called peace party, made up of ministers who did not wish to fight to the death, as the Army leaders did, but still hoped to secure favourable terms, allowing Japan to retain Manchuria and Korea, to avoid any military occupation, and to hold any war crimes trials in Japanese courts. Eventually the Prime Minister, Admiral Suzuki, held a brief press conference on 28 July, claiming that the government had no choice but to ignore the Declaration and fight on. It seems that the Declaration's final threat of 'prompt and utter destruction' was too vague to carry any serious weight.

There followed three hammer-blows against Japan, all delivered within four days between 6 and 9 August. The first was the atomic attack on Hiroshima. On 25 July General Carl Spaatz, commanding the US Army Strategic Air Force in the Pacific, received orders to drop two atomic bombs on cities in Japan, as soon as weather permitted after 3 August. Hiroshima was the first of four possible targets for the first bomb, and was put at the top of the list because it had not suffered from earlier 'conventional' attacks, and so provided a clear demonstration of the destructive power of the bomb; and also because Spaatz had received information that there were no prisoner-of-war camps in the area. So the first atomic bomb, based on uranium, was dropped by parachute from a solitary B-29 bomber at 08.15 on 6 August 1945. Its explosive power was equivalent to 12,500 tons

36 A city destroyed. View from the air of the devastation caused at Hiroshima by the first atomic bomb, dropped on 6 August 1945.

37 Soviet tanks drive into Manchuria, August 1945 – a surprise blow to the Japanese army and government.

of TNT. Its destructive effects were enormous, leaving no more than about 6,000 buildings standing out of a total of 76,000 in the city. Estimates of the dead varied widely between 70,000 and 130,000; and more followed as radiation and other long-term effects took their toll.

Japan then suffered another blow, of a different kind. On 8 August 1945 the Soviet Union declared war on Japan, and in the early hours of 9 August Soviet military attacks began, on a vast front of some 2,700 miles across Mongolia, Manchuria and Korea. The Soviet armies outnumbered their opponents by about three to one in men, and far outmatched them in tanks and guns. Despite these advantages, the Soviets expected heavy fighting, and (just like the Americans as they prepared to invade Japan) anticipated casualties of up to half a million dead and wounded. In the event, the Japanese resistance was patchy, and the Soviet forces made rapid progress, reaching Mukden (the capital of Manchuria) on 20 August. For the Japanese government, this was a political as well as a military disaster. As late as 8 August, the Japanese were still hoping that the Soviet Union would act as a mediator in peace talks with the United States, and the Japanese Ambassador in Moscow was still hoping to pursue this line when Molotov informed him of the Soviet declaration of war.

The third blow was the explosion of another atomic bomb, this time at Nagasaki, again by parachute from a lone B-29, at approximately 11 a.m. on 9 August. (The original target had been the city of Kokura, but thick cloud caused the attack to be diverted to Nagasaki – so thousands of lives were changed by a weather feature.) This second bomb, based on plutonium and of a more complex design, was more powerful than that used at Hiroshima, equivalent to about 22,000 tons of TNT; but the destruction was somewhat less because Nagasaki was split up by ridges and narrow valleys, which mitigated the effects of the blast. Even so, about two-thirds of the city's buildings were destroyed; and deaths were variously estimated at between 30,000 and 74,000. The near-annihilation of a second city conjured up an appalling prospect – how many more of these assaults were yet to come?

The first response in Tokyo to these disastrous events was a strange silence. There was a period of stunned hesitation while the Japanese leaders made up their minds what to do. In this last desperate crisis, the Japanese reactions were largely decided by two key elements: the military cast of mind, and the personal role of Emperor Hirohito. For Japanese officers, surrender was simply out of the question, and the defence of the homeland was a supreme duty. The battles for Iwo Jima and Okinawa had shown what this meant. The Japanese had never understood the British surrender at Singapore, and would never incur that kind of disgrace. Moreover, the armed forces held a powerful position within the government, in that the posts of Army and Navy ministers were by law held by serving officers, who had the right of direct access to the Emperor in case of need.

The Emperor himself held a crucial position, by long custom and also by the immediate force of circumstances. In August 1945, Hirohito was 44 years old. He had been Emperor since 1926, and regent for his predecessor from 1921 to 1926. He was therefore an experienced monarch, and it appears that he was accustomed to following the rules of the political system as he understood them. During the war, he took an active interest in operations, generally on the side of a hard line. In July 1944, when the Americans captured the Mariana Islands and so came within bombing range of Japan, his reaction to defeat was obstinate – in the words of one of his biographers, 'he dug in his heels and refused to accept it'. Similarly, during the battle for Iwo Jima, Hirohito advocated resistance to the last, buying time to prepare for the defence of the home islands. In June 1945, after Germany had been defeated and Japan was left alone, he began to consider the possibility of peace; but only on favourable terms, and not by surrender. If the Japanese military had their own cast of mind, which excluded the idea of surrender, the Emperor too was entrenched in an attitude of resistance to the last. It was therefore of crucial importance that Hirohito changed his mind in the face of the disasters of early August.

It was on 9 August, after the Soviet invasion and the bomb on Nagasaki, that the Japanese Cabinet and Supreme War Council discussed whether to surrender. The hard liners, and especially senior Army officers, were determined to fight on, whereas the peace party, including the former Premier Konoe and the former Foreign Minister Shigemitsu, advocated immediate surrender, conditional only on the maintenance of the status of the Emperor. The debate remained deadlocked, until an Imperial Conference met at ten minutes to midnight on the same day, with the Emperor present in person. At the close of a further discussion, the Foreign Minister, Shigenori Togo, proposed that Japan should surrender, subject to the condition that there should be no change in the status of the Emperor under Japanese laws. The Prime Minister, Suzuki, invited the Emperor to speak, contrary to precedent, which prescribed that he should remain silent. Hirohito declared in favour of surrender, and then left the room. All those present (including the military commanders) then signed their acceptance of the Emperor's decision, though with a stiffening of the Japanese condition, to the effect that there should be nothing to prejudice the Emperor's prerogative as a sovereign ruler.

In Washington, the Secretary of State, James Byrnes, insisted on rejecting the Japanese condition, and instead drew up a statement that, after the surrender, the authority of the Emperor and the Japanese state must be subject to the Supreme Allied Commander, and that a form of government should be established by the will of the Japanese people. This accepted that the Emperor should retain some position, though subject to Allied authority, which offered the Japanese government at least a small part of their condition, and so kept the door open for a compromise. The United States government despatched this reply to their allies in Britain, the USSR and China on 10 August; and then to Tokyo on the 11th, where it was received on the 12th.

In Tokyo, the Emperor himself insisted that the American terms must be accepted, and he actually called a meeting of the imperial family (including no fewer than 13 princes), at which he reaffirmed his conclusion. But in the Cabinet the deadlock between the peace party and the hardliners remained unresolved, and for two days (12 and 13 August) the Japanese government made no reply to Byrnes's note.

The drama came to a head on 14 August, at a meeting of all the members of the Cabinet and the Supreme War Council, in the presence of the Emperor. Hirohito declared that Japan could not continue the war, and asked everyone to respect his decision to accept the Byrnes note, adding that he believed the Americans would in the event retain the essence of the Emperor's position. He instructed the government to prepare an Imperial

Rescript bringing the war to an end. This was signed by all members of the Cabinet, and despatched to the Allied powers by way of neutral countries (Switzerland and Sweden). Hirohito also announced that he would broadcast to the Japanese people; and he wisely ensured that two recordings of this broadcast were made in advance, and concealed in secure hiding places.

The importance of this became plain during the night of 14/15 August, when a clash developed between the 'no surrender' attitude of army officers and the now twice-declared intention of the Emperor to capitulate. In the hours of darkness, some middle-ranking officers attempted a palace coup to prevent a surrender. They also tried to find the recording of the Emperor, to prevent it being broadcast. They failed. The coup collapsed, and its leaders committed suicide. So did General Anami, the Minister for War, who had refused either to approve or disapprove of the conspiracy, but who was fundamentally opposed to surrender.

The Emperor survived the confused events of the night, and his pre-recorded speech was broadcast at noon on 15 August, including the Rescript (imperial statement) declaring the war at an end. It was the first time that the Japanese people had heard the voice of their Emperor, who spoke in a form of old Japanese almost incomprehensible to many of his listeners. Indeed, after the broadcast a radio announcer read the speech again in current speech.

38 After the Japanese surrender. Hirohito, still Emperor of Japan, and General MacArthur, the American Supreme Commander and effectively ruler of the country.

Suicides were expected among the armed forces, and in fact some thousands of Japanese officers took their own lives rather than surrender, even on the authority of the Emperor himself. One dramatic episode may stand as an example. Vice-Admiral Ugaki, the commander of the Navy's 'special attack forces' (including *kamikazes*) led a squadron of 11 dive-bombers from an airfield on Kyushu Island on a flight to certain death. Three pilots turned back, claiming that they were having engine trouble. All the others were shot down by American fighters.

On the whole, however, and in view of the Japanese military mindset at the time, it was striking that the vast majority of the armed services agreed to capitulate and lay down their arms. This could only have been achieved by the express and publicly declared will of the Emperor. In turn, the Emperor would only have acted as he did in the situation created by the atomic bombs and the Soviet intervention in the war. Hirohito himself referred to these different events in two different speeches. In his broadcast of 15 August, to the Japanese people as a whole, he spoke of the Americans using 'a most cruel explosive' – that is, the atomic bombs. In a later broadcast on 17 August, addressed specifically to the armed forces, he did not mention the bombs, but stressed the Soviet entry into the war.

The fact was that events crowded closely on one another. The two atomic bombs, the Soviet intervention, and the almost tacit acceptance by the Americans that the Emperor should keep his position – all occurred in quick succession. And yet affairs also moved with painful slowness. Nine days passed between the explosion of the bomb at Hiroshima on 6 August and the Japanese surrender on 15 August; and *two* imperial interventions were necessary before Hirohito's authority prevailed. Considering the scale and nature of the step that surrender represented for the Japanese, this was not so lengthy a time; and yet it doubtless seemed an eternity to those involved. (Incidentally, this was very close to the same length of time that elapsed between Hitler's suicide on 30 April and the German surrender at Reims on 7 May.)

In the story of these nine days, it is difficult to compare and evaluate the different elements that brought about the Japanese surrender. One Japanese historian emphasises the Soviet entry into the war, arguing that this 'had a greater effect on the decision by Japanese leaders to end the Pacific war' than the atomic bombs. The author of a recent history of the Second World War writes simply that the question of whether the bombs or the Soviet intervention was more important 'cannot be answered'. One of President Truman's most distinguished biographers concludes that: 'In such a welter of events and decisions it is not possible to describe any single factor as a sine qua non.' But despite such testimony, it seems right to single out the two atomic bombs as bearing the greatest weight in the final Japanese decision. The Soviet invasion, however formidable, was after all a military campaign like many others, and it was not directed against the Japanese homeland. The atomic bombs produced a shock of a different order, and had a psychological as well as a material effect. Complete proof cannot be established, but in the balance of probabilities it is surely most likely that the atomic bombs finally brought Japan to the point of surrender and the Second World War to an end.

Moreover, the first atomic bombs were beyond all doubt a turning point in the history of the world. The actual use of the bombs against cities, rather than by a demonstration upon some deserted island, was of crucial importance. The ruins of Hiroshima and Nagasaki, and the long-term effects of the atomic explosions, were a warning that no one has yet dared to ignore. Without the appalling facts of Hiroshima and Nagasaki before the eyes of the world, it is surely likely that at some point in the following years *someone* would have used a nuclear weapon. So far, the events of 6 and 9 August 1945 have saved the world from that disaster.

Since the war, much of the discussion on the use of the atomic bombs against Japan has concentrated on questions of morality; on the possibility of alternative strategies; and on political motives for the use of the bombs. These matters impinge only slightly on the effect of the bombs as a turning point in the Second World War, but they are so important that they require at least brief consideration, which must largely take the form of personal opinion.

On moral issues, it seems likely that *in the circumstances of the time* (especially taking into account the length and nature of the Pacific War) and *in the existing state of knowledge* (notably on the long-term effects of radiation) there was no significant moral difference between the destruction of Japanese cities and the killing of their people by 'conventional' bombing and the use of atomic bombs for the same purpose. The destruction and casualties previously caused by three or four hundred aircraft could now be achieved by one; but that did not constitute a moral issue. Similarly, it is hard to find a *moral* difference between starving people to death by blockade and killing them by bombing. The moral issues were therefore those raised by the waging of total war as a whole rather than by the use of these specific weapons. To deal with this would raise the whole question of morality in warfare, which would require a longer and deeper treatment than can be offered here.

One alternative strategy open to the Americans was to demonstrate the power of the atomic bombs by exploding one over a deserted island or some other uninhabited place. This seems quite unrealistic. The device might have failed, or the aircraft might have been attacked by *kamikazes*. Even if the drop had been successful, it was highly unlikely that the Japanese government would have been brought to the point of surrender by a demonstration. Even the bomb on Hiroshima did not have that effect, so anything less would have been useless.

The principal alternative strategy available was the invasion of the home islands of Japan, and specifically Kyushu and Honshu; and the casualties caused by the atomic bombs are often measured against the likely losses (American and Japanese) that would have resulted from such an invasion. This was of necessity a speculative matter. American estimates of casualties varied according to the information available about the strength of the Japanese defending forces; and their forecasts were also heavily – and very reasonably – influenced by the recent experiences of Iwo Jima and Okinawa. In any case, no one doubted that the death toll of an invasion would have been heavy, and that the losses would have fallen on the Japanese civilian population as well as on the armed forces on both sides. No one can tell how this grim form of accounting would have worked out in practice. In the nature of things, it is hard to compare the actual casualties at Hiroshima and Nagasaki with the hypothetical casualties of an invasion. At the time, the Americans did not wish to put the matter to the proof; and it is surely hard to blame them.

Finally, there has been much discussion, especially among American historians, as to how far the motive behind the use of the atomic bombs was to save lives (and principally American lives), and how far the purpose was to impress the Soviet Union and strengthen the American hand in securing a favourable peace settlement. In this interpretation, the atomic bombs appear as the first shots in the Cold War rather than the final round of the Pacific War. This dispute tells us more about American politics and historiography than about events in August 1945, and has now largely run its course, leaving the way open for a common-sense answer. The bombs were built to be used, and they would have been used against Germany or Japan irrespective of the state of American relations with the Soviet Union – they were 'weapons for victory', as Robert Maddox's book on the matter is entitled. It is also true that the Americans believed that their possession of atomic weapons would impress the Soviet Union and strengthen their diplomatic hand – a significant but essentially secondary purpose.

These various matters, though weighty in their own way, bear only a minor relation to the role of the atomic bombs as a turning point in the defeat of Japan. The main conclusion remains, irrespective of our views on the morality or politics of the use of the bombs. The defeat of Japan was achieved by the cumulative use of conventional force, at sea, on land and in the air. The translation of that defeat into surrender came about by a succession of events in early August 1945: the atomic bombs; the Soviet entry into the war; and a degree of diplomatic flexibility in the American treatment of the status of the Japanese Emperor. Among these influences, it is reasonable, but in the nature of things not certain, to conclude that the atomic bombs had the greatest impact.

CONCLUSION

This review of turning points in the Second World War challenges two widely held impressions of the war: first, that the conflict followed a well-marked, if often rocky, road to an Allied victory which was in the long run inevitable; and second, that the war consisted only of a long and bloody slogging match, punctuated by heroic battles but decided by attrition rather than by any feats of leadership or decisive battles. When we look at turning points, on the contrary, it appears that, so far from an Allied victory being a certainty, there were stages, even as late as 1944, when the balance of the conflict might well have tilted in favour of the other side. And while there were indeed long and gruelling battles, with appalling casualties, notably on the Russian front, there were also distinct events (or sometimes series of events) that reveal a pattern in the war.

First there was a period between mid-1940 and early 1942 that established the geographical shape of the war, and also outlined some of its characteristics. The German victory over France in May and June 1940 set the territorial framework of the war in western and central Europe for the next four years. The Germans dominated the whole of western Europe, and would have to be driven out of their conquered territories if they were to lose the war. But their victory in the west was incomplete. They failed to win the aerial Battle of Britain in the summer and autumn of 1940, and Britain survived, preserving a stronghold of resistance that was a beacon for opposition to Germany in Europe, and eventually offering the United States a base from which they could mount an invasion of the continent.

Next, in Operation BARBAROSSA (in the second half of 1941) Germany conquered vast territories in the Soviet Union, but failed to gain their final objectives – the capture of Moscow proved beyond their reach;

and the Soviet armies, despite terrible losses, remained intact and were able to launch a counter-offensive at the end of the year. As a result, the geography of the war in eastern Europe was settled in its turn, and the great Soviet-German struggle became a permanent feature of the war as a whole.

In the Pacific and East Asia, Japan struck at the American fleet at Pearl Harbor in December 1941, and then exploited its command of the oceans to conquer the whole of South-East Asia, with vast resources of oil, minerals and rubber. Japan also established, through groups of islands stretching from the North to the South Pacific, a long defensive line, which the Americans would have to breach if they were to attack Japan and win the war.

Taken together, these events in Europe and the Pacific marked the initial triumph of Germany in the west and Japan in the east, and also the limits of that triumph. The geographical framework of the war was settled in the almost two years between mid-1940 and early 1942. The Germans and Japanese had conquered territories where their grip would have to be broken if they were to be defeated in the war. But at the same time Britain and the Soviet Union had escaped defeat and begun to strike back; and the Americans too had held on and were setting out to develop their immense industrial and military resources for a counter-stroke. The framework thus set was to last until 1944, and in some cases until 1945.

There followed a period, from mid-1942 to mid-1943, in which the balance of power tilted away from Germany and Japan and in favour of the Allies, and it gradually became clear which side was going to win. Among the turning points that marked this phase of the war, the Battle of Midway Island in June 1942 was the sharpest of all, in that the decisive event could almost be timed to a specific ten minutes on 4 June 1942, when the domination of the Japanese aircraft-carrier fleet was broken, never to be restored. In the German-Soviet conflict, the Battle of Stalingrad between July 1942 and February 1943 destroyed the reputation of invincibility that had so far surrounded the German armies, and established a Soviet superiority which was never subsequently lost. This was a tremendous military and political victory, even though the Germans still held large areas of Soviet territory from which they were hard to dislodge. The Battle of the Atlantic between the Allied convoys and the German U-boats was a long and hard-fought struggle, which in one form or another lasted for most of the war; but its turning point was clearly marked in May 1943, when Admiral Dönitz withdrew his U-boats from the North Atlantic, never to return in any strength. The fruits of this sudden victory were gathered over the following 12 months, as men and supplies crossed the ocean from America and Canada to Britain, building up the forces that were to invade France in 1944.

Meanwhile, a shift in the balance of power of a different character took place in late 1942 and early 1943, when the Germans and Japanese were decisively out-built by the factories and shipyards of their Allied opponents. In numbers of weapons and in the weight of war material and ship-building, the Allies established a superiority that was certain to be decisive *as long as* other non-material factors – morale, determination and unity – held firm.

By the end of this period of shifting balance, it became plain that the Germans and Japanese could certainly not win the war; but it was not yet sure that the Allies would win it, and exactly how they could do so. In Europe there was a severe strategic test to be passed – the seaborne invasion of France in the summer of 1944, an operation of immense difficulty and complexity. The Allies pulled it off, achieving a crucial success when the Germans still had a good chance of defeating the landing forces and driving them back into the sea. Politically, the three Allied powers had to grapple with the difficulties of coalition warfare, which increased in intensity as victory grew closer, and the unifying demands of survival gave way to competition for advantage in the post-war world. It was always possible that the alliance might crack under the strain, as Hitler hoped that it would; but in the event the three-power conferences at Teheran in late 1943 and Yalta in early 1945 enabled the Allies to maintain enough unity to carry the war through to a victorious conclusion.

Finally, the end of the war in the Pacific brought the whole conflict to an end, and marked the great transition from war to peace. The actual change was strangely slow in coming about. Militarily and materially, Japan was defeated by mid-July 1945, but refused to admit this until mid-August. Even the tremendous blows of the atomic bombs at Hiroshima and Nagasaki earlier in August and the Soviet entry into the Pacific war took time to sink in, and Japan was eventually compelled to surrender. But eventually the bombing stopped and the guns fell silent. The world emerged into something that was perhaps not quite peace but was certainly better than war.

Some of the turning points that brought about the Allied victory included a psychological and even a moral dimension of the highest importance. The Battle of Britain, for example, had a profound and lasting effect on the British people, creating within them a confidence and deter-mination that carried them through a long and exhausting war. The great air battle was fought by the few, but its effects were felt by many, and for a long time. In a rather similar way, the Japanese attack on Pearl Harbor instilled in the American people an implacable resolve to punish their assailant, employing the full resources of their armed forces and war production, and using any degree of force that became available. On the Russian front, the Battle of Stalingrad marked a turning point for Soviet morale, breeding a certainty that the war could in fact be won, however great the German successes in the past. In all these cases the elements of public opinion and morale were as important as the material factors – perhaps even more so.

In these ways the apparently separate turning points established a pattern in the war, and determined its outcome – victory for the Allies and defeat for Germany and Japan. But what did it mean to win or lose a war of such an appalling scale and nature? The death of millions, whether soldiers or civilians; the destruction of whole cities; the flight of refugees, again in millions – does it make sense to describe these horrifying events in terms of victory or defeat? On the losing side, Germany and Japan had suffered immense material damage, mainly from air attack. Both were occupied by foreign troops, and both had their political systems reconstructed from outside. For some time, they lost their status as independent states. But in some respects there was only one victor, even on the winning side. The Soviet Union had suffered immense loss of life, and a fall in the number of births, with consequences for the population that inevitably stretched far into the future. Large parts of the country had undergone the ravages of German invasion and Soviet reconquest – some territories became battle-fields four times in the course of the war. Britain was not invaded, but endured bombardment from the air and became the first target in the world for attack by rockets. The British people were worn down and exhausted by six years of war, and the country was left bankrupt and economically dependent upon the United States. Both the Soviet Union and Britain had won the war, but suffered effects that were in some ways as grave as if they had lost it. In the next few years they witnessed the disconcerting sight of their defeated opponents flourishing economically to a degree that they could not match. Even victory began to wear a hollow look.

Only the United States emerged as a material victor from the war. The country had not been invaded or bombed. Military casualties were far smaller than those suffered by the Soviets – 274,000 against at least ten million, probably more. The American economy thrived during the war, largely through the stimulus provided by the demands of war itself. The United States emerged as a great military power, and for a time the only possessor of nuclear weapons. It was all a new and somewhat heady experience.

In the event, most of the victors had to find the fruits of their victory in non-material terms. There was a strong sense among all the Allied peoples that they were fighting in a war of good against evil – a 'good war' in a phrase that embodied an accepted truth. The major purposes of the war in Europe were to destroy Nazi tyranny and liberate the continent from German oppression. These aims were in large part achieved; though this success looked less convincing when the victorious alliance included the Stalinist regime in the Soviet Union, which oppressed its own people and imposed its own form of communist dictatorship on the countries that it controlled. 'Liberation' for the Poles meant that they exchanged one form of domination for another.

Even so, one result of the war was real enough. Over large parts of Europe, to paraphrase one of Churchill's speeches, the curse of Hitler was lifted from the brows of men. The victors had not attained a golden age, or founded a new Jerusalem – though some of them had tried; but in an imperfect world the conclusive defeat of Nazism was no small achievement.

The results of the war, for good or ill, arose from its turning points. The Battle of Britain, the Battle of the Atlantic and the Normandy landings together decided that the British and Americans would control western Europe at the end of the war; while the Battle of Stalingrad and the two conferences at Teheran and Yalta secured the domination of eastern Europe for the Soviet Union. In the Pacific, the American victories over Japan imposed an American peace in that country. Turning points had established the shape of the war and decided its issue, and they then did much to shape the peace.

NOTES

Introduction

p.xii   Figures for deaths in I.C.B. Deare and M.R.D. Foot, eds, *The Oxford Companion to the Second World War* (Oxford, 1995), p. 290, article by Richard Overy on the demography of the war.

p.xv   'It may almost be said . . .', Winston S. Churchill, *The Second World War*, vol. IV, *The Hinge of Fate* (London, 1951), p. 541.

p.xv   'One's imagination boggled . . .', General Quesada, US Army Air Force, quoted in Max Hastings, *OVERLORD: D-Day and the Battle for Normandy, 1944* (London, paperback ed., 1993), p. 212.

Chapter One: Hitler's Triumph

p.3   'the biggest known traffic jam . . .', Karl-Heinz Frieser, *The Blitzkrieg Legend: The 1940 Campaign in the West* (Annapolis, 2005), p. 116.

p.4   'The room was barely half-lit . . .', André Beaufre, *1940: The Fall of France* (London, 1960), p. 189.

p.9   'We're very tired . . .' and 'Everyone is holding on . . .', quoted in Jean-Louis Crémieux-Brilhac, *Les Français de l'An 40*, vol. II, *Ouvriers et Soldats* (Paris, 1990), pp. 643, 646. (My translation.)

p.9   'when we mowed down twenty . . .', quoted in Martin Alexander, 'After Dunkirk: The French Army's Performance against "Case Red", 25 May to 25 June 1940', *War in History*, vol. 14, No. 2, April 2007, p. 245.

p.10.   Figures from Frieser, *Blitzkrieg*, p. 56; Ernest R. May, *Strange Victory: Hitler's Conquest of France* (New York, 2000), pp. 477, 479. May's figures for aircraft are calculated on a different basis from Frieser's – the latter are followed here.

p.10   Steel tip, see Frieser, *Blitzkrieg*, p. 33. Horses, see May, *Strange Victory*, p. 209.

p.11   See Olivia Manning, *The Balkan Trilogy*, vol. I, *The Great Fortune* (Paperback ed., London, 1981), p. 265.

p.11   '. . . in twenty-four hours the unhappy town . . .', quoted in Jean Vidalenc, *L'exode de mai–juin 1940* (Paris, 1957), p. 359.

p.12   'The disaster of 1940 . . .', General Charles de Cossé-Brissac, Preface to Pierre le Goyet and Jean Fousserau, *La corde au cou: Calais, mai 1940* (Paris, 1975), p. 5.

p.12   De Gaulle's broadcast, English translation in Jean Lacouture, *De Gaulle: The Rebel, 1890–1944* (London, 1993), pp. 224–5.

p.13   'a form of government . . .', quoted in P.M.H. Bell, *A Certain Eventuality: Britain and the Fall of France* (Farnborough, 1974), p. 48.

p.13 '. . . if he were told . . .'; 'slippery slope', quoted in *ibid*, pp. 42–3.

p.15 'appeal to reason', quoted in Ian Kershaw, *Hitler*, vol. II, *1936–1945: Nemesis* (London, 2000), p. 304. Halifax's speech, see Andrew Roberts, *'The Holy Fox': A Biography of Lord Halifax* (London, 1991), p. 249.

p.17 'He let fly with some choice Russian curses . . .'. quoted in Ian Kershaw, *Fateful Choices: Ten Decisions that Changed the World, 1940–1941* (London, 2007), p. 260.

p.19 'Seize this golden opportunity. . . .', *ibid.*, p. 111.

Chapter Two: 'Finest Hour'

p.21 Hitler quotation, Militärgeschichtliches Forschungsamt, *Germany and the Second World War*, vol. II, *Germany's Initial Conquests in Europe* (Oxford, 1991), p. 368.

p.21 'What General Weygand called the Battle of France . . .', Winston S. Churchill, *The Second World War*, vol. II, *Their Finest Hour* (London, 1949), p. 198.

p.21 Figures for German losses in D. Boog, *'Luftwaffe* Assault', in P. Addison and J.A. Crang, eds, *The Burning Blue: A New History of the Battle of Britain* (London, 2000), p. 40. RAF losses over Dunkirk in Williamson Murray, *The Luftwaffe, 1933–1945: Strategy for Defeat* (London, 1996), p. 39.

p.22 'I was seized with utter disgust . . .', fighter pilot quoted in R. Hough and D. Richards, *The Battle of Britain: A Jubilee History* (London, 1990), p. 100.

p.22 'The more I see the nakedness of our defences . . .', A. Danchev and D. Todman, eds, *Field Marshal Lord Alanbrooke: War Diaries, 1939–1945* (London, 2001), p. 90, entry for 2 July 1940.

p.23 Fighter Command figures in Peter Fleming, *Invasion 1940* (London, 1957), pp. 214–15.

p.23 Hitler's Directive No. 16, and comment, *ibid.*, p. 42.

p.23 Hitler on 'peace tendency', names, *Germany and the Second World War*, vol. II, p. 368.

p.25 '. . . the best time . . .', in Fleming, *Invasion*, p. 245.

p.26 German estimates of British aircraft production, *Germany and the Second World War*, vol. II, pp. 381–2.

p.26 'the inadequate air defence system . . .', *ibid.*, p. 380.

p.27 'happy possibility', S.W. Roskill, *The War at Sea, 1939–1945*, vol. I, *The Defensive* (London, 1954), p. 249.

p.27 'to destroy an invading Force . . .', *ibid.*, p. 258.

p.27 'while we are predominant . . .', *ibid.*, p. 257.

p.27 'The crux of the matter . . .' Quoted in P.M.H. Bell, *A Certain Eventuality: Britain and the Fall of France* (Farnborough, 1974), p. 50.

p.28 'On virtually every occasion . . .', quoted in Hough and Richards, *Battle of Britain*, p. 221.

p.28 'Never in the field of human conflict . . .', Martin Gilbert, *Finest Hour: Winston S. Churchill, 1939–1941* (London, 1983), p. 742; Battle of Britain clasp, Addison and Crang, p. 247.

p.28 'careful, thorough and thoughtful', description of Dowding by Malcolm Smith, *ibid.*, p. 36.

p.30 'Going out onto the platform . . .', anonymous diary, quoted in Richard Aldrich, ed., *Witness to War: Diaries of the Second World War in Europe and the Middle East* (London, 2004), pp. 145–6.

p.30 Goering's order for Operation Eagle, Hough and Richards, *Battle of Britain*, p. 154.

p.31 'a dive-bomber's dream target', *ibid.*, p. 161.

p.31 'We had been caught stone cold . . .', account by a flight mechanic on the airfield, *ibid.*, p. 161.

p.31 Discrepancies between RAF claims and German losses, Sebastian Cox in Addison and Crang, *Burning Blue*, p. 59; Fleming, *Invasion*, p. 229; Hough and Richards, *Battle of Britain*, pp. 310–1.

p.32 'I was worried daily . . .', Park, in Hough and Richards, *Battle of Britain*, p. 200.

p.32 'Come on in and meet 145 squadron . . .', *ibid.*, p. 202.

p.33 'Dear Mum and Dad . . .', in Addison and Crang, *Burning Blue*, p. 148.

p.33 Figures for RAF and German losses, *ibid.*, p. 232; Fleming, *Invasion*, p. 234; Murray, *Luftwaffe*, p. 50.

p.34 'As we broke through the haze . . .', Squadron Leader Johnstone, Hough and Richards, *Battle of Britain*, p. 258.

p.36 'The gratitude of every home . . .', Gilbert, *Finest Hour*, pp. 741–2.

p.37 'the passing years have only confirmed . . .', Hough and Richards, *Battle of Britain*, p. xv.

Chapter Three: Operation Barbarossa

p.41 Epigraph. Field Marshal Viscount Montgomery of Alamein, *A History of Warfare* (London, 1968), p. 365.

p.42 Figures for German and allied forces, Evan Mawdsley, *Thunder in the East: The Nazi-Soviet War, 1941–1945* (London, 2005), p. 19; Rodric Braithwaite, *Moscow 1941: A City and its People at War* (London, 2006), p. 66.

p.43 'I feel as if I am pushing open the door in a dark room . . .', Joachim Fest, *Hitler* (London, paperback edn, 1977), p. 961.

p.44 'Hitler invaded Russia . . .', Alan Bullock, *Hitler: A Study in Tyranny* (London, 1952), p. 651. 'Operation Barbarossa was not a campaign . . .', Jurgen Forster, in Militärgeschichtliches Forschungsamt, *Germany and the Second World War*, vol. IV, *The Attack on the Soviet Union* (Oxford, 1998), pp. 1,245–6.

p.44 'In every village . . .', Lt Wilhelm Pruller, diary, 30 June 1941, in Richard J. Aldrich, ed., *Witness to War: Diaries of the Second World War in Europe and the Middle East* (London, 2004), p. 228.

p.44 'If it had not been for Hitler's fanatical racism . . .', Robert Service, *A History of Twentieth-Century Russia* (London, 1997), p. 290.

p.45 'England's hope is Russia and America . . .', Halder diary, 31 July 1940, in *Documents on German Foreign Policy*, Series D, vol. X, p. 373. 'The Führer expects . . .', Hewel, in John Lukacs, *Hitler and Stalin* (London, 2006), p. 92. 'Barbarossa: purpose not clear. . . .', Halder, in *Germany and the Second World War*, vol. IV, p. 284.

p.45 '*not* to march on Moscow', Mawdsley, *Thunder in the East*, pp. 7–8.

p.47 'completely in denial', Ian Kershaw, *Fateful Choices: Ten Decisions that Changed the World, 1940–1941* (London, 2007), p. 285.

p.47 'Hitler surely does not know', Braithwaite, *Moscow 1941*, p. 70.

p.48 'an act of treachery . . .', *ibid.*, pp. 74–5.

p.48 'A glorious, wonderful hour . . .', and 'We shall win . . .', Goebbels diary, in James Owen and Guy Walters, eds, *The Voice of War: The Second World War Told by Those Who Fought It* (London, 2004), pp. 126–7.

p.48 Soviet aircraft losses and 'aeroplane panic', Mawdsley, *Thunder in the East*, p. 58; casualties and prisoners, *ibid.*, p. 86.

p.48 'The retreat has caused blind panic. . . .' Report by Ponomarenko, head of Belorussian CP, quoted in Catherine Merridale, *Ivan's War: The Red Army, 1939–1945* (London, 2005), pp. 96–7. Merridale observes that this was a 'frank report'.

p.50 'But they are there', *ibid.*, p. 86. 'If this goes on . . .', Braithwaite, *Moscow 1941*, p. 181.

p.51 Stalin's broadcast, Mawdsley, *Thunder in the East*, p.64. 'Russians and other peoples . . .', Lukacs, *Hitler and Stalin*, p. 126.

p.53 'Everything round about . . .', Field Pastor Sebacher, 29 November 1941, in Aldrich, *Witness to War*, pp. 264–5.

p.55 Prisoners of war, *ibid.*, p. 117; I.C.B. Dear and M.R.D. Foot, eds, *The Oxford Companion to the Second World War* (Oxford, 1995), p. 112.

p.55 Churchill's broadcast, Winston S. Churchill, *The Second World War*, vol. III, *The Grand Alliance* (London, 1950), pp. 331–3.

p.57 Fatalities among prisoners of war, Mawdsley, *Thunder in the East*, pp. 103–4.

p.57 Jews massacred in eastern USSR, *ibid.*, p. 102.

Chapter Four: Pearl Harbor, December 1941

p.59 'We are now at war with Japan . . .', Vere Hodgson, *Few Eggs and No Oranges: The Diaries of Vere Hodgson* (London, 2002), pp. 232–3.

p.59 'I continued to watch the sky . . .', Mitsuo Fuchida, Imperial Japanese Naval Air Service, in James Owen and Guy Walters, eds, *The Voice of War: The Second World War Told by Those Who Fought It* (London, 2004), p. 167.

p.59 'Sick at heart . . .', *The War Diary of Breckinridge Long*, entry for 8 December 1941, in Richard J. Aldrich, ed., *Witness to War: Diaries of the Second World War in Europe and the Middle East* (London, 2004), p. 274.

p.64 For the difficult affair of Roosevelt and the oil embargo, see R.A. Dallek, *Franklin D. Roosevelt and American Foreign Policy* (London, 1979), pp. 274–5; David Reynolds, *From Munich to Pearl Harbor: Roosevelt's America and the Origins of the Second World War* (Chicago, 2001), pp. 142, 150–1.

p.65 'this probably over-valued military power', Eden to Churchill, 12 September 1941, in Antony Best, *Britain, Japan and Pearl Harbor: Avoiding War in East Asia 1936–41* (London, 1995), p. 172.

p.66 'about the worst mistake . . .', Craigie to Eden, 1 November 1941, *ibid.*, p. 179.

p.68 'If I am told to fight . . .', in Gordon W. Prange, *At Dawn We Slept: The Untold Story of Pearl Harbor* (London, 1982), p. 10.

p.69 'I didn't think they could do it . . .', *ibid.*, p. 188.

p.69 'He must be a German', *ibid.*, p. 521.

p.69 'This despatch is to be considered a war warning', Samuel Eliot Morison, *History of United States Naval Operations in World War II*, vol. III, *The Rising Sun in the Pacific, 1931–April 1942* (London, 1948), p. 77.

p.70 Numbers of Japanese aircraft, Morison, *United States Naval Operations*, vol. III, p. 85.

p.72 Colonel Flood's account, Prange, *At Dawn We Slept*, p. 523.

p.72 Lieutenant Dickinson's account, Owen and Walters, *Voice of War*, p. 172.

p.72 US and Japanese losses, I.C.B. Deare and M.R.D. Foot, eds, *Oxford Companion to the Second World War* (Oxford, 1995), pp. 871–2; Ronald Spector, *Eagle Against the Sun: The American War with Japan* (London, 1985), p. 6.

p.74 Sinkings by Nagumo's carrier fleet, Morison, vol. III, *United States Naval Operations*, pp. 385–6.

p.75 'unnerved', *ibid.*, p. 209.

p.75 'aroused the people of the United States . . .', Prange, *At Dawn*, p. 582.

p.76 'In all my fifty years . . .', *ibid.*, p. 554.

p.77 Roosevelt's speech to Congress, James MacGregor Burns, *Roosevelt: The Soldier of Freedom, 1940–1945* (London, 1971), pp. 166–7.

p.79 '. . . now at this very moment . . .', Winston S. Churchill, *The Second World War*, vol. III, *The Grand Alliance* (London, 1950), p. 539.

Chapter Five: The Battle of Midway, 4 June 1942

p.82 Combined Fleet Operation Order, Ronald Lewin, *The Other Ultra* (London, 1982), p. 84.

p.85 Intelligence and code-breaking, *ibid.*, pp. 81–110; Peter C. Smith, *Midway: Dauntless Victory* (Barnsley, 2007), pp. 31–44.

p.86 'to inflict maximum damage . . .', John Keegan, *The Price of Admiralty* (London, 1988), pp. 188–9.

p.87 Times and dates: This follows Samuel Eliot Morison, *History of United States Naval Operations in World War II*, vol. IV, *Coral Sea, Midway and Submarine Actions, May 1942–August 1942* (London, 1949), p. 101 and note 3; S.W. Roskill, *The War at Sea, 1939–1945*, vol. II, *The Period of Balance* (London, 1956), p. 38 and note 1.

p.89 'slaughter of the torpedo-bombers', Morison, vol. IV, p. 116; 'wasted sacrifice', Smith, *Midway*, p. 100. On numbers of torpedo-bombers and their losses, this follows Smith, p. 100, and Lewin, *Other Ultra*, p. 111.

p.89 'without a trace of fighter opposition . . .', Dickinson, in James Owen and Guy Walters, eds, *The Voice of War: The Second World War Told by Those Who Fought It* (London, 2004), p. 236.

p.92 Casualty figures, Keegan, *Admiralty*, p. 211.

p.92 Carrier losses and new building, Richard Overy, *Why the Allies Won* (New York, 1996), p. 43; Max Hastings, *Nemesis: The Battle for Japan, 1944–45* (London, 2007), pp. 102–3.

p.92 'After Midway I was certain . . .', 'The decisive turning point', Overy, *Allies*, p. 43.

p.93 US media and role of heavy bombers, Morison, *United States Naval Operations*, vol. IV, p. 159 and note 38; Dauntless dive-bombers 'airbrushed from history', Smith, *Midway*, p. 124.

p.93 For the impact of ten bombs in ten minutes, see Overy, *Allies*, p. 42.

p.93 'This memorable victory . . .', Winston S. Churchill, *The Second World War*, vol. IV, *The Hinge of Fate* (London, 1951), p. 226; 'will-power and passion', *ibid.*, p. 227.

Chapter Six: The Battle of Stalingrad, July 1942–February 1943

p.95 'Children all over the world . . .', Ronald Matthews, in *Daily Herald*, 10 February 1943.

p.95 'the lands which the Germans have destined . . .', British decrypt of telegram, Turkish Consul in Moscow to Ankara, 15 February 1943, in N. Tamkin, *Britain, Turkey and the Soviet Union 1940–1945* (London, 2009), p. 104.

p.97 'It has become a matter of prestige . . .', Groscurth diary, 3 October 1942, in Antony Beevor, *Stalingrad* (London, paperback ed., 2007), p. 187.

p.97 'You can be sure that nobody . . .', Ian Kershaw, *Hitler, 1936–1945, Nemesis* (London, 2000), p. 536.

p.98 'I wanted to take it . . .', *ibid.*, p. 540.

p.98 'Stalin had committed himself . . .', John Erickson, *The Road to Stalingrad* (London, paperback ed., 1985), p. 506.

p.98 'In the elevator . . .', quoted *ibid.*, p. 555.

p.98 Chuikov, 'The streets of the city . . .', quoted in Catherine Merridale, *Ivan's War: The Red Army, 1939–1945* (London, 2005), p. 150.

p.99 'had absolutely no foundation in truth', Beevor, *Stalingrad*, p. 197. Cf. *Daily Herald*, 29 January 1943.

p.100 'The Führer is amongst us . . .', Anonymous German gunner, in J. Aldrich, ed., *Witness to War: Diaries of the Second World War in Europe and the Middle East* (London, 2004), p. 372.

p.101 Soviet production figures, Beevor, *Stalingrad*, pp. 243, 240.

p.101 'We are surrounded . . .', Anonymous, in Aldrich, *Witness*, p. 372.

p.101 'It was probably the saddest and most desolate place . . .' Joachim Wieder, in James Owen and Guy Walters, eds, *The Voice of War: The Second World War Told by Those Who Fought It* (London, 2004), p. 283.

p.102 Airlift figures, Beevor, *Stalingrad*, pp. 270, 292.

p.102 'Snow, snow . . .', Corporal Schafstein, diary, 2 and 6 December 1942, in Aldrich, *Witness*, p. 370.

p.104 Figures for those killed and surrendering, Beevor, *Stalingrad*, pp. 439–40 – with a discussion of the difficulties in ascertaining any reliable figures. On average over the whole war, about one-third of German prisoners captured by the Soviets did not survive their captivity.

p.104 'it was the biggest defeat . . .', Ronald Matthews, *Daily Herald*, 10 February 1943; 'The disaster was unprecedented . . .', Evan Mawdsley, *Thunder in the East: The Nazi-Soviet War, 1941–1945* (London, 2005), p. 162.

p.104 Half a million killed, Beevor, *Stalingrad*, p. 398.

p.105 'The heroic struggle . . .', Kershaw, *Hitler, Nemesis*, p. 550; see Beevor, *Stalingrad*, p. 380, for interpretation of this sentence.

p.105 German public opinion, Kershaw, *Hitler, Nemesis*, pp. 550–7.

p.106 'You cannot stop an army . . .', Beevor, *Stalingrad*, p. 404.

p.106 Inscription on the Stalingrad Sword, P.M.H. Bell, *John Bull and the Bear* (London, 1990), p. 76. Figures for those viewing the Sword (491,457), *ibid.*, p. 97.

p.106 Overy's views and quotation, Richard Overy, *Why the Allies Won* (New York, 1996), pp. 85, 96, 98.

p.107 'Germany no longer had a grand strategy', Mawdsley, *Thunder in the East*, p. 182.

p.107 'I felt Russia could never hold . . .', Alex Danchev and Daniel Todman, eds, *Field Marshal Lord Alanbrooke, War Diaries, 1939–1945* (London, 2001), p. 355.

Chapter Seven: Convoys and Wolf Packs

p.109 'I am going to proclaim . . .', Winston S. Churchill, *The Second World War*, vol. III, *The Grand Alliance* (London, 1950), p. 107.

p.110 'Happy is the convoy . . .' Marc Milner, quoted in W.J.R. Gardner, *Decoding History: The Battle of the Atlantic and Ultra* (London, 1999), p. 14.

p.112 'one of the great commanders', Martin Middlebrook, *Convoy: The Battle for Convoys SC 122 and HX 229* (London, Penguin edn, 1978), p. 74.

p.113 'the safe and timely arrival . . .', quoted in Gardner, *Decoding History*, p. 86.

p.115 'absolutely ruthless . . .', quoted in Middlebrook, *Convoy*, p. 48.

p.116 'I had got Dönitz where I wanted him . . .', quoted *ibid.*, p. 325.

p.116 'We do not look down onto the sea . . .', quoted in Peter Padfield, *War Beneath the Sea: Submarine Conflict, 1939–1945* (London, 1995), p. 107.

p.116 'North Atlantic weather!', quoted in Richard Woodman, *The Real Cruel Sea: The Merchant Navy in the Battle of the Atlantic, 1939–1943* (London, 2004), p. 429.

p.116 'Gumboots fall upon their sides . . .', quoted *ibid.*, p. 190 – life aboard a corvette.

p.116 '. . . the attitude to convoy work? . . .', quoted in Middlebrook, *Convoy*, pp. 24–5.

p.117 Figures for U-boat successes, June–October 1940, *ibid.*, p. 8. Losses in convoys SC 7 and HX 79, Marc Milner, 'Battle of the Atlantic', in I.C.B. Deare and M.R.D. Foot, eds, *Oxford Companion to the Second World War* (Oxford, 1995), p. 64.

p.119 Sinkings of merchant ships, 1941, Gardner, *Decoding History*, p. 20.

p.119 Numbers of U-boats, 1941, *ibid.*, p. 19.

p.120 'Five Boats versus the United States', J.M. Showell, *U-Boat Command and the Battle of the Atlantic* (London, 1989), p. 91.

p.120 U-boat sinkings, Middlebrook, *Convoy*, pp. 16–17; Gardner, *Decoding History*, p. 20.

p.120 U-boat losses and casualty figures, Padfield, *War Beneath the Sea*, p. 291.

p.121 Liberty ships, *ibid.*, p. 165; article, 'Liberty Ships', in Deare and Foot, *Oxford Companion*, pp. 689–90. For totals of ships built, see Clay Blair, *Hitler's U-Boat War*, vol. II, *The Hunted, 1943–1945* (New York, 1999), p. xi.

p.123 U-boat sinkings in 1942, Middlebrook, *Convoy*, pp. 17–18.

p.123 Merchant-ship losses, November 1942, Marc Milner, *The Battle of the Atlantic* (St. Catherine's, Ontario, 2003), p. 128.

p.123 'a strangle-hold on all offensive operations', quoted in Gardner, *Decoding History* p. 44.

p.123 'to be won and stay won', *ibid.*, p. 7.

p.124 German U-boat strength, January–February 1943, Milner, *Atlantic*, p. 136; Padfield, *War Beneath the Sea*, p. 314.
p.124 Convoy SC 121, Milner, *Atlantic*, p. 146.
p.124 Convoys SC 122 and HX 229, *ibid.*, p. 147; Middlebrook, *Convoy*, gives a graphic account of this battle – not to be missed.
p.124 German successes, March 1943, Milner, in Deare and Foot, *Oxford Companion*, p. 68; Padfield, *War Beneath the Sea*, p. 147; Gardner, *Decoding History*, p. 183.
p.124 Sugar and frozen carcasses, Middlebrook, *Convoy*, pp. 183, 218.
p.124 Naval Staff paper, quoted in S.W. Roskill, *The War at Sea, 1939–1945*, vol. II, *The Period of Balance* (London, 1956), and Roskill's own comment, pp. 367–8.
p.125 ONS 5 losses, Padfield, *War Beneath the Sea*, pp. 330–1; 'In one action . . .', Milner, *Atlantic*, p. 152.
p.125 Summary of British and German losses, 10–24 May, Milner, *Atlantic*, pp. 153–4.
p.125 Dönitz's signal, 21 May, quoted in Padfield, *War Beneath the Sea*, p. 335.
p.126 Horton's signal, quoted in Milner, *Atlantic*, p. 155.
p.126 'I recall the joy . . .', quoted in Middlebrook, *Convoy*, p. 213; the witness was Lieutenant Gravely, USS *Upshur*.
p.127 U-boats sunk by aircraft, Padfield, *War Beneath the Sea*, p. 335.
p.128 U-boat successes and losses, September–October 1943, Milner, *Atlantic*, pp. 172–6; Padfield, *War Beneath the Sea*, p. 369.
p.128 Snorkel U-boats, Padfield, *War Beneath the Sea*, p. 424.
p.129 Average U-boat sinkings, 1944–45, Milner, *Atlantic*, p. 22.
p.129 Last wolf-pack operation, *ibid.*, pp. 228–9.
p.129 Merchant-ship and U-boat losses, and casualty figures, Middlebrook, *Convoy*, pp. 326–7; slightly different figures, Milner, *Atlantic*, p. 230.
p.129 'The only thing that ever really frightened me . . .', Winston S. Churchill, *The Second World War*, vol. II, *Their Finest Hour* (London, 1949), p. 529.

Chapter Eight: 'The Proper Application of Overwhelming Force'

p.130 'So we had won after all! . . .' Winston S. Churchill, *The Second World War*, vol. III, *The Grand Alliance* (London, 1950), p. 539.
p.130 'Modern war is a war of motors . . .', quoted in Evan Mawdsley, *Thunder in the East: The Nazi-Soviet War, 1941–1945* (London, paperback edn, 2007), pp. 185, 193.
p.131 Share of output going to armaments, Adam Tooze, *The Wages of Destruction: The Making and Breaking of the Nazi Economy* (London, paperback edn, 2007), p. 661.
p.131 Aircraft production, article by Richard Overy in I.C.B. Deare and M.R.D. Foot, eds, *The Oxford Companion to the Second World War* (Oxford, 1995), p. 1,060. To avoid repetition, all production figures for the main belligerent countries, unless otherwise indicated, are drawn from this article, or from the tables in Richard Overy, *Why the Allies Won* (New York, 1996), pp. 331–2.
p.132 German oil imports, P.M.H. Bell, *The Origins of the Second World War in Europe* (London, 3rd ed., 2007), p. 177; synthetic production, Tooze, *Wages of Destruction*, p. 411.
p.133 'an almost paranoid sensitivity . . .', Werner Abelshauser, in Martin Harrison, ed., *The Economics of World War II* (Cambridge, 1998), p. 148.
p.133 Hitler Panzer Programme, Tooze, *Wages of Destruction*, p. 594.
p.133 Role of women in the German war economy, *ibid.*, pp. 358–9, 515.
p.134 Decline in production, late 1944, *ibid.*, pp. 638–9.
p.135 Japanese steel and coal production, Akira Hara in Harrison, ed., *Economics of WW II*, pp. 230–1.
p.136 Japanese shipping losses, Nathan Miller, *War at Sea: A Naval History of World War II* (New York, 1995), pp. 483–90.
p.136 Figures for women in industry, the services and Land Army, Overy, in Deare and Foot, eds, *Oxford Companion*, p. 1,277.

p.137 Days lost in strikes, Richard Overy, in D. Reynolds, W.F. Kimball and A.O. Chubarian, eds, *Allies at War: The Soviet, American and British Experience, 1939–1945* (London, 1994), p. 136.

p.138 Evacuation of factories and workers, Richard Overy, *Russia's War: Blood upon the Snow* (New York, 1997), pp. 211–12; Catherine Merridale, *Ivan's War: The Red Army, 1939–1945* (London, 2005), p. 103.

p.139 Six-monthly production figures, Lydia Pozdeeva, in Merridale, *Ivan's War*, p. 154.

p.140 Soviet tank losses, 1944, Mawdsley, *Thunder in the East*, p. 196.

p.141 US military strength, 1940, in Overy, *Allies*, p. 190; Overy, in Deare and Foot, eds, *Oxford Companion*, p. 1,060.

p.141 'Simply asked . . .', Overy, *Allies*, p. 192; Henry Ford and the Democrat-voting county, *ibid.*, p. 196.

Chapter Nine: The Teheran Conference, 28 November–1 December 1943

p.147 Keith Sainsbury's excellent book on the Teheran Conference is entitled *The Turning Point*, though it also has a long subtitle – *Roosevelt, Stalin, Churchill and Chiang Kai-shek, 1943: The Moscow, Cairo and Teheran Conferences* (London, 1986).

p.148 'The men on horseback . . .', Winston S. Churchill, *The Second World War*, vol. V, *Closing the Ring* (London, 1952), p. 302.

p.149 Torpedo near miss, and Arnold's remark, Keith Eubank, *Summit at Teheran* (New York, 1985), pp. 139–41.

p.150 'For this period of time . . .' See Churchill's conversation with Maisky, quoted in Robin Edmonds, *The Big Three: Churchill, Roosevelt and Stalin in Peace and War* (London, Penguin edn, 1992), citing Maisky's telegram reporting the conversation to his government.

p.150 'I know you will not mind . . .', quoted *ibid.*, p. 284.

p.151 '. . . if I had to pick a team . . .', Lord Avon, *The Memoirs of Anthony Eden*, vol. II, *The Reckoning* (London, 1965), pp. 514–15.

p.151 'I rapidly grew to appreciate . . .', Alex Danchev and Daniel Todman, eds, *Lord Alanbrooke, War Diaries, 1939–1945* (London, 2001), p. 483, citing Brooke's 'Notes on my Life'.

p.152 '. . . like carrying a large lump of ice . . .', Winston S. Churchill, *The Second World War*, vol. IV, *The Hinge of Fate* (London, 1951), p. 428.

p.153 Allied shipments via Siberian ports, Evan Mawdsley, *Thunder in the East: The Nazi-Soviet War, 1941–1945* (London, 2007), p. 192.

p.155 'Measures to shorten the war . . .', quoted in Warren F. Kimball, *Forged in War: Churchill, Roosevelt and the Second World War* (London, 1997), p. 31.

p.156 '. . . this meeting looks like being all over the place', David Dilks, ed., *The Diaries of Sir Alexander Cadogan, 1938–1945* (London, 1971), p. 579, entry for 27 November 1943.

p.156 '. . . we are heading towards chaos', Danchev and Todman, eds., *Alanbrooke War Diaries*, p. 482, entry for 28 November 1943.

p.159 Stalingrad Sword. The precise number of visitors was 491,457 – P.M.H. Bell, *John Bull and the Bear* (London, 1990), p. 97.

p.161 'This conference is over . . .', quoted in Dilks, ed., *Diaries of Cadogan*, p. 482.

p.164 Roosevelt's Christmas Eve broadcast, quoted in Edmonds, *Big Three*, p. 367.

p.165 Three-Power Declaration, quoted *ibid.*, p. 358.

p.165 Stalin's speech on New Year's Day, quoted *ibid.*, pp. 361–2.

Chapter Ten: D-Day and the Battle of Normandy, June–July 1944

p.166 'You are to prepare for the invasion of Europe . . .', quoted in Carlo D'Este, *Decision in Normandy* (London, paperback edn, 1984), p. 21.

p.166 'If they attack in the west . . .', quoted in Max Hastings, *OVERLORD: D-Day and the Battle for Normandy, 1944* (London, paperback edn, 1993), p. 70.

p.166 'If this is successful . . .', quoted in *ibid.*, p. 65.

p.166 'Well, sergeant . . .', quoted in Jonathan Bastable, *Voices from D-Day* (London, 2004), p. 61.

p.166 'The struggle for Normandy . . .', Hastings, *OVERLORD*, p. 13.

p.167 'You must remember . . .', quoted in Samuel Eliot Morison, *History of United States Naval Operations in World War II*, vol. XI, *The Invasion of France and Germany, 1944–1945* (Boston, 1957), p. 10 and note 15.

p.167 'ingrained dread', quoted in D'Este, *Normandy*, p. 29.

p.168 'It is very hard to believe . . .', Alex Danchev and Daniel Todman, eds, *Field Marshal Lord Alanbrooke, War Diaries 1939–1945* (London, 2001), p. 554.

p.168 'I am under no delusions . . .', Richard J. Aldrich, ed., *Witness to War: Diaries of the Second World War in Europe and the Middle East* (London, 2004), p. 524.

p.168 Eisenhower's note, quoted in W.G.F. Jackson, *'Overlord': Normandy 1944* (London, 1978), p. 180. Bastable, *Voices*, p. 69, draws attention to the misdating.

p.168 'I knew too well . . .', Danchev and Todman, eds, *Alanbrooke War Diaries*, p. 554.

p.169 'What Stalin would think of this . . .', quoted in Carlo D'Este, *Bitter Victory: The Battle for Sicily, 1943* (London, paperback edn, 1989), p. 86.

p.169 Figures for troops and supplies, Morison, *United States Naval Operations*, vol. XI, pp. 51, 146.

p.173 Figures for German aircraft losses, Hastings, *OVERLORD*, p. 51.

p.175 'How, in God's name . . .', quoted in Bastable, *Voices*, p. 67.

p.178 'At H-Hour the tide had been low . . .', Anthony Di Stephano, 111th Field Artillery, in Robin Neillands and Roderick de Normann, *D-Day 1944: Voices from Normandy* (London, 1993), p. 149.

p.178 'Our forces had suffered . . .', quoted in Hastings, *OVERLORD*, p. 110.

p.180 Figures for German and Allied divisions, *ibid.*, p. 43.

p.180 Figures for Allied strength, 16 June, S.W. Roskill, *The War at Sea, 1939–1945*, vol. III, *The Offensive*, part II (London, 1961), p. 63.

p.180 'like Margate on a Bank Holiday', *ibid.*, p. 63; 'If the ship on your port bow . . .', *ibid.*, p. 64.

p.181 'Now we are absolutely safe . . .', quoted in D'Este, *Normandy*, p. 239.

p.182 'Almost single-handedly . . .', Hastings, *OVERLORD*, p. 183.

p.183 'Monty is a good man . . .', quoted in D'Este, *Normandy*, p. 51, note.

p.183 V-1 attacks, I.C.B. Deare and M.R.D. Foot, eds, *Oxford Companion to the Second World War* (Oxford, 1995), p. 1,249.

p.184 'The whole of June . . .', Katherine Moore, quoted in Aldrich, *Witness*, p. 551.

p.185 'One's imagination boggled . . .', quoted in Hastings, *OVERLORD*, p. 212.

p.186 Rommel's losses, *ibid.*, p. 208.

p.186 'Someone has to tell the Führer . . .', quoted in D'Este, *Normandy*, p. 407.

Chapter Eleven: 'A Fateful Conference'

p.188 'This may well be a fateful conference . . .', Churchill to Roosevelt, 8 January 1945, in Warren F. Kimball, ed., *Churchill and Roosevelt: The Complete Correspondence*, vol. III, *Alliance Declining, February 1944–April 1945* (London, 1984), p. 502.

p.190 'I am not going to give way about this . . .', Churchill to Ismay, 6 July 1944, National Archives, PREM 3/271/9.

p.190 'If my departure from the scene . . .', Kimball, vol. III, pp. 225–6, draft not sent, 30 June 1944.

p.190 'looked like he wanted to fight the President', Alex Danchev and Daniel Todman, eds, *Field Marshal Lord Alanbrooke, War Diaries 1939–1945* (London, 2001), p. 565, entry for 30 June 1944.

p.191 'Both PM and AE . . .', John Harvey, ed., *The War Diaries of Oliver Harvey* (London, 1978), pp. 347, 364; Churchill, 'I was naturally surprised . . .', Churchill to Roosevelt, 23 October 1944, Kimball, vol. III, p. 367.

p.192 'a common mind about the Balkans', Churchill to Roosevelt, 11 October 1944, Kimball, vol. III, p. 353.

p.193 '. . . take a stand with you', Roosevelt to Churchill, 13 Dec. 1944, *ibid.*, p.456.

p.193 'Stalin . . . adhered strictly . . .', Winston S. Churchill, *The Second World War*, vol. VI, *Triumph and Tragedy* (London, 1954), p. 255.

p.197 'slender contact with life', quoted in Robin Edmonds, *The Big Three: Churchill, Roosevelt and Stalin in Peace and War* (London, paperback edn, 1992), p. 368.

p.197 Molotov quotation in Thomas Parrish, *Roosevelt and Marshall: Partners in Politics and War* (New York, 1989), pp. 472–3.

p.199 'As we crossed the mountains . . .', Churchill, *Second World War*, vol. VI, p. 301.

p.199 'they had laid on the most terrific show . . .', diary kept by Maureen Stuart-Clark, a Wren officer on Admiral Somerville's staff, quoted in Richard J. Aldrich, ed., *Witness to War: Diaries of the Second World War in Europe and the Middle East* (London, 2004), p. 605.

p.205 'It would be a great pity . . .', *ibid.*, p. 327.

p.205 'he didn't care . . .', quoted in David Reynolds, *Summits: Six Meetings that shaped the Twentieth Century* (London, 2007), p. 102.

p.206 'The Provisional Government . . .', US Department of State, *Foreign Relations of the United States: The Conferences at Malta and Yalta, 1945* (Washington, DC, 1955), pp. 971–5.

p.207 'We can deal with it in our own way . . .', V. Molotov, *Molotov Remembers: Inside Kremlin Politics*, ed. Albert Resis (Chicago, 1993), p.51.

p.208 *Yalta! Yalta!*, Timothy Garton Ash, 'A Lesson to Learn from Yalta', *The Times*, 11 February 1995.

p.208 Churchill's speech, *HC Deb.*, 5th Series, Vol. 408, cols 1,267–95; the quotation is from col. 1267.

Chapter Twelve: The Defeat of Japan and the Atomic Bombs, 1945

p.210 'The hour was early . . .', Michiko Hachiya, *Hiroshima Diary: The Journal of a Japanese Physician, August 6 – September 30, 1945*, in James Owen and Guy Walters, eds, *The Voice of War: The Second World War Told by Those Who Fought It* (London, 2004), p. 593.

p.211 Japanese losses at Leyte Gulf, Max Hastings, *Nemesis: The Battle for Japan* (London, 2007), p. 151.

p.212 Casualties at Iwo Jima and Okinawa, I.C.B. Deare and M.R.D. Foot, eds, *The Oxford Companion to the Second World War* (Oxford, 1995), pp. 604, 836.

p.215 Japanese losses of merchant ships and tankers, *ibid.*, pp. 628-9; Operation STARVATION, Hastings, *Nemesis*, p. 334.

p.215 Rations and calories, *ibid.*, p. 46.

p.216 Figures for Tokyo raid, Deare and Foote, *Oxford Companion*, p. 1,077. 'The whole city . . .', quoted in Hastings, *Nemesis*, p. 320.

p.216 'digging through the rubble . . .', quoted in Herbert P. Bix, *Hirohito and the Making of Modern Japan* (London, 2001), p. 491.

p.217 Differing figures for Japanese casualties, Hastings, *Nemesis*, p.339; *Oxford Companion*, p.1,078.

p.219 Leahy's estimates of casualties, Ronald Spector, *Eagle Against the Sun: The American War with Japan* (London, 1985), p. 543. Cf. higher contemporary estimates in Robert James Maddox, *Weapons for Victory: The Hiroshima Decision Fifty Years Later* (Columbia, Missouri, 1995), pp. 53–6, 59–61, 118–26; Robert H. Ferrell, *Harry S. Truman: A Life* (Columbia, MO, 1994), pp. 212–13.

p.220 Figures for MANHATTAN PROJECT, Deare and Foot, *Oxford Companion*, p. 73 (article by R.V. Jones).

p.221 Potsdam Declaration, Hastings, *Nemesis*, p. 511.

p.222 Hiroshima, Deare and Foot, *Oxford Companion*, pp. 530–1; Nagasaki, *ibid.*, p. 773.

p.224 'he dug in his heels . . .', Bix, *Hirohito*, p. 476.

p.226 Reading of broadcast in current Japanese, *ibid.*, p. 527.

p.227 Suicide flight by Ugaki and his squadron, Hastings, *Nemesis*, p. 561.

p.227 'had a greater effect . . .', Hatano Sumio, in Deare and Foote, *Oxford Companion*, p. 637; 'cannot be answered', Evan Mawdsley, *World War II: A New History* (Cambridge, 2009), p. 429.

p.228 'In such a welter of events . . .', Ferrell, *Truman*, p. 216.

p.229 'weapons for victory', Maddox, *Weapons for Victory*.

FURTHER READING

Historical writing on the Second World War is vast in scope and often remarkably high in quality. The following notes do no more than indicate a few books that the reader may find particularly interesting and helpful.

General Books on the War

Evan Mawdsley, *World War II: A New History* (2009) provides a clear and well-balanced survey of the whole war, within a manageable compass. Gerhard L. Weinberg, *A World at Arms: A Global History of World War II* (1994) is much longer, packed with detail and full of insights, especially on links between different aspects of the conflict. Richard Overy, *Why the Allies Won* (1996) is a masterly analysis of an intriguing problem. John Lukacs, *The Last European War, September 1939–December 1941* (1977) offers an individual and illuminating study of the first period of the war. In *Fateful Choices: Ten Decisions that Changed the World, 1940–1941* (2007), Ian Kershaw trains his own searchlight on a number of turning points in the war. I.C.B. Deare and M.R.D. Foot, eds, *The Oxford Companion to the Second World War* (1995) is a comprehensive and enlightening work of reference.

Hitler's Triumph: The Collapse of France

Alistair Horne, *To Lose a Battle: France 1940* (new ed., 1990) provides a vivid narrative of fast-moving events. Karl-Heinz Frieser offers a well-documented German account, under the challenging title of *The Blitzkrieg Legend: The 1940 Campaign in the West* (2005). Julian Jackson, *The Fall of*

France: The Nazi Invasion of 1940 (1995), and Ernest R. May, *Strange Victory: Hitler's Conquest of France* (2000), are valuable modern studies of an old problem. Irène Némirowski, *Suite Française* (English translation, 2006) is a fictional yet realistic description of the flight of French refugees escaping from the advancing German armies. John Lukacs, *Five Days in London, May 1940* (1999) tells the story of the hidden British crisis that accompanied the defeat of France.

'Finest Hour': The Battle of Britain

Richard Hough and Denis Richards, *The Battle of Britain: The Jubilee History* (1989) is a splendid narrative. A more recent joint work, Paul Addison and Jeremy Crang, eds, *The Burning Blue: A New History of the Battle of Britain* (2000) casts its net wide and makes a good haul of fresh insights. Peter Fleming, *Invasion 1940* (1957) gets the atmosphere of the time just right, and should not be missed. Williamson Murray, *Strategy for Defeat: The Luftwaffe, 1933–1945* (1983) illuminates the German side. Peter Stansky's *The First Day of the Blitz: September 7, 1940* (2007) brings the events of a single crucial day to life.

Operation BARBAROSSA and the Battle of Stalingrad

A number of excellent books deal with both the German invasion of the Soviet Union in 1941 and the Battle of Stalingrad in 1942–43. Evan Mawdsley, *Thunder in the East: The Nazi-Soviet War, 1941–1945* (2005) covers its vast subject in a single well-organised volume. Richard Overy's *Russia's War: Blood upon the Snow* (1997) is a vivid account. John Erickson's two volumes, *The Road to Stalingrad* (1975) and *The Road to Berlin* (1983), are packed with detail and driven along by an intense narrative power. The vast background to the struggle between Hitler and Stalin is covered at length in Richard Overy's *The Dictators: Hitler's Germany and Stalin's Russia* (2004). John Lukacs, *June 1941: Hitler and Stalin* (2006) takes a short, sharp look at one episode in that rivalry. Geoffrey Roberts, *Stalin's Wars: From World War to Cold War 1939–1953* (2006) provides a view from the top; while Catherine Merridale, *Ivan's War: The Red Army, 1939–1945* (2005) tells the extraordinary story of the 'ordinary' Russian soldier. On the campaign of 1941, Rodric Braithwaite, *Moscow 1941: A City and its People at War* (2006) is incisive and wide-ranging. Antony Beevor's *Stalingrad* (1998) is a masterpiece – the one book to read on the battle if you read no other.

Pearl Harbor

Ronald Spector, *Eagle Against the Sun: The American War with Japan* (1985) sets Pearl Harbor in the context of the whole Pacific war, while H.P. Willmott, *The Second World War in the Far East* (2004) achieves a similar result with admirable brevity and clarity. Gordon W. Prange's *At Dawn We Slept: The Untold Story of Pearl Harbor* (1982) is full of detail but still carries the reader along at a lively pace. Samuel Eliot Morison, *The Rising Sun in the Pacific, 1931–April 1942* (1948), a volume in his official *History of United States Naval Operations in World War II*, is still well worth reading. Political and diplomatic aspects are well covered in Robert A. Dallek, *Franklin D. Roosevelt and American Foreign Policy, 1932–1945* (1979), and David Reynolds, *From Munich to Pearl Harbor: Roosevelt's America and the Origins of the Second World War* (2001). Ronald Lewin, *The Other Ultra* (1982) gives a clear and lively account of its subject.

The Battle of Midway

The Battle of Midway is set in context in the books by Ronald Spector and H.P. Willmott under 'Pearl Harbor', above. John Keegan, *The Price of Admiralty: War at Sea from Man of War to Submarine* (1988) has a first-rate chapter on Midway – the best short treatment. Samuel Eliot Morison, *Coral Sea, Midway and Submarine Actions, May 1942–August 1942* (1980) is still valuable. Gordon W. Prange, *Miracle at Midway* (1982), and Jonathan Parshall and Anthony Tully, *Shattered Sword: The Untold Story of the Battle of Midway* (2005), offer detailed and vivid accounts; while Peter C. Smith, *Midway: Dauntless Victory* (2007) stresses the part played in the battle by the Dauntless dive-bombers.

Convoys and Wolf Packs – Decision in the Atlantic

Marc Milner, *Battle of the Atlantic* (2003), and Peter Padfield, *War Beneath the Sea: Submarine Conflict, 1939–1945* (1995), provide first-rate general accounts of the Battle of the Atlantic, including the turning point of March–May 1943. Martin Middlebrook, *Convoy: The Battle for Convoys SC122 and HX229* (1978) tells the gripping story of two convoy battles, followed in detail day by day – not to be missed. W.J.R. Gardner, *Decoding History: The Battle of the Atlantic and Ultra* (1999) is an absorbing technical analysis. Tony Lane, *The Merchant Seamen's War* (1990) is a vivid account of a sometimes neglected aspect of the war at sea. J.P.M. Showell, *U-Boat Command and the Battle of the Atlantic* (1989) looks at the battle from the German point of view.

War Production – The Battle of the Factories

Much of the story has necessarily to be told in statistics, but behind every statistic lies a human story, as the following books bring out. The main framework is set out in Mark Harrison, ed., *The Economics of World War II: Six Great Powers in International Comparison* (1998). The economic efforts of the Allied powers are dealt with in D. Reynolds, W.F. Kimball and A.O. Chubaryan, eds, *Allies at War: The Soviet, American and British Experience, 1939–1945* (1994). On individual countries, Adam Tooze, *The Wages of Destruction: The Making and Breaking of the Nazi Economy* (2007) is massive and readable on Germany. Mark Harrison, ed., *Guns and Rubles: The Defense Industry in the Stalinist State* (2008) repays careful attention. Donald M. Nelsen, *Arsenal of Democracy: The Story of American War Production* (1946), and W.K. Hancock and M.M. Gowing, *British War Economy* (1949), remain indispensable.

The Teheran Conference

There is an excellent detailed account of the Teheran Conference and its context in Keith Sainsbury, *The Turning Point: Roosevelt, Stalin, Churchill and Chiang Kai-shek, 1943: The Moscow, Cairo and Teheran Conferences* (1986). Keith Eubank, *Summit at Teheran* (1985) is another first-rate discussion, offering an American perspective. Robin Edmonds, *The Big Three: Churchill, Roosevelt and Stalin in Peace and War* (1991) is an illuminating survey by a diplomat turned historian. Warren F. Kimball, who edited the complete Churchill-Roosevelt correspondence, offers his reflections in *Forged in War: Roosevelt, Churchill and the Second World War* (1997). For Stalin, see also the book by Geoffrey Roberts, *Stalin's Wars: from World War to Cold War 1939–1953* (2006).

D-Day and the Battle of Normandy

There is no shortage of fine books on D-Day and the Normandy campaign. One of the most recent and best-informed is Antony Beevor, *D-Day: The Battle for Normandy* (2009). Max Hastings, *OVERLORD: D-Day and the*

Battle for Normandy, 1944 (1984) remains a classic. Carlo-D'Este, *Decision in Normandy: The Unwritten Story of Montgomery and the Allied Campaign* (1983) has a case to argue as well as a story to tell. Ralph Bennett's *Ultra in the West: The Normandy Campaign, 1944–45* (1979) is the fruit of personal experience as well as historical study, while a fascinating selection of first-hand accounts are gathered by Jonathan Bastable in his *Voices from D-Day* (2004).

The Yalta Conference

The books by Robin Edmonds and Warren F. Kimball, noted under 'Teheran' above, and Geoffrey Roberts, under 'BARBAROSSA', above, are also valuable for this subject. David Reynolds, *Summits: Six Meetings that Shaped the Twentieth Century* (2007) includes a perceptive chapter on Yalta. Diane S. Clemens, *Yalta* (1970) provides a shrewd general account, still well worth reading. S.M. Plokhy, *Yalta: The Price of Peace* (2010) appeared too late to be used in this study.

The Defeat of Japan and the Atomic Bombs

Max Hastings, *Nemesis: The Battle for Japan, 1944–45* (2007) is the single best book on the whole subject, and not to be missed. Ronald Spector, *Eagle Against the Sun: The American War with Japan* (1985), as in 'Pearl Harbor', above, puts the final act in perspective. On the atomic bombs, Robert James Maddox, *Weapons for Victory: The Hiroshima Decision Fifty Years Later* (1995), and Martin J. Sherwin, *A World Destroyed: The Atomic Bomb and the Grand Alliance* (1975), offer different views on the use of atomic weapons against Japan. Herbert P. Bix, *Hirohito and the Making of Modern Japan* (2001) sheds light on Japanese decision-making.

INDEX

Note: Page numbers in bold refer to illustrations, maps and tables

ACKNOWLEDGEMENTS

Many people have helped in the writing of this book, and I am glad to take this opportunity to express my thanks. At Yale University Press, Heather McCallum first suggested the idea of a book on turning points in the Second World War, and then followed the work in progress with much encouragement and wise advice. Rachael Lonsdale has taken immense care in seeing the manuscript through the complicated stages leading towards publication. I am most grateful to them both. My friends David Dutton, Ralph White and Geoffrey Blades have read drafts with critical yet sympathetic eyes, saving me from errors and sharpening my prose. Warren Reed provided valuable advice at crucial points. David Annett has been generous with his time and expertise, rescuing me repeatedly from computer calamities.

It scarcely needs to be said that this book is a work of synthesis and interpretation, dependent on the research and scholarship of other historians. Some of my debts are acknowledged in the notes, and among the books suggested for further reading; but most are to be found in the gleanings of a life-time's reading, and my thanks must remain general, though none the less heart-felt for that. The London Library, with its vast holdings, remains a haven for scholars – even when it has been partly given over to builders! I am most grateful to the librarian and the ever-helpful staff.

As ever, my greatest debt is to my wife, who has lived closely with this book, reading drafts in their messiest state, and keeping me going when I needed it most. To her, and to all my helpers, I offer my warmest thanks.

P.M.H. BELL
Kew, August 2010